Memorable Psychopharmacology

Second Edition

Jonathan Heldt, M.D.

Also available from the same author:
Memorable Psychiatry
Memorable Neurology

The content of this book is not intended to be a replacement for proper medical training, nor is it intended to substitute for professional medical advice, diagnosis, or treatment. Always seek the advice of your physician or other qualified health provider with any questions you may have regarding a medical condition.

Editing and behavioral consultation provided by **Juliane Heldt, BCBA (Board Certified Behavior Analyst)**.

Copyright © 2017 Jonathan Heldt.

All rights reserved.

Revision 2.0. Last revised June 18, 2021.

ISBN: 1737210800
ISBN-13: 978-1-7372108-0-1

DEDICATION

To **Dr. Aubyn Fulton**. Thank you for introducing me to the wonders of the human mind and for setting the standard of courage to which I continue to aspire.

CONTENTS

	Acknowledgments	i
1	Introduction	1
2	Neurotransmitters	3
3	Antidepressants	27
4	Antipsychotics	51
5	Mood Stabilizers	71
6	Anxiolytics and Hypnotics	91
7	Stimulants	105
8	Analgesics	117
9	Antidementia	129
10	Recreational Stimulants	139
11	Recreational Depressants	153
12	Hallucinogens	165
13	Cannabis and Others	173
14	Drug-Drug Interactions	185
15	Other Modalities	195
16	Final Review	209

ACKNOWLEDGMENTS

A world of gratitude to **Dr. Frank Randall** who supported me in starting this project. Without him, this would not have been possible.

Special thanks to **Dr. Katrina DeBonis** who generously applied her knowledge and expertise to the crafting of this book.

1 INTRODUCTION

Psychopharmacology is the field of science that studies the effects that specific medications, drugs, and other substances can have on the mind, including their influence on a person's thoughts, feelings, and behaviors. Psychopharmacology can be daunting, but it doesn't have to be! Unlike other fields of medicine like cardiology or endocrinology (which tend to involve processes that are easily visualized and follow a logical order), the concepts in psychopharmacology can seem random, illogical, and abstract. This can lead to frustration or boredom on the part of the learner.

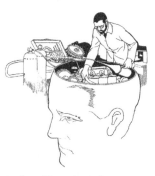

This book aims to correct that. It pursues the goal of making the information stick with reckless abandon. It is shameless in its use of mnemonics and other memory aids. It wants to (and believes it can!) make psychopharmacology interesting or even *fun*. This approach should make the book helpful to healthcare providers from various disciplines and at various stages of training (including medical students, doctors, nurses, nurse practitioners, pharmacists, psychologists, physician assistants, social workers, and others). The only prerequisites are a basic knowledge of **physiology** (including organ systems and cell biology), **neurology** (such as action potentials, synapses, and the autonomic nervous system), and **pharmacology** (agonists, antagonists, half-lives, and the like).

We'll begin with a quick overview of neurotransmitters which are the biological target of many psychoactive substances. From there, we will go over the prescription medications used to treat common mental illnesses such as depression, bipolar disorder, and schizophrenia. We will then discuss recreationally used drugs, including how to recognize the clinical syndromes they produce and how to treat cases of substance abuse. Finally, for a balanced view of the field we will finish with a brief overview of non-drug treatment options for psychiatric disorders.

Before we start, it can be good to remind yourself of exactly *why* you are sitting through this material, especially if you aren't planning on becoming a psychiatrist. There are a few reasons. First, the vast majority of psychoactive drugs are being prescribed not by psychiatrists but by doctors, nurse practitioners, physician assistants, and healthcare professionals in other fields, with primary care forming the bulk of that. Therefore, it's important for *all* prescribers to have a solid foundation in the subject to be able to practice responsibly. Second, even if you will not be prescribing psychiatric medications yourself, you will almost certainly encounter patients using psychoactive substances (whether prescribed or not). And finally, being able to talk knowledgeably about brain stuff is always popular at parties!

While studying, look for the following boxes to identify **high-yield** concepts! You should remember these well for both tests and clinical practice. The most high-yield information has been collected together in a few pages at the end of this book which you can reference this as you progress throughout the text. You may even consider snapping a photo to take with you for future reference!

Concepts in boxes are particularly **high-yield**!

An ***easy way*** to remember them will be in ***italics*** below.

Finally, a warning that the language and content in this book may occasionally be a bit salty. While every effort has been taken to avoid unnecessarily offensive language or concepts, certain mnemonics simply do not work in a more sanitized form. In addition, we should note that nothing in this book is intended to disrespect or trivialize the experiences of people suffering from mental illness. The hope is that, by making the information as memorable and accessible as possible, we can be better equipped to provide the best quality of care for our patients.

If you're **short on time**, you can fly through the chapters reading **only the boxes**.

Try to ***come back later*** to make sure you understand any **complex concepts**.

Now, let's begin...

2 NEUROTRANSMITTERS

Let's start with a discussion of the primary **neurotransmitters** which are involved in the mechanism of action of the vast majority of psychoactive substances. We will briefly review basic principles of neurology and pharmacology before moving on to discuss each of the major neurotransmitters one by one.

Neurotransmitters are **chemical messengers** that transmit signals across a junction (or **synapse**) between neurons. Neurotransmitters are stored in **vesicles** prior to being released. Here is a basic schematic of a synapse:

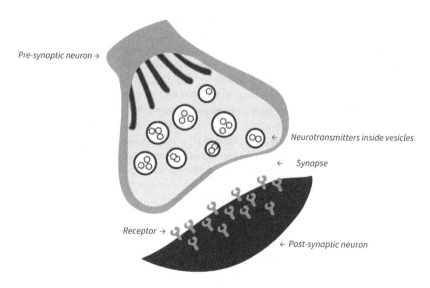

A visual schematic of a **neurochemical synapse**.

When the first (**pre-synaptic**) neuron is activated, it releases neurotransmitters, which then diffuse across the synapse to activate **receptors** on the receiving (**post-synaptic**) neuron. This depolarizes the post-synaptic neuron and causes it to "fire." A visual representation of this process is found below, going from left to right:

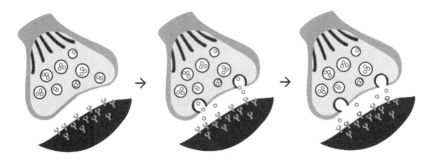

Neurotransmitters diffusing across a chemical synapse.

The post-synaptic neuron then propagates a wave of depolarization (known as an **action potential**) down to the next neuron, and this process repeats. This is the central mechanism by which one neuron can transmit information to another neuron, creating a method for different cells in the brain to communicate with each other.

The neurotransmitters released into the synapse cannot simply remain there (otherwise the post-synaptic neuron would continue to fire even when the original signal is gone). There are several mechanisms by which the synapse can "reset" itself: the neurotransmitter can **diffuse** away, it can be broken down by an **enzyme**, or it can be pumped back into the pre-synaptic neuron by **transporter proteins** for storage and reuse (a process known as **reuptake**).

The post-synaptic neuron can also make itself more or less sensitive to future stimulation. For example, if a neuron is being activated too often, it can reduce the number of receptors available on its membrane, thereby making itself less sensitive to activation (this process is known as **downregulation**). The opposite is true as well: cells can make themselves *more* sensitive to stimulation by increasing the number of receptors available on their membranes, which is known as **upregulation**.

While this is an oversimplified overview of neurotransmission, it is important to understand each of these concepts because they will all come into play during our study of psychopharmacology. Each step in this process is a potential target for drug effects, as different medications can increase the overall amount of neurotransmitter released from the synapse (methamphetamines), interfere with the reuptake process (antidepressants), block post-synaptic receptors (antipsychotics), or slow down action potential propagation (mood stabilizers). These are only a few examples, and there are more to come in the chapters ahead!

As a final note, neurotransmitters are not the only type of chemical messenger that can enable communication between neurons. **Hormones** exert similar effects, but instead of crossing the synaptic cleft, they instead travel through the bloodstream where they can exert influence on more distant parts of the body. The downside of this wider reach is that hormone effects are slower than the near-instantaneous speed of neurotransmission.

DRUG EFFECTS

When discussing the specific ways that a drug can interact with receptors, it can be helpful to have a standardized vocabulary to use. You should recall from your study of pharmacology that a **full agonist** mimics the effect of a neurotransmitter while a **partial agonist** mimics it but only to a lesser extent. Conversely, an **antagonist** blocks the effect of a neurotransmitter, while an **inverse agonist** produces the opposite effect. (If any of this feels unfamiliar, take a few moments to review the basics of pharmacology before moving on!)

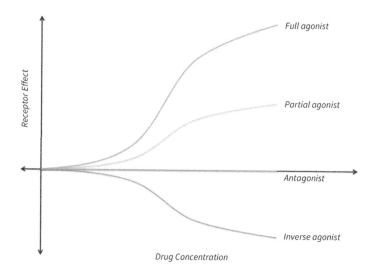

A visual representation of the various effects a drug can have on a receptor.

TWO RULES OF NEUROTRANSMISSION

To simplify our study of psychopharmacology, consider the following Rules of Neurotransmission. These aren't laws in the sense of the "law of gravity." Rather, they are core principles that will help you to make sense of a lot of what you'll be learning.

The First Rule of Neurotransmission is: "**What goes up must come down**." This rule explains the concepts of intoxication and withdrawal. Each drug has its own unique effects during intoxication. When someone is withdrawing from that drug, however, the *opposite* effects will be observed. For example, someone who has taken a stimulating drug will often experience a low-energy "crash" during withdrawal. Conversely, "**What goes down must come back up**," and withdrawal from depressant drugs is characterized by a state of hyperarousal and excitation. Mechanistically, this is due to the dual processes of downregulation and upregulation. The brain strives for homeostasis and will act to counterbalance any perceived excesses.

The Second Rule of Neurotransmission is: "**With great power comes great responsibility**." This refers to the fact that the efficacy of a drug is often intrinsically linked to its adverse effects. If a drug is powerful, it is more likely to have severe side effects. In contrast, if a drug has a more benign side effect profile, it probably won't work quite as well either. Within psychopharmacology, there are several examples of this (such as clozapine and lithium, to be discussed further in Chapters 4 and 5). Because of this, we can't always use the big guns right off the bat. It's always best to attempt treatment with the least powerful option that will still produce good results.

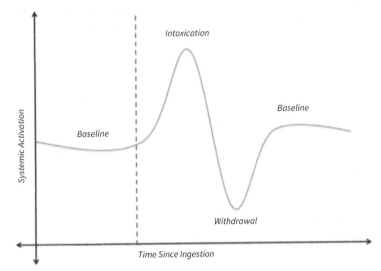

A graphical representation of the **First Rule of Neurotransmission**.
This graph shows a **stimulant** such as cocaine or amphetamines.

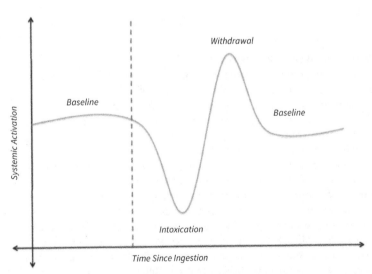

Another graphical representation of the **First Rule of Neurotransmission**.
This graph shows a **depressant** such as alcohol or benzodiazepines.

SEROTONIN

Okay, now onto the individual neurotransmitters! We will start by talking about three **monoamines** that each play a big role in psychopharmacology: serotonin, dopamine, and norepinephrine. (We will refer to these as the "big three monoamines" from time to time.) These neurotransmitters share some characteristics (including a prominent role in mood disorders like depression), but they each have a unique set of both psychological and physiologic effects that must be memorized separately.

Let's first look at **serotonin** (also known as 5-hydroxytryptamine or 5-HT). Drugs that boost serotonin in the brain are often used as **antidepressants**, with the most popular class being **selective serotonin reuptake inhibitors (SSRIs)**. However, serotonergic medications have many uses beyond just depression! SSRIs have proven to be helpful for conditions ranging from anxiety and OCD to bulimia and PTSD. Truly, serotonergic medications can be thought of as "**broad-spectrum antineurotics**!" This is because serotonergic drugs are not "happy pills" but instead help to modulate **emotional processing** in response to one's life experiences (more to come on this in Chapter 3!).

> **Serotonergic medications** are commonly referred to as **antidepressants**, but they are effective in a **wide range** of other psychiatric disorders as well.
>
> *Serotonergic medications are "**broad-spectrum antineurotics!**"*

While serotonin can be very effective at improving emotional processing, it does come with some downsides as well. Most of these adverse effects are related to the fact that serotonin receptors are found not only in the brain but throughout the rest of the body as well! You can use the mnemonic **SPAROW**-tonin (pronounced "sparrow-tonin") to keep these side effects in mind when talking to patients about starting serotonergic medications:

S is for Sleep and energy. Serotonin is involved in regulating sleep and energy. However, the exact effect differs from one drug to the next! Some medications can be quite sedating, while others are more activating. We'll discuss these differences more in Chapter 3, but for now just associate serotonin with sleep and energy!

P is for Platelet dysfunction. Despite its association with the brain, only around 1% of all the serotonin in your body is actually in your head! Around 10% of serotonin is found in platelets where it is involved in blood clotting. SSRIs can interfere with this process, putting patients at higher risk of bleeding. However, the overall risk of bleeding is quite low, so it's really only a concern in patients who are already taking other medications (like anticoagulants) that can thin their blood.

A is for Abdominal upset. While 1% of serotonin is in your brain and 10% is in your platelets, the other 90% is in your gut! For this reason, abdominal symptoms are among the most common side effect of SSRIs, with nausea, diarrhea, and stomach discomfort all being frequently seen (most often in the first few weeks after starting).

R is for Reproductive effects. Many people taking SSRIs report that their desire for sex, their ability to maintain arousal, and their capacity to reach orgasm are all impacted. Some studies suggest that sexual side effects are the number one reason why patients stop taking SSRIs, so it's important to assess this on an ongoing basis with your patients and to consider non-serotonergic options if needed!

O is for Overdose. It's possible to have too much of a good thing! Too much serotonin can lead to a potentially life-threatening condition known as **serotonin syndrome**. We will talk about serotonin syndrome in more detail on the next page, so hold tight for now! Generally speaking, however, it's worth noting that most SSRIs are actually quite safe in overdose, especially compared with older antidepressants.

W is for Weight gain. While initial studies on SSRIs did not show significant amounts of weight gain, longer term studies have suggested that some (though certainly not all) patients taking serotonergic medications do put on weight when taking these medications over months or years.

Serotonin's functions involve **multiple organ systems**, including the **brain**, **abdomen**, and **platelets**.

SPAROW-tonin:
Sleep and energy
Platelet dysfunction
Abdominal upset
Reproductive effects
Overdose (serotonin syndrome)
Weight gain

NEUROANATOMY

One bit of trivia that sometimes gets tested is the fact that serotonin is produced in the **raphe nuclei** (pronounced "ray-fee") of the brain. The raphe nuclei are located in the brain stem but have projections to almost every part of the brain, which further explains serotonin's wide-reaching effects. You can remember this by linking the **ray**-phe nuclei to the bright **rays** of  the sun bringing light and hope to people suffering from depression!

Serotonin is produced in the **raphe nuclei**.

The **ray**-phe nuclei bring **rays** of light to people suffering from depression!

SEROTONIN SYNDROME

Let's look at serotonin syndrome in more depth, as this will give us another way to remember the effects of serotonin in the body and brain. Patients with serotonin syndrome often present with a specific constellation of signs and symptoms which you can remember using the mnemonic **shits and SHIVERS**. This will remind you of **d**iarrhea (which makes sense given what we learned about 90% of serotonin being in the gut!), **S**hivering, **H**yperreflexia, **I**ncreased temperature, **V**ital sign instability (including tachycardia, hypertension, and  respiratory distress), **E**ncephalopathy (changes in mental status), **R**estlessness, and **S**weating. Together, these signs and symptoms are highly suggestive of serotonin syndrome!

Serotonin syndrome is a complication of prescribing **too many serotonergic drugs**.

Shits and SHIVERS:
Shits (diarrhea)
Shivering
Hyperreflexia
Increased temperature
Vital sign instability
Encephalopathy
Restlessness
Sweating

The severity of serotonin syndrome can vary. In subacute forms it produces only mild discomfort, while in more extreme forms many patients will require admission to the ICU. It can even be lethal, with a significant mortality rate between 2 and 12%. In fact, the death of an 18 year-old college student named Libby Zion in 1984 from serotonin syndrome after she was prescribed two serotonergic drugs (phenelzine, a monoamine oxidase inhibitor, and meperidine, an opioid with significant serotonergic activity) by an overworked intern is what led directly to the federal regulations imposing work-hour restrictions during residency.

After learning about serotonin syndrome, diligent providers will often try to avoid combining *any* two medications that have serotonergic effects. However, this is probably not necessary. In fact, decades of clinical experience tell us that in *most* cases we can safely prescribe multiple medications that interact with serotonin at the same time. It appears that a particular class of antidepressant known as **monoamine oxidase inhibitors** (which we will learn about further in Chapter 3) is the biggest culprit here! As long as an MAOI is not involved, you can safely use two serotonergic drugs at the same time in most cases.

DOPAMINE

Like serotonin, **dopamine** has diverse functions throughout the body, including acting as a neurotransmitter in the brain, inhibiting gastric motility, increasing urine output, and modulating blood vessels. These actions are mediated by various receptors, with D_1, D_2, D_3, D_4, and D_5 receptor subtypes having been identified so far. For our purposes, we will primarily focus on dopamine's effects in the **central nervous system**.

Psychoactive drugs involving dopamine tend to either *increase* its effects (either by acting as an agonist at the receptor, inhibiting its reuptake, or causing its release from pre-synaptic vesicles) or *oppose* its action (such as by acting as an antagonist at the receptor). To understand the effects that you will see with use of dopaminergic medications, use the word **DOPAMINE** itself:

D is for Drug addiction. Dopaminergic pathways play a key role in cases of **addiction** and substance use disorders, and many recreational drugs such as methamphetamine and cocaine directly involve dopamine. In fact, the extent to which a drug releases dopamine seems to correlate directly with how addictive it is!

O is for Outcomes. Anytime you consider the outcome of any particular behavior (whether that's making food so you can eat it, studying for a test so you can do well, or grabbing an umbrella on a rainy day to avoid getting drenched), dopamine is released. In this way, dopamine governs **motivation and goal-oriented behavior**. Contrary to popular beliefs, dopamine is much more involved in the *wanting* of something than it is in the feeling of *liking* it once it's been obtained!

P is for Psychosis. Dysregulation of dopamine is implicated in psychosis. Accordingly, dopamine antagonists that block the effect of this neurotransmitter are typically used as **antipsychotics** to treat disorders like schizophrenia and seem to lessen symptoms such as delusions and hallucinations.

A is for Attention. Dopamine is involved in determining what information gets our attention. For this reason, drugs that boost dopamine are used as **stimulants** to treat disorders like attention deficit hyperactivity disorder (ADHD).

M is for Movement. Dopamine does not *directly* cause muscle contraction. Rather, dopamine makes movements *more likely* to happen. In this way, dopamine is like grease: it doesn't *move* the hinges, it just makes them *easier* to move! This explains why people taking dopaminergic drugs often appear hyperactive as well as why patients who have Parkinson's disease (which involves a loss of dopamine-releasing neurons) or who take dopamine-blocking drugs  often have difficulty initiating movements (more to come on this in Chapter 4).

I is for Inhibition of prolactin. Dopamine directly inhibits the release of the hormone **prolactin** which is involved in breast growth, lactation, menstruation, sex drive, and other reproductive functions.

N is for Nausea. For reasons that aren't completely understood, drugs that block dopamine (such as prochlorperazine) seem to be effective at reducing nausea.

E is for Energy. Drugs that boost dopamine in the brain are known to increase levels of energy, which can be helpful in treating specific symptoms of depression.

Pack this information into the part of your brain labeled "Very Important." Think about how well you want to do on the test or how much you want to impress others with your knowledge of psychopharmacology! By engaging in outcome appraisal, you are using dopamine to motivate yourself, and you will learn the information better.

Functions of **dopamine** include **cognition**, **movement**, and **inhibition of prolactin**.

DOPAMINE:
Drug addiction
Outcomes
Psychosis
Attention
Movement
Inhibition of prolactin
Nausea
Energy

DOPAMINE RECEPTORS

While 5 dopamine receptor subtypes have been identified, many antipsychotics work primarily on the **D₂** receptor subtype (abbreviated D$_2$R) . You'll notice that D$_2$R sounds a bit like "detour," so you can think of a **psychotic** person taking a **D$_2$R from reality**.

Antipsychotics are thought to work by **blocking** the **D$_2$ receptor**.

Psychotic patients sometimes take a D$_2$R from reality.

NEUROANATOMY

Unlike serotonin (which is produced primarily in a single part of the brain), dopamine exerts various effects depending on the specific area or pathway in which it is acting. While there are eight dopaminergic pathways, we will only review the ones that are the highest-yield clinically here.

First, patients with schizophrenia have **positive symptoms** such as auditory hallucinations, paranoid delusions, and disorganization of both speech and behavior. The ability of antipsychotics to reduce positive symptoms appears to be related to opposing dopamine's action in the meso**limb**ic pathway. You can remember this association by thinking that you need **limb**s in order to do a "**thumbs-up**" sign to indicate that you feel **positive** about something.

Blocking dopamine reduces **positive symptoms** via the **mesolimbic pathway**.

*You need **limbs** to show **positivity** with a thumbs-up!*

Second, the **negative symptoms** of schizophrenia (such as apathy, blunted affect, cognitive impairment, and poverty of thought) appear related to hypofunction of dopaminergic neurons in the meso**cortical** pathway. This association makes sense, as the higher thought processes that are impacted are localized in the cerebral **cortex**.

Third, opposing the release of prolactin is a function of dopamine's effects in the **T**ubero**I**nfundibular **P**athway, which you can remember as "**T**his **I**nhibits **P**rolactin." When dopamine is blocked (such as in a patient taking antipsychotics), a side effect can be hyperprolactinemia resulting in breast development and milk release (even in males).

Dopamine inhibits prolactin via the **tuberoinfundibular pathway**.

***T**uberoInfundibular Pathway = **T**his **I**nhibits **P**rolactin.*

Fourth, dopamine's involvement in addictive disorders stems from its action in the reward pathway located in the **ventral tegmental area**. Drugs that act on this pathway (such as heroin and methamphetamines) are often highly addicting. The ventral tegmental area connects to the limbic system, which (as you will recall from neurology) contains many of the structures involved in emotion, learning, and memory. You can remember the association of the **V**entral **T**egmental **A**rea to drug addiction by thinking of the phrase "**V**ery **T**iring **A**ddiction."

Dopamine is involved in the **reward** pathway via the **ventral tegmental area**.

Ventral Tegmental Area = Very Tiring Addiction.

Finally, dopamine's effects in the **N**igro**S**triatal **P**athway primarily have to do with involuntary movement. Clinically, conditions involving the nigrostrial pathway include Parkinson's disease, stuttering, and the extrapyramidal side effects of antipsychotic medications. Fortunately, these three things can be packed away easily in the name of the pathway itself: the **N**igro**S**triatal **P**athway is involved in i**N**voluntary movements, **S**tuttering, and **P**arkinsonism.

Dopamine's effects on **movement** are linked to its role in the **nigrostriatal pathway**.

NigroStriatal Pathway = iNvoluntary movements, Stuttering, and Parkinsonism.

NOREPINEPHRINE

Norepinephrine is a key player in the **sympathetic nervous system** and its "**fight or flight**" response. (Norepinephrine is also called noradrenaline, especially in Europe. We will use the word norepinephrine in this book, although it's helpful to know both terms since certain words like "noradrenergic" are based on the other name.)

We can learn the effects of norepinephrine by imagining that we are surrounded by our enemies! In response to this threat, your body will go into sympathetic nervous system overdrive, releasing both norepinephrine and its hormone counterpart epinephrine. You may say to yourself, "Oh **FFFFFF**!" which can help you remember the functions of norepinephrine which include activating the **F**ear response, **F**ocusing your attention on the moment at hand, getting you feeling energetic and **F**ired up, shutting down less urgent functions like eating on hold (leading to a **F**asting state), reducing pain sensation through **F**eedback inhibition, and engaging a **F**ull body "fight or flight" response by raising your heart rate, upping your blood pressure, and releasing energy stores.

> **Norepinephrine** is both a neurotransmitter and a hormone that is involved in **sympathetic nervous system** activation.
>
> Think of being **surrounded by your enemies** and saying, "Oh **FFFFFF**!":
> *Fear*
> *Focus*
> *Fired up*
> *Fasting*
> *Feedback pain inhibition*
> *Full body response*

NEUROANATOMY

Let's use this situation to help us remember another fact about norepinephrine. Like serotonin and the raphe nuclei, the fact that **norepinephrine** is produced in the **locus ceruleus** is frequently tested. You can link these two things together by thinking that being **cer**-rounded makes your locus **cer**-uleus jump into action!

> **Norepinephrine** is produced in the **locus ceruleus**.
>
> Being **cer**-rounded makes your locus **cer**-uleus jump into action!

ADRENERGIC RECEPTORS

Norepinephrine mediates its effects via several adrenergic receptors, including α-1, α-2, β-1, β-2, and β-3. Each of these receptors plays a unique role which will come into play when using any of the drugs that involve norepinephrine.

α-1 adrenergic receptors are distributed throughout the body and mediate much of the **F**ull body response to norepinephrine including vasoconstriction, sweating, and release of glucose as well as the **F**ear and **F**ocusing effects in the brain. You can remember the widespread distribution of α-1 receptors by thinking that **α-1 receptors** are found **α-11 over the place**.

> **α-1 adrenergic receptors** are **widely distributed** throughout the body and brain.
>
> *α-1 receptors are found α-11 over the place.*

α-2 adrenergic receptors are unique in that they *in*activate the sympathetic nervous system (rather than activating it). This works as part of a **negative feedback loop** where release of norepinephrine not only signals the body to enter "fight or flight" mode but also prepares it for the inevitable cool down. You can remember this unique function of α-2 receptors by noting how **α-2** looks like **A–Z** to remind you that they take the sympathetic nervous system **from beginning to end** (A to Z).

> **α-2 receptors** are unique in that they **inhibit** the **sympathetic nervous system**.
>
> *α-2 takes the SNS from A–Z (it ends its effects).*

β-1 adrenergic receptors are mostly found in the **heart** where they act to increase cardiac output by raising both heart rate and stroke volume. In contrast, β-2 receptors are found primarily in the **lungs** where they work to relax the bronchioles and increase airflow. Both of these changes are helpful physiologically, as the fight or flight response requires not only extra oxygen for stressed tissues but also the ability to move this oxygen around the body quickly.

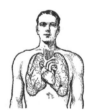

> **Beta adrenergic receptors** are located primarily in the **heart** (β-1) and **lungs** (β-2).
>
> *You beta have 1 heart and 2 lungs.*

In general, norepinephrine tends to cause constriction of smooth muscles (such as in blood vessels, the skin, and the gastrointestinal tract). In contrast, the effects of β-2 receptors are unique in that they cause *relaxation* of smooth muscles in the bronchioles. You can remember this unique effect by thinking that "it's β-2 relax."

> While **adrenergic receptors** generally cause **constriction** of smooth muscle, **β-2 receptors** cause **relaxation** of the bronchioles.
>
> *It's β-2 (better to) relax.*

ACETYLCHOLINE

Like norepinephrine and its various receptors, the different effects of **acetylcholine** (ACh) are mediated by several types of receptors. For acetylcholine, the two types to know are muscarinic and nicotinic receptors. You can remember that two different types of receptors bind to acetylcholine by thinking of it as "**I see two cholines**."

> **Acetylcholine** binds to two different receptors: **nicotinic** and **muscarinic receptors**.
>
> Think of **acetylcholine** as *I-see-two-cholines*.

MUSCARINIC RECEPTORS

Muscarinic receptors are primarily found in **peripheral organs** throughout the body. Just as the sympathetic nervous system uses norepinephrine as its neurotransmitter in the body, so too does the **parasympathetic nervous system** use acetylcholine to enact its "**feed and breed, then rest and digest**" agenda. By binding to muscarinic receptors, acetylcholine causes specific signs and symptoms that can be remembered using the kind of gross mnemonic **SLUDG-E BM** which stands for **S**alivation, **L**acrimation (tearing), **U**rination, **D**iaphoresis (sweating), **G**astrointestinal motility, **E**mesis (vomiting), **B**radycardia (slow heart rate), and **M**iosis (pupil constriction).

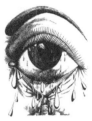

> The **parasympathetic nervous system**'s peripheral effects are largely mediated by **acetylcholine** acting at **muscarinic receptors**.
>
> *SLUDG-E BM:*
> *S*alivation
> *L*acrimation
> *U*rination
> *D*iaphoresis
> *G*astrointestinal motility
> *E*mesis
> *B*radycardia
> *M*iosis

Parasympathetic nervous system overactivation, as can occur in cases of drug overdose or pesticide exposure, make these signs and symptoms appear in excess. In these cases, an **anticholinergic medication** like **atropine** can result in improvement.

> **Atropine** is an **anticholinergic medication** that opposes the effects of acetylcholine.
>
> *At-rope-in* tries to *rope in* the effects of Acetylcholine.

NICOTINIC RECEPTORS

Nicotinic receptors are found both in the central nervous system and in the rest of the body. When acetylcholine binds to nicotinic receptors in the central nervous system it acts to promote cognitive processes such as **learning, memory, and attention**. In contrast, when acetylcholine binds to nicotinic receptors in the periphery, it acts as the neurotransmitter at the **neuromuscular junction** to lead to contraction of skeletal muscles. You can remember the two core functions of acetylcholine at nicotinic receptors ("muscle" and "memory") by visualizing a guy named **Nic** working out at the gym and using his **muscle memory**. On a clinical level, drugs that affect acetylcholine are used to treat cognitive disorders like Alzheimer's disease as well as neuromuscular diseases like myasthenia gravis.

> **Nicotinic receptors** are responsible for acetylcholine's role in **muscle contraction** and **cognition**.
>
> *Visualize **Nic** using his **muscle memory**.*

ANTICHOLINERGIC STATES

Many of the drugs used in psychiatry are antagonists at the muscarinic receptor, so it can be helpful to memorize what happens during *anti*cholinergic states as well. These signs and symptoms are the *opposite* of what is seen in the **SLUDG-E BM** mnemonic, such as dry mouth instead of salivation and constipation instead of diarrhea. Blocking nicotinic receptors can also lead to impairments in cognition and thought. A common way of remembering these wide-ranging effects is using this poem: "*Blind as a bat, dry as a bone, hot as a hare, stuck on the throne, red as a beet, heart in the zone, mad as a hatter when ACh goes.*"

Let's break this down bit by bit. "Blind as a bat" refers to blurry vision (from inability to constrict the pupil or change lens shape, both of which are done by the parasympathetic nervous system), "dry as a bone" refers to dry eyes, dry mouth, and decreased sweating, "hot as a hare" refers to fever, "stuck on the throne" refers to urinary retention and constipation, "red as a beet" refers to flushing of the skin, "heart in the zone" refers to tachycardia, and "mad as a hatter" refers to delirium and cognitive impairment.

> **Anticholinergic states** present with signs of **parasympathetic nervous system inactivation** and **delirium**.
>
> *Remember "**Blind as a bat…**"*

NEUROANATOMY

We've talked about serotonin and the raphe nuclei and norepinephrine and the locus ceruleus already, but it's time for one more! Acetylcholine is produced in a region of the brain known as the **nucleus basalis of Meynert**. Accordingly, damage to this region is seen in disorders like Alzheimer's disease that are characterized by memory dysfunction.  To remember the association of **memory** and the nucleus basalis, picture a scene from a hypothetical action movie in which the villain has started a countdown timer to launch nukes from his **nuclear base**. A secret agent is sweating while trying to **remember** the codes to cancel a nuclear launch as a countdown timer ticks away behind him (only 90 seconds left!). This scenario can help you link the **nucleus basalis** to the concept of **memory** as well as the neurotransmitter acetylcholine.

> The **nucleus basalis of Meynert** is rich in **acetylcholine** and is involved in **memory**.
>
> Picture a secret agent trying to **remember** cancel codes on a **nuclear base**.

HISTAMINE

When most people hear **histamine**, they think of **allergies**, not neurotransmitters. While it's true that histamine is the key molecule involved in the inflammatory response to allergens, once you first see the effect of using **antihistamines** like diphenhydramine (Benadryl) to make a dog **sleep** through a long car trip, you'll never forget that histamine is also a neurotransmitter with effects on the brain and behavior!

Histamine's mental effects primarily involve alertness and the sleep-wake cycle. The cerebral cortex depends upon a constant stream of histamine for activation, so if you cut off that supply by taking an antihistamine, the cortex shuts down and a feeling of tiredness is produced. For this reason, several antihistamines are available as **hypnotics** or drugs that help someone sleep.

The effects of histamine on both sleep and allergies occur at the H_1 **receptor** in particular. (Other histamine receptors exist as well, such as the H_2 receptor which is involved in **stomach acid** production. For this book, we'll look primarily at the psychoactive effects of histamine at the H_1 receptor.) You can remember the two clinically relevant functions of histamine at this receptor by writing it as H_1**S+A**-mine to remind you that the H_1 receptor is involved in **S**leep + **A**llergies.

> Drugs that block **histamine at the H_1 receptor** are helpful for **sleep** and **allergies**.
>
> H_1**S+A**-mine: the H_1 receptor is involved in **S**leep + **A**llergies.

Histamine's cognitive effects are due to histamine receptors located **centrally** in the brain, while its role in allergies occurs at histamine receptors distributed **peripherally** in the body. First generation antihistamines such as diphenhydramine work *both* peripherally and in the central nervous system, so they are used not only to combat allergies but also for their sedative effect. In contrast, newer antihistamines such as loratadine (Claritin) do not cross the blood-brain barrier and are selective for only peripheral sites, making them "non-drowsy" allergy fighters.

OPIOIDS

Opioids are a group of compounds that bind to the opioid receptors in the brain. There are many naturally occurring opioids such as endorphins or enkephalins which help to regulate **pain perception**. (A runner's high is a well-known example of your body attempting to regulate pain perception in response to stress.) However, there are many exogenous drugs which bind strongly to the opioid receptor, and these are used both clinically for pain control as well as recreationally for their narcotic effect.

The human race enjoys opioids so much that entire wars have been waged over access to them. One example is the Opium Wars which took place in China in the 1800's. While opioids were far from the only factor in the war, this association can help us to remember their functions. Let's focus on one guy in the following picture, the **ARMED C**olonialist, to help us remember the functions of opioids:

A is for Analgesia. Analgesia (pain relief) is the best known function of opioids. Drugs that hit the opioid receptor are used both medically and recreationally to relieve pain.

R is for Respiratory depression. Opioids slow the breathing rate, especially in higher doses. This makes opioid overdose a potentially lethal situation.

M is for Miosis. Miosis (or constriction of the pupils) is a sign of opioid intoxication. A finding of **pinpoint pupils** in an obtunded patient is concerning for opioid overdose.

E is for Euphoria. Opioids cause a feeling of bliss and well-being. However, in some people the desire for this feeling can become all-consuming and lead to an addiction.

D is for Drowsiness. Sedation and slowing of mental speed can occur with opioid use.

C is for Constipation. Opioids cause constipation as a side effect, so people taking opioids for chronic pain will often need stool softeners to have a bowel movement.

> **Opioids** are best known for their **painkilling** effects, although they have other **physical and psychological functions** as well.
>
> **ARMED** Colonialist:
> **A**nalgesia
> **R**espiratory depression
> **M**iosis
> **E**uphoria
> **D**rowsiness
> **C**onstipation

Like most neurotransmitters, there are a variety of opioid receptors in the brain that each have their own functions, including δ, κ, μ, nociceptin, and ζ. Morphine and most of the other opioids we will cover seem to exert their analgesic effect by binding to the **mu** (μ) receptor subtype. Try to remember "**mu** for **m**orphine!"

> Many **opioids** exert their **analgesic effect** by binding to the **mu opioid receptor**.
>
> **Mu** for **m**orphine!

GABA

The next two neurotransmitters we will talk about are, in essence, a neuron's "on" and "off" switches. We'll start with the "off" switch GABA. When you hear **GABA**, think **inhibitory**! GABA acts to *lower* excitation of the post-synaptic neuron. Clinically, this leads to a state of **sedation** and **relaxation**. To get this into your mind, picture the most boring lecturer you have ever had and how they would just **gab** on and on and on. Next, picture

Gab gab gab...

yourself falling asleep while listening to this **gabber**. As you fall asleep, you relax both physically and mentally. You feel more at ease, and a feeling of calm comes over you. Your muscles unclench, your breathing slows, and your mind is free of racing thoughts. If you can hold this image in your mind, you can remember the effects of GABA on the body and mind!

By inducing calmness and relaxation, GABAergic drugs such as **barbiturates** and **benzodiazepines** are useful for short-term treatment of insomnia, anxiety, and agitation. Their inhibitory properties have also made them useful for treating seizures. In addition to their clinical use, substances that hit the GABA receptor (like alcohol) are also used on a recreational basis to reduce anxiety, as can be seen whenever someone pours themselves a drink to de-stress after a long day at work.

> **GABA** is the primary **neuronal inhibitory neurotransmitter**.
>
> *GABA is like a **gabber** who just goes on and on and puts everyone to **sleep**.*

GLUTAMATE

If GABA is a neuron's "off" switch, then glutamate is its "on" switch! Glutamate binding to a post-synaptic neuron almost always leads to **excitation** of that cell. How this translates clinically is still unclear, however. It would be wrong to think that glutamate  causes effects that are exactly opposite to what is observed with GABA (even though one is excitatory and the other is inhibitory), as these terms refer specifically to the effect that these neurotransmitters have on the post-synaptic neuron, not to their more general cognitive and physiologic effects. Overall, just like you can associate **GABA** with a long-winded **gabber** who puts you to sleep, you should link gluta**mate** to the idea of **mate**-ing which (most people would likely agree) is quite excitatory!

> **Glutamate** is the primary **neuronal excitatory neurotransmitter**.
>
> *Glutamate-ing is **excitatory** for most people!*

Like many of the neurotransmitters we have discussed, glutamate binds to various receptors, each with their own functions. Specifically, glutamate can bind to **NMDA** receptors, **AMPA** receptors, and **kainate** receptors. NMDA and AMPA receptors are the best understood and have the most clinical applications, so we will focus our attention there for now!

NMDA receptors are clinically significant for their involvement in a variety of drugs and diseases that all involve higher cognitive processes such as consciousness, thought, and memory. You can remember the main classes of drugs that bind to the NMDA receptor by packing them into the name **NMDA** itself: **N**itrous oxide (an anesthetic commonly known as "laughing gas"), **M**emory enhancers (like those used to treat dementia), **D**issociative hallucinogens (like ketamine and phencyclidine which induce dream-like mentation with distortions of sight and sound), and **A**lcohol (which is a notoriously "dirty drug," binding not only to GABA receptors as previously discussed but also to NMDA and other receptors as well!).

NMDA receptors are involved in **consciousness, thought, and memory**.

*Drugs that bind to **NMDA** receptors:*
Nitrous oxide
Memory enhancers
Dissociative hallucinogens
Alcohol

In contrast, AMPA receptors are clinically important for their role in propagating seizures. For this reason, AMPA receptor antagonists can be used as **anticonvulsants**, including a few that are commonly used in psychiatry (such as lamotrigine and topiramate).

OXYTOCIN

Oxytocin is a neuropeptide hormone that plays an important role in interpersonal bonding, sexuality, and reproduction. It is released during many forms of social interaction (and particularly during skin-to-skin physical contact and sex!). While it is sometimes called the "love hormone," this is an oversimplification and undersells the many other functions that oxytocin plays in the brain and body. You can remember the roles that oxytocin has by calling it **BLOC**-ytocin:

B is for Birth. Oxytocin stimulates uterine contractions and helps to speed along the process of childbirth. Medications that bind to oxytocin receptors can help to induce labor, while drugs that block oxytocin will suppress premature labor.

L is for Lactation. Following childbirth, oxytocin helps to release milk during breast feeding. (This is in comparison to prolactin, which we talked about in the context of dopamine, that helps with milk *production*.)

O is for Orgasm. Oxytocin plays a role in human sexuality, including initial arousal, stimulation, and orgasm.

C is for Connection. Oxytocin's role in non-reproductive socialization is increasingly being recognized. Oxytocin is released in greater amounts during many forms of social interaction, including talking with a friend to skin-to-skin contact (even petting a dog seems to increase it!). While oxytocin has historically been associated with prosocial emotions such as trust, bonding, and altruism, recent research suggests that it is  implicated in feelings like envy, disgust, and even *schadenfreude* (the happy feeling one gets when seeing the misfortune of others). The more accurate understanding of oxytocin is that it plays a role in *all* **social emotions**, not just positive ones!

Oxytocin is a neuropeptide that is involved in **reproduction** and **social connection**.

BLOC-ytoxin:
Birth
Lactation
Orgasm
Connection

OREXIN

Orexin (also named hypocretin) was only recently discovered in the late 1990s. As one of the newest kids on the block, orexin's effects are still being worked out. However, it seems pretty clear at this point that orexin makes you **hungry** and **awake**. Orexin will only pop up a few times in this book, but it's possible that with more time and research it will find its own niche in pharmacology! You can remember the effects of **go-rex**-in by thinking that it helps you to be on-the-**go** (rather than sleeping) and makes you hungry like a T. **rex**!

Orexin is a neuropeptide that increases **appetite** and **wakefulness**.

Go-rex-in keeps you on-the-go (awake) and hungry like a T. rex.

PUTTING IT ALL TOGETHER

And that's it for the neurotransmitters! There are many more neurotransmitters than this, but we'll stick to just the most clinically significant ones discussed here. Because they are so foundational to the study of psychopharmacology, take a moment to review each of the neurotransmitters we've discussed and try to embed them into your mind one more time. It can seem like a lot of memorizing (and it is), but having a solid foundation in the basics of serotonin, dopamine, norepinephrine, acetylcholine, GABA, glutamate, histamine, opioids, oxytocin, and orexin will serve you well during your studies!

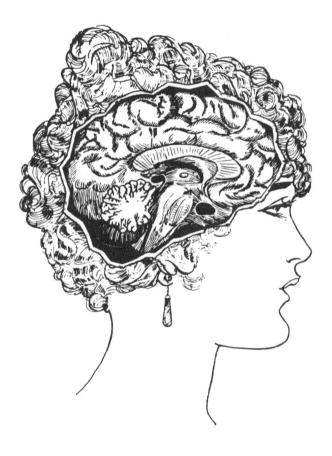

REVIEW QUESTIONS

1. A 20 y/o F is prescribed a drug intended to treat depression by augmenting a specific neurotransmitter in the brain. Side effects of this drug include nausea, diarrhea, and decreased libido. The neurotransmitter affected by this drug is produced primarily in which area of the brain?
   A. Locus ceruleus
   B. Raphe nuclei
   C. Nucleus accumbens
   D. Basal ganglia
   E. Ventral tegmental area

2. A 28 y/o M is released from the psychiatric hospital following an acute psychotic episode. Several months later, he comes into clinic complaining that he is developing breasts, as pictured below:

   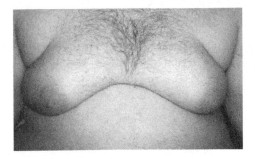

   This is likely due to a medication's effects on which of the following areas of the brain?
   A. Mesolimbic pathway
   B. Mesocortical pathway
   C. Tuberoinfundibular pathway
   D. Ventral tegmental area
   E. Nigrostriatal pathway

3. A 31 y/o M is brought into the hospital by paramedics who report that the patient was found non-responsive in his bathroom with an empty unlabeled bottle of pills nearby. Vital signs are normal except for a respiratory rate of 4 breaths per minute. On exam, the patient has notable pupillary constriction in both eyes. An EKG is normal. What medication did the patient most likely take?
   A. An antidepressant
   B. An antipsychotic
   C. A mood stabilizer
   D. A stimulant
   E. An analgesic

4. An 18 y/o F college student is brought into the hospital complaining of feeling "like my head is going to explode." She is profoundly confused. On exam, she has noticeable facial flushing and profuse sweating. Loose feces are noted in her pants. Vital signs show HR 110 and T 101.7°F. Neurological exam reveals muscular twitching and hyperreflexia. What neurotransmitter is most likely in excess?
    A. Acetylcholine
    B. Serotonin
    C. Norepinephrine
    D. GABA
    E. Glutamate

5. A 72 y/o M is diagnosed with Alzheimer's disease and prescribed a drug which boosts levels of acetylcholine not only on the brain but throughout the body as well. Which of the following is *least* likely to be seen once he begins taking this drug?
    A. Slowed gastrointestinal motility
    B. Decreased heart rate
    C. Lower blood pressure
    D. Prolonged muscle contraction
    E. Improved memory

6. A 35 y/o F is experiencing recurrent difficulty falling asleep at night. She goes to see her primary care doctor and requests a prescription for a medication that will help to induce sleep. Which of the following neurotransmitters is *least* likely to be involved in a drug that helps to induce sleep?
    A. Histamine
    B. Opioids
    C. GABA
    D. Orexin
    E. Oxytocin
    F. All of the above are likely to be involved in a drug that induces sleep

1. **The best answer is B.** Based on the drug's side effect profile and the fact that it is being used to treat depression, you can infer that the drug works on serotonin which is released in the raphe nuclei. Locus ceruleus (answer A) is the source of norepinephrine. The nucleus accumbens and ventral tegmental area are both associated with dopamine (answers C and E). Several neurotransmitters, including GABA, dopamine, and acetylcholine, are active in the basal ganglia (answer D), but it is not the site of serotonin production.

2. **The best answer is C.** Given the patient's recent psychotic episode, an antipsychotic which blocks dopamine was likely given. Blocking dopamine results in increased prolactin. This can result in gynecomastia and/or milk letdown, which can be confusing or embarrassing for the patient. This is due to dopamine's effects in the tuberoinfundibular pathway. The mesolimbic pathway (answer A) is involved in positive symptoms, while the mesocortical pathway (answer B) is implicated in negative symptoms. The ventral tegmental area (answer D) is thought to be related to the addictive potential of certain substances, while alterations in the nigrostriatal pathway (answer E) are involved in involuntary movements such as parkinsonism.

3. **The best answer is E.** There are a couple of things in the question stem that should point you to an excess of opioids in the brain, specifically the slowed breathing rate and the pupillary constriction. None of the other medication classes are associated with respiratory depression and pupillary constriction in overdose.

4. **The best answer is B.** This is a classic picture of serotonin syndrome that you should know, including flushing, diaphoresis, altered mental status, tachycardia, fever, tremor, and hyperreflexia. In particular, the loose feces is a sign of diarrhea which is one of the hallmark findings of serotonin syndrome. Excesses in the other neurotransmitters would not result in the clinical picture seen here.

5. **The best answer is A.** Given that it is part of the parasympathetic nervous system, acetylcholine will tend to *increase* the rate of digestion, not slow it down (remember "feed and breed, then rest and digest"!). A slow heart rate (answer B) and lower blood pressure (answer C) are both mediated by acetylcholine at muscarinic receptors, while muscle contraction (answer D) and memory (answer E) are related to acetylcholine acting at nicotinic receptors.

6. **The best answer is E.** Oxytocin does not have effects on sleep and is instead involved in reproductive events such as birth, lactation, and orgasm as well as social emotions. GABA inhibits neuronal activity and will often produce feelings of sedation (answer C). Histamine antagonists are also used to induce sleep (answer A). Orexin promotes wakefulness, so blocking this receptor is a potential target for sleep induction (answer D). Opioids produce drowsiness as a side effect and could be used for sleep induction, although this should not be done in real-world clinical settings due to the dangers of addiction and abuse (answer B).

3 ANTIDEPRESSANTS

Now that you have been introduced to each of the major neurotransmitters, we're ready to talk about the drugs themselves. The first class we will cover are **antidepressants** which are among the most widely prescribed drugs in all of medicine, with over 10% of all adults in the United States reporting having taken an antidepressant in the past month.

Almost all antidepressants impact **serotonin** to some degree, which makes sense given this neurotransmitter's key role in emotional processing and feelings of satisfaction. The most common class of antidepressants are the **selective serotonin reuptake inhibitors** (SSRIs) which increase the amount of serotonin that is available in the synaptic cleft. In addition to SSRIs, there are also a few of other antidepressant types including **serotonin-norepinephrine reuptake inhibitors** (SNRIs), **tricyclic antidepressants** (TCAs), and **monoamine oxidase inhibitor** (MAOIs) as well as a grab bag of "atypical" antidepressants that don't fit neatly into any of these categories.

In this chapter, we'll first introduce the most commonly used medications in each class. When we talk about specific drugs, we will try to focus on what sets it apart from its peers (like why you would want to use one drug over another). From there, we will talk about the overall principles that you should consider when starting a patient on antidepressants.

One final note: from time to time, you may see additional terms like serotonin reuptake inhibitor (SRI) or norepinephrine reuptake inhibitor (NRI) used as well. These are broader terms that encompass *all* medications that inhibit the reuptake of that particular neurotransmitter, as opposed to terms like SSRI which are more specific to drugs that *only* involve serotonin. Keep in mind that these terms are related, but ultimately distinct, concepts.

And with that, let's get to know the antidepressants!

ANTIDEPRESSANT EFFECTS

So what do antidepressants *do* exactly? This is a much trickier question than it initially appears, but let's start with what we know. Most antidepressants work by increasing synaptic levels of serotonin in the brain. While there is no evidence that depression results from any sort of "**chemical imbalance**," the fact remains that medications that boost serotonin are effective at reducing depression symptoms in the majority of people who take them.

How does serotonin do this? One theory suggests that it has to do with the way that depressed people process information. To put it simply, people with depression see the world differently. Depression causes a tendency to focus on negative, rather than positive, stimuli. When presented with a list of words, for example, people with depression are more likely to focus on words like "hate" or "pain" rather than "love" or "comfort." When shown a variety of faces, a depressed person will fixate on people with negative facial expressions while blocking out those with positive expressions. This phenomenon is referred to as a **negative affective bias**: *negative* for sad, *affective* for emotional, and *bias* for being drawn to certain stimuli over others.

Example of a **negative affective bias** in a patient with **depression**.

What is perplexing about serotonergic medications is that they increase serotonin within *minutes* of taking the drug, but the effect on depression isn't seen until weeks or months later. Why do antidepressants take so long to work? While antidepressants don't instantly cure depression, they *do* cause an immediate decrease in negative affective biases. Tellingly, this change in perception perfectly coincides with the drug's serotonin-boosting effect in the brain. Within minutes of taking an antidepressant, people with depression are more able to remember positive words and are less fixated on sad parts of images. These effects are seen even when people *without* depression are given these medications, suggesting a primary drug effect.

By targeting the negative affective biases found in depression, antidepressants set the stage for a *gradual* unlearning of depressive thought patterns. Like any form of learning, this process will not happen overnight. Rather, it will take days, weeks, months, or (in cases of severe depression) even years to learn to see the world as a more hopeful, less threatening place. In fact, studies have found that the extent to which an antidepressant will ultimately help someone can be predicted by how much it changes their emotional processing within even the first few days of treatment.

Ultimately, there is no getting around the fact that antidepressants are not simple, one-shot drugs that target depression like a silver bullet. They don't work in the way that many people think, leading to dashed hopes and unmet expectations. While this can be frustrating, there is a silver lining in knowing that, by catalyzing the process of learning new ways of thinking and interpreting the world, antidepressants can create lasting changes in a way that one-shot drugs rarely can.

So what are the downsides of using serotonin? Let's review its other functions using our **SPAROW**-tonin mnemonic so we know what side effects to expect here. These include changes in **S**leep and energy, **P**latelet dysfunction (mostly in patients already at high risk), **A**bdominal upset including nausea and diarrhea, **R**eproductive effects like low libido and anorgasmia, the risk of **O**verdose and serotonin syndrome, and finally the possibility of **W**eight gain when used long-term. Some side effects, like nausea and diarrhea, are most noticeable in the first few weeks of starting the drug and can be reduced by starting at a low dose and gradually increasing. In contrast, other side effects, like sexual dysfunction, will generally persist as long as the patient keeps taking the drug.

ANTIDEPRESSANT DISCONTINUATION SYNDROME

Serotonergic medications are also associated with a **discontinuation syndrome** when the drug is stopped abruptly. You can use the word **FINISH** to remember the unpleasant symptoms that this syndrome involves, including **F**lu-like symptoms and a general sense of malaise, **I**nsomnia and disturbed sleep, **N**ausea and upset stomach, **I**mbalance including light-headedness and vertigo, **S**ensory disturbances such as tingling and electrical sensations in the head (sometimes called "brain zaps"), and **H**yperarousal including increased  energy and anxiety. These symptoms generally appear quickly after the drug is stopped and then resolve slowly over the next few weeks. While not everyone experiences a discontinuation syndrome, it is common enough that it is worth counseling your patients to avoid abruptly stopping their medications and instead aim for a slow taper over several weeks or even months!

Serotonergic medications can be associated with a **discontinuation syndrome**.

FINISH:
Flu-like symptoms
Insomnia
Nausea
Imbalance
Sensory disturbances
Hyperarousal

SEROTONIN-SPECIFIC REUPTAKE INHIBITORS

Now that we have a better understanding of serotonin's role in treating depression, let's take a look at the individual SSRIs to understand what makes each one unique!

FLUOXETINE

Fluoxetine (Prozac) is one of the more **activating** SSRIs, with patients often feeling increased energy and at times even some jitteriness. In addition, fluoxetine has one of the **longest half-lives** of any SSRI. Why is this important? Because fluoxetine (as well as its metabolite norfluoxetine) stay in the bloodstream longer than other SSRIs, it can be a good option for people who aren't great at remembering to take medications regularly. There also tend to be fewer rebound side effects because the drug effectively tapers itself. On the other hand, because it lingers in the system so long, you have to be careful not to add another serotonergic drug too fast to avoid causing serotonin syndrome. By focusing on the "flu" part of the name, you can remember that fluoxetine, like the flu, generally lasts about 1 to 2 weeks. So when you see **flu**oxetine, think of the **flu** and the **week** you spent in bed when you got it.

Fluoxetine has a very **long half-life**.

Like the **flu**, **flu**oxetine generally lasts about **1-2 weeks**.

PAROXETINE

Paroxetine (Paxil) is more **sedating** than most SSRIs, so try to dose it at bedtime. In addition, paroxetine has been linked to birth defects, so it should be avoided in pregnant patients. Finally, in contrast to fluoxetine, paroxetine has a very **short half-life** of less than 24 hours! This means that any rebound effects will likely happen much faster and will be more uncomfortable than, say, fluoxetine. How to remember this important fact? When traveling by wagon, you will move much **faster** with a **pair** of **ox**en than with a single ox. Use this to remember that **parox**etine is a **fast** SSRI.

Paroxetine has a **short half-life** (less than 1 day) and is very **rapidly absorbed**.

A **pair** of **ox**en moves **faster** than a single ox.

SERTRALINE

The serotonergic effect of sertraline (Zoloft) should be is easy to remember, as the "**ser**" of **ser**otonin is built right into the name! Interestingly, sertraline also appears to inhibit the dopamine transporter, so some have argued that it should be classified as an SDRI. In general, however, it is classified as an SSRI.

In terms of what makes this drug unique, two things stand out. First, sertraline can have harsher **gastrointestinal** side effects such as nausea and diarrhea compared to other SSRIs, which has earned it the endearing nickname of "**squirt**-raline" among  patients. Tell patients to take it with a meal to help aid absorption and decrease GI effects. Second, sertraline is one of the safest SSRIs for **pregnant** or **breastfeeding** patients, as less of the drug gets into the fetal circulation or breast milk. If you use your imagination, the mnemonic **squirt**raline can help you this connection as well!

> **Sertraline** has **more GI side effects** but is safer when **pregnant** or **breastfeeding**.
>
> *Think **squirt**-raline to remember **diarrhea** and **breast milk**.*

CITALOPRAM AND ESCITALOPRAM

These next two SSRIs are basically twins. Citalopram (Celexa) is the base drug, with escitalopram (Lexapro) being a purified version of its S-enantiomer which is the active form. This means that a 10 mg dose of escitalopram is equivalent to a 20 mg dose of citalopram. Dosing aside, citalopram and escitalopram is basically the same. Both are very "**clean**" SSRIs that don't have many drug interactions. However, the downside is that they can **prolong the QTc interval** which is a marker of the electric properties of the heart. Theoretically, QT prolongation can increase the risk of arrhythmias and even sudden death, although there is a lack of data linking either of these drugs to *actual* cases of harm. Nevertheless, it is still recommended to track EKGs for patients taking these drugs and to avoid prescribing it to anyone with pre-existing arrhythmias. You can remember this association by thinking of a **car seat** to remind you that **seat**-alopram and es-**seat**-alopram require an electro-**car**-diogram.

> **Citalopram** and **escitalopram** can cause **QTc prolongation**.
>
> *Think of a **car seat** to remind you that **seat**-alopram and es-**seat**-alopram require an electro-**car**-diogram.*

FLUVOXAMINE

The last SSRI we will talk about is fluvoxamine (Luvox). In contrast to other SSRIs (and especially citalopram and escitalopram), it is very "**messy**" and has many drug-drug interactions. Because of the complications this introduces (such as having to re-dose other medications that the patient is taking), it is not frequently used these days.

SEROTONIN-NOREPINEPHRINE REUPTAKE INHIBITORS

While serotonin is commonly used during treatment of depression, it is not the only neurotransmitter at our disposal. As you will recall from Chapter 2, norepinephrine is associated with increased **F**ocus and energy from getting **F**ired up, both of which could be helpful in treating depression. Indeed, drugs that boost both norepinephrine and serotonin (known as **serotonin-norepinephrine reuptake inhibitors** or SNRIs) do appear to be effective antidepressants while also having positive effects on other conditions like anxiety.

However, you might be asking yourself why increasing norepinephrine is helpful for treating anxiety. After all, isn't **F**ear one of the effects that norepinephrine has in the brain? Couldn't this make anxiety and depression *worse*? While this is a completely logical conclusion, for whatever reason norepinephrine reuptake inhibitors actually *help* anxiety and depression. There are no good explanations for this "noradrenergic paradox" yet, although it is possible that norepinephrine may have different effects depending on whether it is arrives in a "flash flood" (as in sympathetic nervous system activation) or as a "steady trickle" (as in long-term medication administration).

The downside of norepinephrine involvement is that the **F**ull body response can add some additional side effects over what is seen from serotonin alone. Increases in **heart rate** and **blood pressure** can be seen with norepinephrine reuptake inhibitors which requires careful monitoring, especially at higher doses.

VENLAFAXINE AND DESVENLAFAXINE
The next two drugs we will talk about boost not only norepinephrine but serotonin as well, making them serotonin-norepinephrine reuptake inhibitors or SNRIs.

We'll first go over venlafaxine (Effexor) You can remember the involvement of **N**orepinephrine by focusing on the **en** sound of v**en**lafaxine. So how does the presence of norepinephrine impact treatment? When venlafaxine first came out, there was excitement that the dual mechanism would result in a more effective antidepressant, or at least one with a unique profile of positive effects. Despite the hype, it has become increasingly clear that venlafaxine is more similar to most SSRIs than it is different. In fact, at low to moderate doses, this drug is **basically an SSRI**, as the norepinephrine transporter is only affected at higher doses.

If anything, the main way that venlafaxine has differentiated itself is in terms of new side effects, with **hypertension** being seen at higher doses. In most cases, the vascular effects are short-lived, but in some cases venlafaxine can induce sustained hypertension. Because of this, close monitoring of blood pressure is a requirement.

> **Venlafaxine** is an **serotonin-norepinephrine reuptake inhibitor** that can cause **hypertension** at higher doses.
>
> **Ven**lafaxine impacts **n**orepinephrine at higher doses and can cause hyper**ten**sion.

Like paroxetine, venlafaxine has a **short half-life** of less than 24 hours, even in extended release formulations! Because of this, it tends to produce more severe discontinuation side effects than, say, fluoxetine. In some patients, the rebound syndrome can be so severe that it takes months to fully taper them off of the drug. Keep this in mind if you will be taking someone off venlafaxine, and be prepared to go very slowly! To remember this side effect, focus on the **fax** part of venla-**fax**-ine. This should remind you that it is **faster** to send a **fax** compared to regular mail. However, even with the availability of newer and better technology like emails, fax machines are still around, showing that they **take a long time to go away**!

> **Venlafaxine** is **rapidly metabolized** with unpleasant **discontinuation effects**.
>
> Like a **fax** machine, venla-**fax**-ine is **fast** but **takes a long time to go away**!

Most of the venlafaxine that a patient takes is converted to its active metabolite desvenlafaxine which is itself available as a drug (marketed as Pristiq). Like citalopram and escitalopram, the efficacy and side effects of these drugs are basically the same.

DULOXETINE

Another common SNRI is duloxetine (Cymbalta). Unlike venlafaxine (which is basically an SSRI until you hit higher doses), duloxetine impacts serotonin and norepinephrine more evenly at all doses! This means that the same warnings about blood pressure apply here as with venlafaxine. Focus on the **dual** part of **dual**-oxetine to remind you of the **dual** mechanisms at play. Duloxetine has another unique feature which helps to differentiate it from other antidepressants. In addition to treating depression, duloxetine can also help with **chronic pain** conditions such as neuropathic pain or fibromyalgia, as it seems to lessen pain sensation to some degree. You can remember this **dull**ing effect by thinking of it whenever you see **dull**-oxetine.

> **Duloxetine** is a **serotonin-norepinephrine reuptake inhibitor** that not only treats depression but can be used for **chronic pain** as well.
>
> **Dual**-oxetine has a **dual** mechanism.
> **Dull**-oxetine helps to **dull** the pain.

MILNACIPRAN AND LEVOMILNACIPRAN

The final two SNRIs we will talk about are milnacipran (Savella) and levomilnacipran (Fetzima). (Like escitalopram, levomilnacipran a purified enantiomer of milnacipran, but the two can generally be treated similarly.) Compared to other SNRIs, milnacipran has **strong effects on norepinephrine** (versus the weak effects of venlafaxine and the moderate effects of duloxetine). However, this doesn't translate into much clinically, with the same benefits (pain relief) and same side effects (high blood pressure), so there is not much reason to use (levo)milnacipran over its less expensive alternatives.

"ATYPICAL" ANTIDEPRESSANTS

In addition to SSRIs and SNRIs, there are several other medications that have been useful as antidepressants. They don't fit as neatly into discrete mechanistic classes as SSRIs or SNRIs, so they are often referred to as "other" or "atypical" antidepressants.

BUPROPION

If adding norepinephrine into the mix works for depression, why not try dopamine as well? As you'll recall from Chapter 2, **motivation** and **attention** are core functions of dopamine which are both lost in depression. Could boosting dopamine help to reverse these symptoms? Out of this thought came a drug called bupropion (Wellbutrin).

Unlike the other antidepressants we've studied thus far, bupropion doesn't have significant effects on serotonin receptors. Instead, it works as an **norepinephrine-dopamine reuptake inhibitor** (NDRI). Despite the lack of serotonin involvement, studies show that it is equally effective at treating depression as its SSRI and SNRI counterparts. You can remember this mechanism by focusing on the "**bu**" part of **bu**propion and associate it with the word "**bu**tane". The word "**bu**tane" (if you misspell it slightly) will help you to link "**bu**" to "**DA-NE**," which represents **D**op**A**mine and **N**or**E**pinephrine.

Bupropion boosts **dopamine** and **norepinephrine** but lacks serotonin involvement.

*Bu*propion = *D*op*A*mine + *N*or*E*pinephrine = *Bu-DA-NE* (butane).

"**Budane**" can also help us remember two unique features of bupropion. First, the fire from a butane lighter should make you think of something **hot** and **steamy**: sex! Use this to remind yourself that bupropion does not have significant sexual side effects (owing to its lack of serotonin involvement) and may even improve sexual function for some patients! Given that sexual side effects are the number one reason why people stop treatment with an antidepressant, this is an incredibly valuable option for some patients.

Second, bupropion has been shown to help people **quit smoking** (it is marketed for this indication under the trade name Zyban). Bupropion and its metabolites have effects at the nicotinic receptors as well, which may account for this action. Visualize using a butane lighter to **light a cigarette** to remember this important association (more on this in Chapter 10).

Bupropion has **no sexual side effects** and can be used for **smoking cessation.**

A *butane lighter* is *hot*, like bupropion's lack of *sexual side effects*.
It can also be used to *light cigarettes.*

So what's the downside to all of this depression-busting, sex-crazed, cigarette-quitting excitement? By virtue of its excitatory properties, bupropion has a tendency to lower the **seizure** threshold. This is particularly troublesome for patients with bulimia nervosa who are engaging in frequent vomiting, as this can cause electrolyte imbalances that further raise the risk of seizure. For that reason, giving bupropion to a bulimic patient is **absolutely contraindicated**.

> **Bupropion** has **no sexual side effects** and can be used for **smoking cessation**. However, it can also increase risk of the **seizures in patients with bulimia**.
>
> *Bupropion should be avoided in patients with bulimia.*

MIRTAZAPINE

Mirtazapine (Remeron) has a unique mechanism of action for an antidepressant, as it works as an **α-2 receptor antagonist**. This means that it *inhibits* an *inhibitor* of the sympathetic nervous system, resulting in *increased* sympathetic output overall. You can remember this unique mechanism by thinking of it as mirt-**α-2**-apine to remind yourself that it is an **α-2** receptor antagonist.

> **Mirtazapine** is an **α-2 receptor antagonist** that works as an **antidepressant**.
>
> *Mirt-**α-2**-apine is an **α-2** receptor antagonist.*

Mirtazapine has two major side effects to know. **Sedation** is common due to mirtazapine's interactions with histamine receptors. While this is an inconvenient side effect for some, for other patients (such as those struggling with insomnia) it can be a major selling point! Paradoxically, sedation is more prevalent at *lower* doses, as the antihistamine effect is seen at *lower* doses while the **F**ired up effect of norepinephrine is mostly seen at *higher* doses.

The second major side effect of mirtazapine is **increased appetite**. Like sedation, this side effect is a double-edged sword: some people won't appreciate the weight gain, while others (such as patients with cancer or AIDS who struggle to keep weight on) will welcome the effects on appetite. (Mirtazapine also tends to decrease nausea, in contrast to most SSRIs!)

You can remember both of these associations if you change the name to **meal**-ta**zzz**apine! This will remind you that this drug makes you want to eat a **meal** and that it will help patients to catch some **zzz**'s.

> **Mirtazapine** can cause increased **appetite**, **weight gain**, and **sedation**.
>
> *Meal-ta**zzz**apine makes you want to eat a **meal** and is **sedating**.*

TRAZODONE

While trazodone (brand name Desyrel, but everyone just calls it trazodone) was initially marketed as an antidepressant, it is now used primarily as a **sleeping aid**. This is because its sedative effects are seen at lower doses (starting at around 25 mg), while its antidepressant potential is not realized until at least 150 mg. Therefore, to get any effect on depression, patients are on such high doses that they are often too sedated to get much done. Even dosing at night does not fully prevent this, as many people report a "hangover" effect the next day. Its effects on sleep seem to work best in patients with depression, but it can also be used as all-purpose sleeping pill.

Aside from sedation, trazodone has a particularly dreaded side effect: **priapism**, which is defined as an erection lasting at least four hours. Priapism is a **medical emergency**, as blood flow to the engorged organ gets compromised after a while, leading to ischemia, tissue loss, and even gangrene in some cases. Because of the emergent nature of priapism, it's worth counseling your patients (even your female patients – priapism can happen in either sex) to go to the nearest emergency room should they experience this side effect. You can remember the association of trazodone with both sedation and priapism by thinking of it as tra**zzz**o-**bone**.

The Greek god Priapus. Eek.

Trazodone is useful as a **sleep aid** but can cause **priapism**, a medical emergency.

*Think of trazodone as tra**zzz**o-**bone** to remember **sedation** and **priapism**.*

Mechanistically, trazodone is a very "messy" drug, as it appears to not only inhibit serotonin reuptake but also act as either an agonist or an antagonist at various 5-HT receptors directly. You will likely never be asked about the mechanism.

NEFAZODONE

Nefazodone (Serzone) is another "messy" drug that, like trazodone, not only inhibits serotonin reuptake but also interacts with various 5-HT receptors in various ways. Nefazodone is not used much anymore, as it is associated with a rare but potentially deadly side effect of **liver failure**. Even for patients who survive, a liver transplant may be needed. Because there are so many other antidepressants with equal efficacy that *don't* involve the risk of death, nefazodone is rarely prescribed. You can think of **nefa**-zodone as having **nefa**-rious intentions towards the liver to remember this side effect.

VILAZODONE

Vilazodone (Viibryd) is a newer antidepressant that works not only as an SSRI but also as a **partial agonist** at the serotonin receptor. (Recall from Chapter 2 that partial agonists activate receptors but to a lesser degree than a full agonist.) This means that it increases the amount of serotonin in the synapse while also ensuring that the receptors don't get oversaturated. You can remember this unique effect by thinking of this drug as **villain**-zodone: while it appears to be helping serotonin (by inhibiting its reuptake), it's secretly stabbing it in the back and preventing it from reaching its full potential by acting as a partial agonist!

Hard-working serotonin

Back-stabbing vilazodone

So what does this mean clinically? Vilazodone's partial agonist activity appears to block some of the side effects seen with full saturation of serotonin receptors, with **sexual side effects** in particular being less noticeable with vilazodone compared to "pure" SSRIs. On a mechanistic level, you can basically think of vilazodone as "**SSRI + buspirone**." (We haven't talked about buspirone yet, but it is another drug that works as a partial agonist at the serotonin receptor. We will cover it more in Chapter 6 as it is primarily used for treatment of generalized anxiety disorder.)

> **Vilazodone inhibits serotonin reuptake** while also acting as a **partial agonist** at the serotonin receptor, leading to **fewer serotonergic side effects**.
>
> **Villain**-zodone seems to be **helping serotonin** but is actually **holding it back**!

VORTIOXETINE

The final atypical antidepressant we will talk about is vortioxetine (Trintellix). This is a newer antidepressant that not only acts as an SSRI but also modulates serotonin receptors. Vortioxetine is even more complex than vilazodone as it can be an agonist, partial agonist, or even antagonist depending on the particular 5-HT receptor subtype! You can associate this drug with a "swirl" of different effects on serotonin by calling it **vortex**-etine. However, this doesn't appear to translate into any clinically meaningful differences. Vortioxetine is often advertised as being better at improving cognition in patients with cognitive deficits secondary to depression, but with each passing year it seems clearer that this is more marketing hype than actual effect. Overall, vortioxetine is not prescribed regularly due to its high cost and the lack of clinically meaningful differences from standard antidepressants.

TRICYCLIC ANTIDEPRESSANTS

We just got done talking about some of the newest antidepressants on the market, so let's travel back in time and talk about the oldest: the **tricyclic antidepressants** (often shortened to just "tricyclics" or "TCAs"). You can generally recognize TCAs by their name, as they usually have either the suffix **–triptyline** (as in amitriptyline and nortriptyline) or **–ipramine** (as in clomipramine and imipramine).

Tricyclics have incredibly complex mechanisms of action which result both in their efficacy as well as their increased side effect burden. The complexity of TCAs should remind you of the Second Rule of Neurotransmission: "With great power comes great responsibility." The more things you mess with in the brain, the higher chances of having an effect, but also the higher chance of causing serious side effects. Consistent with this, there is some evidence to suggest that TCAs are more effective than more modern antidepressants, but given their side effect profile they generally should not be first-line options.

To better understand TCAs, let's take a moment to review their pharmacologic effects. TCAs act as *ag*onists at two neurotransmitters, *antag*onists at another two, and inhibitors of two ion channels. We can consolidate this into the mnemonic **Trans, Chans, and Ans** which, conveniently, spells out **TCAs**! The "s" at the end of each word reminds us that there are two of each.

T is for Transmitters. TCAs inhibit reuptake of both **serotonin** and **norepinephrine** (similar to SNRIs). This is what is primarily responsible for their antidepressant effects.

C is for Channels. TCAs work as **sodium** and **calcium** channel inhibitors. Clinically, this property may account for some of their analgesic properties. However, it may also account for their **toxicity in overdose**. TCAs are some of the most potentially deadly drugs that are still prescribed in psychiatric, with a therapeutic index of 7 (meaning that taking just 7 times the normal amount of the drug could cause death). Slowing these ion channels affects electrical conduction in both the brain and the heart. In the brain, this leads to altered mental status or even coma. In the heart, this leads to arrhythmias, with a **widened QRS complex** on an EKG being highly specific for a TCA overdose. This is very high yield, enough that it bears repeating: a wide QRS in the context of a suspected overdose is highly specific for TCA toxicity! An equally high-yield fact is that **sodium bicarbonate** is the treatment for TCA overdose. To remember this association, picture a car running into a tricycle. It's no contest: the **car** is going to absolutely *destroy* that **tricycle**. If you extend this to the idea that sodium bi-**car**-bonate beats a **tricycle**, you'll remember the antidote for TCA poisoning.

A **wide QRS** on an EKG in the context of **suspected overdose** is likely **TCA overdose**. Treatment involves **sodium bicarbonate**.

*Sodium bi-**car**-bonate runs over a **tricycle**.*

A is for Antagonists. Finally, TCAs antagonize **acetylcholine** and **histamine** which accounts for much of their side effect profile. The anticholinergic effects that were captured in the "Blind as a bat..." rhyme all apply here, with blurry vision, dry mouth, constipation, urinary retention, tachycardia, and cognitive impairment all being seen to some degree. Antagonism of histamine results in a soporific effect, with drowsiness and sedation being common complaints while on a tricyclic.

TCAs increase **serotonin** and **norepinephrine**, inhibit **sodium** and **calcium** ion channels, and antagonize **acetylcholine** and **histamine**.

TCAs affect Trans, Chans, and Ans.

While the overall pattern captured in "Trans, Chans, and Ans" holds true for most TCAs, it would be a mistake to assume that every medication in this class has the *exact* same neurotransmitter profile. In fact, some TCAs boost serotonin more than norepinephrine, others do the opposite, and still others hit them both equally. The same holds true for anticholinergic and antihistaminergic effects as well! The nuances here really are what set one TCA apart from its peers, as we'll discover now as we talk about each of the individual TCAs. Keep in mind that we won't be covering every single TCA, as many are no longer commonly prescribed. Instead, we will focus on those that are used most often or have unique effects!

IMIPRAMINE

Imipramine (Tofranil) is a prototypical TCA which also has the distinction of being the first antidepressant ever discovered! One thing that sets imipramine apart is that it is sometimes used for treating **nocturnal enuresis** (bed wetting). The anticholinergic effect of imipramine prevents the bladder from contracting, thus holding the urine. Because of its significant side effects, it is not used as a first-line option for bed wetting but can be useful in refractory cases. You can remember **imipramine** as "**I'm-peeing-ramine**" to associate it with bedwetting.

Imipramine is a TCA that is useful for treating **nocturnal enuresis**.

*I'm-i-P-ramine can be thought of as I'm-**pee**ing-ramine.*

CLOMIPRAMINE

Like any TCA, clomipramine (Anafranil) can be used to treat depression. However, in the modern day it is most often used to treat **OCD**. In fact, clomipramine is considered to be the **gold-standard** for medication treatment of OCD, as it was found in several randomized controlled trials to be more effective than any other antidepressants. Clomipramine is one of the strongest serotonin reuptake inhibitors known, which most likely accounts for its incredible efficacy in treating OCD. Due to its higher side effect burden, however, it should be reserved for more severe or treatment-refractory cases of OCD, with SSRIs as the first-line option.

> **Clomipramine** is the gold-standard treatment for **obsessive-compulsive disorder**.
>
> Use **clom**-ipramine for obsessive-**clom**pulsive disorder.

AMITRIPTYLINE AND NORTRIPTYLINE

Two other commonly prescribed TCAs are amitriptyline (Elavil) and nortriptyline (Pamelor). Amitriptyline is actually converted to nortriptyline is the liver, which is why the two are grouped together. In addition to treating depression, you will also see them prescribed for chronic pain issues, such as diabetic peripheral neuropathy, chronic low back pain, or pelvic pain. Amitriptyline is fairly balanced in its effects on serotonin and norepinephrine, while nortriptyline  is much more selective for norepinephrine. In addition, nortriptyline tends to have fewer anticholinergic effects and is less associated with sedation and orthostatic hypotension. For these reasons, it is preferred for elderly patients for whom sedation and falls can be very big deals!

> **Nortriptyline** is associated with **less sedation** or **orthostatic hypotension** compared to other tricyclics.
>
> Elderly patients will fall less on **no-trip**-tyline than other TCAs.

DOXEPIN

The final TCA we will talk about is doxepin (Sinequan). Compared with most TCAs, doxepin has extremely strong **antihistaminergic** effects, and at lower doses it is basically a pure antihistamine. This property makes it a useful option for insomnia as well as for severe cases of allergies. However, generally speaking there are better options for both of these indications that don't come with the same side effect burden (like trazodone for insomnia and second-generation antihistamines for allergies), so doxepin is generally reserved for cases where other things haven't worked yet.

MONOAMINE OXIDASE INHIBITORS

We now move onto another old class of antidepressants: the **monoamine oxidase inhibitors** or **MAOIs**. Rather than inhibiting the *reuptake* of neurotransmitters out of the synaptic cleft, MAOIs instead act upon an enzyme known as monoamine oxidase (MAO) that *breaks down* the neurotransmitter. Overall, though, the effect is the same: the drug makes the amount of monoamine in the synapse increase!

There are two distinct types of the MAO enzyme that each have different levels of ability when it comes to breaking down monoamines. MAO-**A** is an **A**dvanced operator and is capable of inactivating all three of the monoamines implicated in depression (serotonin, norepinephrine, and dopamine). In contrast, MAO-**B** is much more **B**asic and can only handle one (dopamine).

> There are **2 subtypes of monoamine oxidase** that each **break down** the three monoamines implicated in depression to different degrees.
>
> *MAO-**A** is **A**dvanced (all 3), MAO-**B** is **B**asic (dopamine only).*

There are four MAOIs that are used to treat depression. Phenelzine (Nardil), tranylcypromine (Parnate), and isocarboxazid (Marplan) all inhibit both MAO-A and MAO-B, making them some of the only antidepressants capable of increasing synaptic levels of **all three monoamines**. In contrast, **sele**giline (Emsam) is unique in that it is **sele**ctive for MAO-B, meaning that only dopamine is increased. For this reason, you may see selegiline being used not only to treat depression but also other disorders (such as Parkinson's disease) where only dopamine needs boosting.

> **Phenelzine, tranylcypromine,** and **isocarboxazid** inhibit **both** MAO-A and MAO-B, while **selegiline** is **selective** for MAO-B.
>
> ***Sele**giline is **sele**ctive for MAO-B.*

MAOIs are among the most effective of all antidepressants, especially in a particular form of depression known as **atypical depression**. Atypical depression is characterized by mood reactivity, interpersonal rejection sensitivity, increased appetite, hypersomnia, and leaden paralysis (the sensation that one's arms are too heavy to lift). For reasons that are still not clear, atypical depression responds better to MAOIs than other types of treatments like SSRIs, SNRIs, or TCAs. Remember to use **MAWIs** when your patients tell you, "**M**y **A**rms' **W**eight **I**ncreased!"

> **MAOIs** are particularly effective for **atypical depression** which features **mood reactivity** and specific symptoms such as **leaden paralysis**.
>
> *Use **MAWIs** when patients tell you, "**M**y **A**rms' **W**eight **I**ncreased!"*

In line with the Second Rule of Neurotransmission, MAOIs are very effective but can also have some very severe side effects, including a few that can be life-threatening. Because of this, MAOIs are not prescribed often in modern psychiatry and are typically used as a "**last resort**" after a patient has failed multiple other medications from several different classes first.

There are two main life-threatening side effects to be aware of here. The first is known as a **hypertensive crisis** which can occur when someone who is taking an MAOI ingests anything with **tyramine** in it. Tyramine is found naturally in many **aged foods** such as cheeses or wine. Once ingested, it causes the release of norepinephrine and dopamine from pre-synaptic vesicles. Ordinarily, this wouldn't cause too much trouble, but in the presence of an MAOI, the released norepinephrine and dopamine can build up to dangerous levels, leading to widespread vasoconstriction and incredibly high blood pressures. This is a **medical emergency** and needs to be recognized promptly. Because of this, all patient's taking MAOIs need to be counseled on how to recognize and avoid foods which contain tyramine. To remember this severe interaction, imagine a young man on a romantic vacation with his girlfriend **Tyra Mine** at a beachside resort on **Maui** (MAOI). He takes her out on a picnic over fine **aged wines and cheeses**. As he nervously prepares to pop the question, you can bet that his **blood pressure** would be **sky high**! This mental image will help you associate these disparate words and concepts (MAOIs, tyramine, aged food and drink, blood pressure, and "last resort" antidepressants) together.

> **MAOIs** can cause a **hypertensive crisis** when combined with **tyramine**, Which occurs naturally in **aged food and drink**.
>
> *Picture a young man about to propose to his girlfriend **Tyra Mine** at a **(last) resort** on **Maui** over **wines and cheeses**. He would probably have **sky high blood pressure**!*

In addition to hypertensive crisis, the other potentially lethal side effect of MAOIs to be aware of is **serotonin syndrome**. While hypertensive crisis results from MAOIs causing an excess of dopamine and norepinephrine, serotonin syndrome results from MAOIs causing an excess of serotonin. Recall from Chapter 2 that, while any two serotonergic medications can theoretically cause serotonin syndrome, the biggest risk by far comes when one of those drugs is an MAOI. To prevent this, it is recommended to have a "washout" period of at least 2 weeks when switching from a serotonergic drug to an MAOI. (The exception to this is fluoxetine which, due to its long half-life, requires a 5 week washout!)

KETAMINE

Is ketamine (Ketalar) an antidepressant? It's certainly the strangest drug we will learn about in this chapter. It's not a pill that you take by mouth (it must either be injected or taken intranasally), it doesn't inhibit the reuptake of anything, and it doesn't even involve serotonin, norepinephrine, or dopamine! Instead, ketamine is classified as an **NMDA receptor antagonist**, although it appears to have other actions as well.

From the time that clinical use of ketamine first began in 1970, it has primarily been used as an **anesthetic**, as it induces a state of **dissociation** characterized by pain relief, sedation, memory loss, perceptual disturbances, and hallucinations (remember that **D**issociative hallucinogens are the **D** in NM**D**A mnemonic!). Its analgesic and amnestic properties make it ideal for emergency pain relief (such as treating wounded soldiers on the battlefield), while its hallucinatory properties make it a popular recreational drug as well.

While ketamine has been in use for over 50 years, it is only in the last decade or two that its antidepressant effects have been noted. Depressed patients who received ketamine for other reasons often noted a total resolution of depressive symptoms within days or even hours of taking it. The **speed and extent of improvement** in depression was remarkable, especially considering that most traditional antidepressants can take weeks or months to work! The downside, however, is that these improvements disappear just as quickly as they come, with improvements **rarely lasting beyond a few days** and almost never past a week. In this way, ketamine is the poster child for the phrase "**easy come, easy go.**" Different strategies for extending the initial antidepressant effect of ketamine, such as repeat infusions or combination with more traditional antidepressants, are still being explored. For now, there is insufficient evidence to recommend ketamine as a routine treatment for depression, but with additional time ketamine's place in our treatment algorithms may become more clear. We'll talk more about ketamine in Chapter 12!

ADDITIONAL OPTIONS

While the drugs we have covered so far make up the bulk of treatment options for depression, there are some additional options as well. Some of these (like psychotherapy) can be used instead of medications as a first-line treatment, while others are typically reserved for patients who have not responded to several trials of antidepressants.

PSYCHOTHERAPY

Medications are not the only treatment option for depression! There are several highly effective psychotherapies for depression such as cognitive behavioral therapy (CBT). Medications and therapy are both equally effective on their own, and they can both be considered good first-line options. However, research has shown that the best outcomes are seen when the two are combined!

ANTIPSYCHOTICS
Several antipsychotics have been shown to treat unipolar depression when added to existing antidepressants, including aripiprazole (Abilify), quetiapine (Seroquel), and ziprasidone (Geodon), among others. Not all antipsychotics are helpful for treating depression! These antipsychotics all have greater action at serotonin receptors than most others, which likely accounts for their increased utility in depression. However, they are all associated with significant side effects (to be explored in more detail in Chapter 4) that make them unsuitable as a first-line treatment. The only exception to this is cases of depression with psychotic features, as adding an antipsychotic results in a better and faster response than an antidepressant alone. For this reason, combined therapy with an antidepressant and an antipsychotic is the standard of care for patients who have psychotic depression.

LITHIUM
Lithium (Eskalith) is primarily known for its use in patients with bipolar disorder. However, there is good evidence that lithium can be an effective treatment for unipolar depression as well, both on its own and when combined with traditional antidepressants. Because of its side effects (to be covered more in Chapter 5), it tends not to be used very frequently for this purpose despite its efficacy.

THYROID HORMONE
Pharmaceutical-grade forms of thyroid hormone such as liothyronine (Cytomel) can be used to treat residual symptoms of depression even in patients with normal thyroid function. In essence, your goal is to induce a state of subclinical hyperthyroidism, which can be helpful for addressing the low energy and anhedonia that are commonly seen in depression.

STIMULANTS
Stimulants such as methylphenidate (Ritalin) and amphetamine (Adderall) (which will be discussed further in Chapter 7) can be used to address certain symptoms of depression (such as fatigue and difficulty concentrating). However, repeated studies have failed to show that they actually improve the course of depressive illness.

ELECTROCONVULSIVE THERAPY
This will be covered in much more detail in Chapter 15, but in brief, electroconvulsive therapy is the **single most effective treatment** for treatment-resistant depression, with a response rate of approximately 50%. It should be considered for patients with severe depression who have failed to respond to multiple trials of medication.

TRANSCRANIAL MAGNETIC STIMULATION
Transcranial magnetic stimulation (TMS) is a type of brain stimulation where magnetic coils are placed on the head in order to generate an electric current in the brain. While not nearly as effective as ECT, TMS does have the benefit of being non-invasive and generally safe, with the main downside being its time-consuming nature.

HOW TO USE ANTIDEPRESSANTS

As their name implies, antidepressants are most often used to treat **major depressive disorder**, a disorder characterized by depressed mood as well as a variety of signs and symptoms including poor **S**leep, decreased **I**nterest in activities, feelings of **G**uilt or hopelessness, low **E**nergy, impaired **C**oncentration, decreased **A**ppetite, **P**sychomotor retardation, and **S**uicidal thoughts (which can be easily recalled using the mnemonic **SIGECAPS**). Having **at least 5** of these symptoms for **2 or more weeks** qualifies the patient for major depressive disorder per current standards. (You can remember the timeframe for depression using the phrase "**two blue weeks**.")

When considering an antidepressant for one of your patients, there are some key principles to keep in mind:

1. Antidepressants don't work overnight.
Decades of research and clinical practice have established that antidepressants do not fully "bloom" until 4 or even 8 weeks after being started. Patients can sometimes feel like stopping the drug early, as the side effects (like diarrhea) are immediate while the positive effects are still catching up. It's important to counsel patients on the need to do a full trial period of a month or two before saying that the drug is or isn't working.

2. Remember the Rule of Thirds!
If patients do stay on the antidepressant for the full 8 weeks, a "**Rule of Thirds**" is generally observed, with one-third of patients getting completely better with no symptoms remaining (**remission**), an additional third getting somewhat better but still with some residual symptoms (**response**), and a final third not getting any better at all (**treatment resistance**). While it can be frustrating that such a large percentage of patients do not respond to treatment (after all, we want to get 100% of our patients feeling better!), it is reassuring that *most* patients do benefit from treatment to some degree.

3. All antidepressants are about equally effective.
It's worth noting that the Rule of Thirds is seemingly independent of the particular drug that is chosen. Because of this, most of the medications discussed under SSRIs, SNRIs, or "atypical" antidepressants would be a reasonable first-line treatment. (TCAs or MAOIs would, in general, not be used until other options have been exhausted due to their higher side effect burden and higher lethality in overdose.) Because all antidepressants are equally effective, you should...

4. Choose based on side effect profile.
If efficacy does not differ significantly, then choose based on side effects, as these *do* differ significantly between the drug classes and even within the specific drugs in each class. For example, if a patient is worried about weight gain, then mirtazapine might not be the best option. If they are concerned about sexual side effects, we should avoid SSRIs. If they often forget to take medications, fluoxetine may be a good choice. If they are pregnant, sertraline might be a good option. By keeping our patients' lives and preferences in mind, we can be savvy with our treatments and increase their chances of getting better.

5. Know your options for treatment resistance.
So you've started your patient on an antidepressant and waited the full month or two to see if it is working. However, your patient is not feeling any better. What then? You have a few options: staying the course, increasing the dose, switching to another drug, or adding a new medication. While it is standard practice to increase the dose, the fact is that most studies have found that (provided the drug was within the therapeutic dosing range) increased doses *don't* result in better outcomes and, if anything, only seem to increase the side effect burden! Switching antidepressants also doesn't seem to work much better than staying the course. In fact, the only option that's been shown to be any good is adding a new medication, with the combination of an SRI and mirtazapine appearing to be particularly effective. However, this has to be balanced with the high risk of new side effects as well. Ultimately, the decision on what to do should be based on the patient's desires and preferences, as there is no "one size fits all" approach that works for treatment-resistance.

6. Don't "set it and forget it."
In most cases, antidepressants are not life-long drugs. Research suggests that patients should continue taking antidepressants for **at least 6 months** from the time they first feel better, as stopping earlier than this involves a higher risk of relapsing back into depression. However, as long as your patient has cleared this threshold, you can and *should* try to taper off the medication. For most patients, their depression will not return (at least not for a long while). In a minority of patients (typically those with severe depression), you may need to continue medication treatment for longer, with some needing to be on the drugs for life. This is the exception rather than the rule, however, and you should try to taper after 6 months for most of your patients.

7. Antidepressants don't inherently prevent suicide.
While it is tempting to think that you are helping to prevent suicide just by prescribing an antidepressant, the fact of the matter is that antidepressants do not lower the risk of suicide in and of themselves. In fact, in certain populations (such as people under the age of 25), thoughts of suicide can even *increase* in the period after starting an antidepressant. The reasons for this are complex. For some patients, the increase in energy from the drug can happen before any improvement in hopelessness or other negative thought patterns, making for a dangerous situation where someone who is still depressed now has the energy to act upon their thoughts. On the other hand, some have argued that the association between suicidality and antidepressants is a statistical artifact rather than a true increase in suicidality. Regardless of which side is true (it's likely that both are to some degree), the fact remains that you should not rely on antidepressants as your only form of suicide prevention. Instead, work with your patients and their families to come up with a safety plan for if they start to feel unsafe.

8. Pair antidepressants with psychotherapy for best results.
Don't forget about psychotherapy! We'll talk about specific types of psychotherapy in Chapter 15, but for now it is enough to know that therapy is just as effective as drugs and that the two of them together are better than either one alone. For this reason, you should always have a discussion about therapy with any patient you are treating for depression!

PUTTING IT ALL TOGETHER

In some ways, antidepressants are incredibly easy, especially if you avoid older classes like TCAs and MAOIs. Pick any one you want, they all have the same odds of working! If the first one doesn't work, try another! Don't worry about side effects, none of them will kill the patient!

And the worst part is, most of these things are true! This means that it is remarkably easy to do a bad job of choosing antidepressants, as the consequences are not always obvious and likely won't happen for a long time. However, we need to set our sights higher than simply "not killing the patient." While it's true that most antidepressants are equally effective at reversing the symptoms of depression, that doesn't account for the rest of someone's experience. For example, if a patient's depression has improved but they are horribly unhappy with their sex life, struggling to keep focus at work, concerned about their appearance after gaining 15 pounds, or unable to eat the foods that they want, then it's not as clear that their life has improved for the better. By taking our patient's preferences and combining that with a detailed knowledge of the unique aspects of these medications, we can help our patients at a higher level than if we just throw random drugs at them.

Ultimately, these medications can be incredibly helpful, but they are not the only solution for depression. Other interventions like therapy can be just as effective and result in longer lasting changes in mood and self-esteem. Always keep an eye on the patient's overall goals in seeking treatment, and try to use (or not use) these drugs in a way that maximizes the patient's chances of success.

REVIEW QUESTIONS

1. A 47 y/o M with a history of depression comes into his doctor's office reporting that he stopped taking his fluoxetine after "a couple of embarrassing nights" where he was unable to get an erection with his wife, which he finds intolerable. What is the most reasonable replacement for fluoxetine in this patient?
    A. Citalopram
    B. Sertraline
    C. Venlafaxine
    D. Bupropion
    E. Imipramine
    F. Nortriptyline

2. A 24 y/o M presents with a five year history of severe anxiety over having forgotten to lock the door. It has gotten to the point where he must wake up 4 hours early so that he can repeatedly check the locks before leaving for work. He describes his behavior as "extremely upsetting" to him but says he is unable to stop. He has never before been in treatment for this condition. What is the most reasonable medication to suggest?
    A. Clomipramine
    B. Trazodone
    C. Bupropion
    D. Fluoxetine
    E. Phenelzine

3. A 26 y/o G2P1 single mother who recently gave birth brings her baby boy in for a 1-month check. The baby is back to his birth weight and seems to be doing well. She has been exclusively breastfeeding. During the interview, she lets on that she has been feeling sad and tearful since delivering. A complete history is consistent with post-partum depression. What medication is most often recommended to treat this condition?
    A. Sertraline
    B. Paroxetine
    C. Fluoxetine
    D. Escitalopram
    E. Trazodone

4. A 36 y/o F with a long history of treatment-refractory depression and OCD is found passed out on the floor with an empty bottle of medications nearby. She is non-responsive. Vital signs are HR 138 and BP 92/58. EKG is shown below:

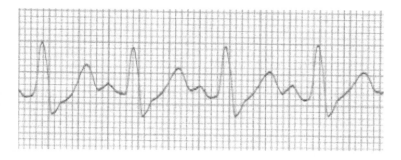

Cardiac enzymes are normal x1. What is the most appropriate treatment after hydration and supportive measures?
   A. N-acetylcysteine
   B. Atropine
   C. Propranolol
   D. Sodium bicarbonate
   E. Flumazenil

5. A mother brings her 7 y/o boy into his pediatrician's office with complaints of bed wetting. She states that this behavior has been present since he was 4, but she believed that he would soon outgrow it. Now that he is 7, she worries that it will be an issue at sleepover parties. She requests treatment. What is a reasonable therapy to try?
   A. No therapy (continue to wait)
   B. Bedwetting alarms
   C. Citalopram
   D. Imipramine
   E. Amitriptyline

6. A 51 y/o M comes to his psychiatrist's office for a follow-up appointment. He was initially diagnosed with major depressive disorder 9 months ago and started on citalopram at a therapeutic dose. He noticed minor improvements but overall did not feel that this medication was working for him, so his psychiatrist switched him to mirtazapine 6 months ago. Within 2 months, he felt that his depression had "gone away completely" and that he was "back to my old self." During his appointment today, he asks his psychiatrist, "How long do I need to stay on this drug? It's worked wonders, but I'm not used to taking medication and don't really want to take it if I don't need it." What is the best response?
   A. "There's no reason to keep taking it! We can stop today."
   B. "Let's wait at least another couple of months before stopping."
   C. "It's best if we give it another year."
   D. "Ideally you should be taking this medication for at least a few years."
   E. "You will likely need to take this medication for life."

1. **The best answer is D.** Serotonergic drugs are known to cause sexual side effects. Of all the listed options, bupropion is the only medication with no significant serotonergic effects. It is a useful antidepressant for patients who experience sexual side effects with traditional serotonergic drugs.

2. **The best answer is D.** Fluoxetine is the most reasonable option listed, as all SSRIs are helpful in treating OCD. Clomipramine may be tempting as it is the gold standard for pharmacologic treatment of OCD, but because of the high amount of side effects it should be reserved until the patient has failed therapy with an SSRI (answer A). Trazodone is serotonergic, but it is not a good first-line option due to its sedating nature (answer B). Bupropion does not have serotonergic effects and is unlikely to improve OCD symptoms (answer C). The side effect profile of MAOIs makes phenelzine an inappropriate initial pharmacotherapy (answer E).

3. **The best answer is A.** Sertraline is often recommended for post-partum depression, as little of it gets into the breast milk. Paroxetine (answer B) would be a particularly bad choice, as it is rapidly absorbed and could result in uncomfortable withdrawal symptoms if discontinued. Fluoxetine (answer C), escitalopram (answer D), and trazodone (answer E) are not entirely incorrect, as all can be used to treat post-partum depression, but given that the patient is actively breastfeeding sertraline is a better option.

4. **The best answer is D.** The question stem describes a patient who has likely overdosed on TCAs, as wide QRS complexes on an EKG in the context of a medication overdose is very likely to be TCA overdose. Sodium bicarbonate is the treatment for tricyclic overdose. N-acetylcysteine (answer A) can be used to treat acetaminophen overdose, while flumazenil (answer E) can at times be used to treat benzodiazepine overdose; however, neither are antidotes for TCA overdose. Atropine (answer B) will only contribute further to tachycardia, while propranolol (answer C) will further lower the blood pressure.

5. **The best answer is B.** The patient is certainly at the age where some form of therapy should be considered (answer A). While TCAs such as imipramine (answer D) and amitriptyline (answer E) are effective at inhibiting urination via their anticholinergic effects, behavioral therapies should always be pursued before medications to avoid their significant side effects. Should the patient fail behavioral therapy, then imipramine or desmopressin could be considered. Citalopram has no significant effect on nocturnal enuresis (answer C).

6. **The best answer is B.** Current guidelines recommend waiting at least 6 months from the time that the patient is in remission from their depression before tapering off of an antidepressant, as stopping before this time is associated with a higher rate of relapse. While the patient has been taking the medication for 6 months, he has only been in remission for 4 months so waiting another 2 months is best at this time.

4 ANTIPSYCHOTICS

We now move onto the next class of psychoactive drugs. As their name implies, **antipsychotics** are typically used to treat schizophrenia and other psychotic disorders. However, just like antidepressants are not only used to treat depression but are actually "broad-spectrum antineurotics," so too are antipsychotics used for more than just psychosis, as they have found use in a wide variety of psychiatric disorders including depression, bipolar disorder, anxiety disorders, and delirium. For this reason, they rival antidepressants in the sheer extent of their use and have at times been the single most popular drug class in the United States.

If antidepressants were a showcase for all the roles that serotonin has in the brain and body, antipsychotics will do the same for **dopamine**, as both the efficacy and the side effects of antipsychotics largely derive from their modulation of dopamine receptors. In contrast to antidepressants and serotonin, however, most antipsychotics generally *block* dopamine rather than increase it.

Antipsychotics are often divided into two general categories: **first generation antipsychotics** (also known as FGAs or "typical" antipsychotics), which were first discovered in the 1950s, and **second generation antipsychotics** (SGAs or "atypical" antipsychotics), which appeared a few decades later starting in the 1980s and 1990s. However, this is a *historical* distinction rather than a *clinical* one. While there are some broad patterns to be found here, the fact is that there are no consistent differences in either efficacy or side effects between the two categories. For this reason, we will not make this distinction here for anything other than historical purposes.

ANTIPSYCHOTIC EFFECTS

As is consistent with the Second Rule of Neurotransmission ("With great power comes great responsibility"), antipsychotics are potent and potentially very helpful drugs, but they must be treated with respect to avoid doing more harm than good!

When learning about antipsychotics, we will repeatedly come across different actions of dopamine, so it will be helpful to review a few key effects of dopamine using our **DOPAMINE** mnemonic:

P is for Psychosis. By blocking dopamine in the mesolimbic pathway, antipsychotics reduce the positive symptoms of schizophrenia, including hallucinations, delusions, and thought disorganization.

A is for Attention. Because dopamine plays a key role in attention and concentration, people taking antipsychotics often report that their ability to focus and is impaired.

M is for Movement. Dopamine antagonists are known to cause a variety of movement abnormalities which are known as **extrapyramidal side effects** (EPS). We will learn more about these soon!

I is for Inhibition of prolactin. Antipsychotics that block dopamine have the side effect of *un*inhibiting prolactin via the tuberoinfundibular pathway. This leads to an overall *increase* in prolactin which can then cause enlargement of the breasts and milk release. (As you can imagine, this is not a popular side effect, especially for men!)

E is for Energy. People taking antipsychotics can often appear sedated or apathetic. Sometimes this can be a good thing (such as a patient in a state of agitated psychosis who is at risk of hurting themselves or someone else), but for the most part it is a sad and unfortunate side effect of blocking dopamine.

While dopamine explains much of what we see when using antipsychotics, it doesn't tell the whole story, as many antipsychotics interact with other receptors as well. You can remember the most common receptors involved in antipsychotic effects using the word mish-**MASH** to remember that **M**uscarinic acetylcholine receptors, **α**-1 norepinephrine receptors, **S**erotonin receptors, and **H**istamine receptors are all involved to some extent depending on the specific drug:

M is for Muscarinic. Some antipsychotics act as antagonists at muscarinic receptors, leading to the specific signs and symptoms of the "Blind as bat" rhyme such as constipation, urinary retention, blurry vision, dry mouth, tachycardia, and cognitive impairment.

A is for α-1. Recall from Chapter 2 that α-1 receptors are found all over the place, including in the peripheral vascular system where they help to regulate blood vessel tone and blood pressure. Antagonism of α-1 receptors can therefore lead to an inability to increase blood pressure tone in response to standing up, a condition known as **orthostatic hypotension**, as well as to **reflex tachycardia** as a result.

S is for Serotonin. Modulation of serotonin by certain antipsychotics is believed to be responsible for their efficacy in treating depression and bipolar disorder. However, it may also contribute to sedation and weight gain to some extent as well (remember that **S**leep and **W**eight gain are some of **S**PAR**OW**-tonin's known side effects!).

H is for Histamine. Finally, some antipsychotics block the histamine receptor, leading to sedation (remember H$_1$**S**+A-mine!). In addition, the strength of an antipsychotic's histamine blockade appears to correlate with its propensity to cause a variety of serious **metabolic side effects** including weight gain, insulin resistance, diabetes, and hyperlipidemia, especially for people taking the drugs long-term.

> Many **antipsychotics** are not just **dopamine antagonists** but interact with receptors for **other neurotransmitter** as well.
>
> *Antipsychotics hit a mish-**MASH** of different receptors:*
> **M**uscarinic
> **α**-1 (norepinephrine)
> **S**erotonin
> **H**istamine

EXTRAPYRAMIDAL SIDE EFFECTS

Now that we have covered the effects of antipsychotics, let's learn more about some of the specific side effects that are seen. We'll start by talking about extrapyramidal side effects (EPS) which are the movement abnormalities brought up earlier.

You may recall from your study of neurology that the nerves carrying voluntary motor signals from your brain to your muscles travel in bundles known as **pyramidal tracts** through a region known as the **medullary pyramids** in your midbrain. In contrast, nerves that carry *in*voluntary motor impulses (such as those that help to fine-tune movements and make them appear smooth and coordinated) travel *outside* of this system and are known as **extrapyramidal** tracts. This is where the dopamine-blocking effects of antipsychotics come into play! By interfering with the ability of extrapyramidal tracts to fine-tune movements, antipsychotics cause EPS and lead to **rough, uncoordinated, or jerky movement patterns**.

There are four main types of EPS. Remember these well, because they will definitely show up on boards and on wards! You can use the mnemonic **AD-A-P-T** to help you remember each of these as well as the order in which they appear:

AD is for Acute Dystonia. Acute dystonia is a sustained and often painful **involuntary contraction** of a muscle group, often involving muscles in the face or neck. It typically strikes in the first few **hours** after giving an antipsychotic. Young adult males are at highest risk for this reaction. Treatment involves giving an anticholinergic drug such as diphenhydramine (Benadryl) or benztropine (Cogentin), usually with dramatic improvement within a few minutes and no long-term effects. When a patient cannot **bend** due to acute dystonia, consider di-**bend**-hydramine or **bends**-tropine.

> Treat **acute dystonia** with an **anticholinergic** like diphenhydramine or benztropine.
>
> *When a patient cannot **bend**, consider di-**bend**-hydramine or **bends**-tropine.*

A is for Akathisia. The second form of EPS is akathisia which is experienced as a constant **restlessness or jitteriness** of the muscles. Patients may report being "on edge" or unable to sit still. You may even see them restlessly moving their legs back and forth as if they're waiting to use the bathroom or perpetually rocking back and forth while in a chair. They will often report an internal sense of anxiety. (If you would like to experience something similar to akathisia for yourself, drink four shots of espresso and then force yourself to sit still while not doing anything for the next few hours. If you find yourself physically unable to do so, you're on your way to feeling similar to patients with akathisia!) Akathisia tends to occur a **few days** after starting an antipsychotic, although some notice it immediately. Treatment involves stopping or lowering the antipsychotic and/or starting either propranolol (Inderal), a benzodiazepine, or an anticholinergic. Akathisia is usually reversible, though in some cases it can become permanent.

P is for Parkinsonism. Parkinsonism is exactly what it sounds like: motor deficits resembling the signs and symptoms seen in patients with **Parkinson's disease**. Recall from Chapter 2 that dopamine's actions in the nigrostriatal pathway affect involuntary movements. It sounds weird to think of it this way, but when you prescribe your patients an antipsychotic, you are effectively giving them a form of pharmacologically-induced Parkinson's disease, with all the motor and cognitive effects that go along with that. (You can remember the association of Parkinson's disease with decreased dopamine by thinking that **Pa**rkinson's **D**isease is caused when do**Pa**mine is **D**own.)

> **Parkinsonism** and **Parkinson's disease** is caused **insufficient dopamine**.
>
> *Pa*rkinson's *D*isease happens when do*Pa*mine is *D*own.

The core abnormalities seen in parkinsonism include **bradykinesia** (decreased movements and/or troubling initiating movement), **tremor**, **rigidity**, **postural instability**, and a **shuffling gait** (which was colloquially known as the "Thorazine shuffle" after the introduction of the first antipsychotic). These effects are generally indistinguishable from Parkinson's disease. Parkinsonism tends to occur **several weeks** after the drug is started. Unlike acute dystonia, older patients are at the highest risk. Parkinsonism tends to be stable (it doesn't progressively get worse like in

Parkinson's disease), and the effects usually go away after stopping the medication. Treatment involves switching to an antipsychotic with less potent dopamine blockade or stopping antipsychotics completely. Unfortunately, no other medications have been shown to be effective at relieving the symptoms of Parkinsonism.

T is for Tardive dyskinesia. One of the most feared outcomes of long-term use of an antipsychotic is tardive dyskinesia. Tardive dyskinesia is characterized by **constant involuntary rhythmic movements**, generally involving the **perioral muscles**. They tend to resemble grimacing, lip smacking, chewing, tongue flicking, or excessive eye blinking. They occur slowly over time, with the highest risk coming **years** after starting (hence the name "tardive," as in being "tardy" or late). The risk goes up with every year of continuous treatment, with an additional 3-5% chance of developing tardive for every year of being on a strong dopamine antagonist. (This means that patients on some antipsychotics for 15 years have a 50% chance of developing tardive!)

Unlike the extrapyramidal side effects we have discussed thus far (which will usually disappear once the antipsychotic is stopped), tardive dyskinesia does not always go away so easily and, indeed, can become **irreversible** if it goes on for too long. As with parkinsonism, older patients are at highest risk. Treatment consists of discontinuing the antipsychotic or replacing it with something with less of a dopamine blockade. New medications such as valbenazine (Ingrezza) and deutetrabenazine (Austedo), which reduce dopamine release through a completely different mechanism than antipsychotics, can help to reduce the severity of tardive dyskinesia, although none of them are completely curative.

Extrapyramidal side effects include **acute dystonia, akathisia, parkinsonism,** and **tardive dyskinesia.**

AD-A-P-T:
*A*cute *D*ystonia (hours)
*A*kathisia (days)
*P*arkinsonism (weeks)
*T*ardive Dyskinesia (years)

NEUROLEPTIC MALIGNANT SYNDROME

The final adverse effect of antipsychotics that we will discuss, and arguably the most tragic, is **neuroleptic malignant syndrome** (NMS). To help understand this syndrome, let's break it down word by word:

Neuroleptic. While the term is pretty dated now, antipsychotics were once called "neuroleptics" (roughly meaning "seizing the nerves"). Since that was the terminology when neuroleptic malignant syndrome was first recognized, the word got stuck in there and has never been updated. It follows that NMS is more common with the older first generation antipsychotics than with the newer second generation drugs.

Malignant. As "malignant" implies, NMS is a serious event, with a 15% mortality rate.

Syndrome. Patients with NMS present with a characteristic pattern of symptoms. You can remember the core symptoms using the mnemonic **FEVER** which stands for **F**ever (often quite pronounced, with temperatures soaring above 105°F), **E**ncephalopathy, **V**ital sign instability, **E**levated WBC and CPK, and extreme **R**igidity of the muscles.

> **Neuroleptic malignant syndrome** is a **life-threatening antipsychotic side effect** that presents as fever, muscle rigidity, unstable vital signs, and delirium.
>
> *FEVER:*
> *Fever*
> *Encephalopathy*
> *Vital sign instability*
> *Elevated WBC and CPK*
> *Rigidity*

Take some time to compare the symptoms of neuroleptic malignant syndrome with what we learned about serotonin syndrome in Chapter 2. They are easy to confuse, as both are associated with the use of psychiatric medications, both have a significant mortality rate, and both present with confusion, hyperthermia, and vital sign instability. To differentiate the two, remember that the unique symptoms of **NMS** are **fever** (often extreme) and **rigidity**, while the unique symptoms of **serotonin syndrome** are **diarrhea**, **hyperreflexia**, and **shivering**. The mnemonics for each ("FEVER" and "shits and SHIVERS," respectively) should also help to point you in the right direction, as the key distinguishing features are highlighted in each.

How do you go about treating NMS? First things first: stop the antipsychotic, admit the patient to the ICU, and take steps to control the hyperthermia (typically through cooling blankets and ice packs). The best medication treatment is still debated, but for the purposes of boards the answer is either dantrolene (Dantrium) or bromocriptine (Parlodel). It can be difficult to remember these medications, as they're not used very often anymore. To help you out, picture in your mind a **bro** named **Dan** who has a **fever** for dance and **N**ever **M**isses a **S**tep. This will help you to correlate **NMS** (and its associated **FEVER**) with **bro**mocriptine and **dan**trolene.

> Treat **neuroleptic malignant syndrome** by **discontinuing the antipsychotic**, initiating **cooling measures**, and using either **dantrolene** or **bromocriptine**.
>
> Remember **Dan** the **Bro** who has dance **FEVER** and **N**ever **M**isses a **S**tep.

DOSING FORMS

Because medication compliance plays such a large role in treatment of schizophrenia (with less than half of patients consistently taking medications as prescribed), there are some additional dosing forms that may be worth considering.

Oral. Taking medications by mouth is the most common and straightforward way, but it is dependent upon the patient being willing and able to take them regularly, which you cannot assume in this (or frankly *any*) patient population.

Oral dissolvable. Several antipsychotics have dissolvable forms which can help to prevent "cheeking" where a patient pretends to take the pill but hides it in their cheek to spit out later. These formulations dissolve on the tongue and are absorbed in seconds. This can help more of the drug to be administered, though they are often more expensive than traditional pills.

Intravenous. IV antipsychotics are the gold standard as, by definition, they have 100% bioavailability. However, given that they can only safely be administered in a hospital setting, they are mostly used for inpatient management of acute agitation or delirium.

Intramuscular. IM injections, which can be given without the patient's consent, are only administered in emergent situations where a patient's behavior puts themselves or others at risk of immediate harm. They take effect very quickly (often within several minutes of administration) and often result in rapid sedation.

Intramuscular depot. There are several antipsychotics with IM depot forms. One injection contains a few weeks' or months' worth of the drug which will diffuse slowly into the bloodstream, negating the need for any oral medications during this time. IM depot formulations are associated with lower rates of psychiatric hospitalization than traditional pills, making them a good option to consider for patients who repeatedly end up in the hospital! When considering using the depot form of an antipsychotic, make sure that the patient has been tried on the oral form of that particular drug first! Once you give a depot injection, the patient 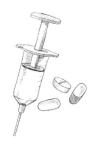 is stuck with it in their bloodstream for several weeks. If your patient happens to be allergic, they will have a few awful weeks and you will have a malpractice lawsuit on your hands. You can remember this using the rhyming phrase "**PO** before **depot**" (PO being Latin for *per os*, or by mouth).

Always give the **oral form** of an antipsychotic **before** administering it as an **IM depot**.

*PO before **depot**!*

FIRST GENERATION ANTIPSYCHOTICS

Let's move on to the individual antipsychotics and talk about the highest-yield facts for each, starting with the older "first generation" antipsychotics. While there are more FGAs than the three we will talk about here, the fact of the matter is that FGAs have all but been **replaced by SGAs** in modern psychiatry. While this is due in no small part to aggressive marketing, there is also the fact that patients seem to be able to tolerate metabolic side effects much better than the uncomfortable and stigmatizing nature of extrapyramidal side effects and are ultimately **more likely to stay on SGAs** than FGAs.

There are really only a few FGAs that are still used on a regular basis, so let's focus our discussion to just those. You may come across other FGAs from time to time (many of which have difficult-to-pronounce names like perphenazine, trifluoperazine, thiothixene, and loxapine). However, if you can remember that FGAs in general have high potency at the D_2 receptor and come with a high risk of EPS, you should be okay!

HALOPERIDOL

Haloperidol (Haldol) is the most famous of the FGAs and, despite its age, is still used to treat schizophrenia today. Haloperidol is a **strong antagonist** of the D_2 receptor with few anticholinergic effects like dry mouth. However, because it blocks the D_2 receptor so strongly, there is a significant risk of EPS including tardive dyskinesia.

In addition to its use as an antipsychotic, haloperidol is commonly combined with lorazepam (Ativan) and diphenhydramine (Benadryl) to make a "cocktail" which is administered intramuscularly when a patient is agitated or violent. (Lorazepam, a GABAergic drug, helps with sedation, while diphenhydramine, an antihistamine, both increases sedation and prevents acute dystonia.) Haloperidol also remains popular on medical and surgical floors due to the availability of an intravenous formulation. Patients who become delirious will often be given IV haloperidol for symptomatic control. However, every patient receiving IV haloperidol needs to be on **cardiac monitoring**! IV haloperidol (much more than oral or intramuscular haloperidol) has been shown to prolong the QTc interval which, as mentioned in Chapter 3 when discussing (es)citalopram, is a significant risk factor for **torsades des pointes** and sudden death. *Unlike* with (es)citalopram, where the risk of progressing to torsades is not clearly established, IV haloperidol *has* been shown in studies to have a **clear link** to torsades and sudden death. If you remember nothing else from this section, remember this: every patient on IV haloperidol needs cardiac monitoring! To make the link, think of the **twisting** vines of an **ivy** whenever you see **IV** haloperidol to remind you of the "**twisting of the points**" you see in **torsades des pointes**.

IV haloperidol can cause **QTc prolongation** and **torsades des pointes**.

*Think of **twisting ivy** to remind you of the risk of **torsades** with **IV haloperidol**!*

CHLORPROMAZINE

Chlorpromazine (Thorazine) is the very first antipsychotic that was ever discovered, dating all the way back to 1950! While it is a relatively weak *dopamine* blocker, it has strong effects on the mish-**MASH** receptors, resulting in a wide range of side effects. Notably, chlorpromazine is one of the **most sedating** of all antipsychotics due to its effects at the histamine receptor and is often used in cases where this sedating effect is desired (like in highly agitated patients).

> **Chlorpromazine** is a **typical antipsychotic** that is **highly sedating**.
>
> **Snore**-*promazine will put you to sleep.*

FLUPHENAZINE

The last typical antipsychotic we will discuss is fluphenazine (Prolixin) which, like haloperidol, is a high-potency dopamine blocker. While not as common as it once was, fluphenazine is still used today, mostly because it has both an IM depot formulation as well as a short-acting IM for agitation.

> **Fluphenazine** is a **typical antipsychotic** with both **short and long-acting IMs**.
>
> **Flu**-*phenazine can* **knock you out** *(short-acting) and* **lasts a few weeks** *(long-acting)!*

SECOND GENERATION ANTIPSYCHOTICS: THE "-APINES"

Let's move on to the learn about the newer "second generation" antipsychotics. While they are frequently lumped together, in reality each of the SGAs are more different than they are alike! Rather than treating SGAs as a single homogeneous group, let's divide them up into three groups that share some basic similarities. We'll call these groups the "-apines," the "-idones," and the "IPRs."

We'll start with the -**apines** (like olanz**apine** and queti**apine**). The -apines have much weaker dopamine blocking effects than most other antipsychotics which makes them excellent choices for when you want to avoid EPS! They also tend to interact strongly with **serotonin** receptors, making them useful for treating mood disorders. However, the downside is that they tend to be **heavily sedating** and are associated with severe **metabolic side effects** such as weight gain, diabetes, and dyslipidemia. You can remember this association by pronouncing these drugs with "peanut butter" at the end (as in "olanza-peanut butter") to associate it with a highly fattening food.

> -**Apines** have **less EPS** and can **improve mood** but cause **sedation** and **weight gain**.
>
> *Convert "a-pine" to "a-***peanut butter***" to link it with a* ***fattening food****!*

OLANZAPINE

Olanzapine (Zyprexa) is one of the most popular antipsychotics, and there is good reason for this. Not only is it a "heavy-duty" option that is very effective at rapidly reversing psychotic symptoms, but studies have also shown it to be among the best tolerated of all antipsychotics, with patients sticking on it for longer.

So what's the downside? For one, like all -apines, olanzapine is very **sedating**, so aim for nighttime dosing. More concerning, however, is the fact that olanzapine is one of the absolute worst in its class for causing metabolic side effects. Patients on olanzapine have a propensity to **gain weight** independently of caloric intake. It's not a trivial amount either: many patients gain upwards of 10-20 pounds, and some gain much more than that. The significant risk of developing insulin resistance and even diabetes mellitus also cannot be ignored. Because of this, some clinicians argue that olanzapine should not be a first-line agent despite its effectiveness and tolerability. The jury is still out on that, but at the very least, patients and their families should be counseled on the potential for metabolic effects with olanzapine. You can remember this association by emphasizing the "**O**" in **O**lanzapine to remind you of **O**besity (like this chubby **O**-shaped bird).

Olanzapine is **highly effective** but often causes **sedation** and **weight gain**.

*Think **O** for **O**lanzapine and **O** for **O**besity.*

QUETIAPINE

Quetiapine (Seroquel) is similar to olanzapine but has a few key differences. Quetiapine has strong serotonergic properties which makes it helpful for treating mood disorders like depression and bipolar disorder. While it can cause metabolic effects like weight gain, it tends to be to a lesser extent than olanzapine. Notably, quetiapine is a very weak dopamine blocker, so it can be good for patients who  are highly sensitive to EPS or who cannot tolerate a dopamine blockade (such as a patient with Parkinson's disease). The downside of this is that you tend to need much higher doses to get any sort of antipsychotic effect, and with higher doses come more side effects. Most notably, therapeutic doses of quetiapine tend to be **very sedating** for patients. Some clinicians will even use quetiapine as an anxiety or sleep medication on an as-needed basis, although given its side effect profile, it should not be a first-line agent for this purpose. You can remember the association of quetiapine with sedation by thinking that **queti**-apine is for **quiet** time.

Quetiapine is a **weak dopamine blocker** that is highly **sedating**.

Queti-apine is for quiet time.

CLOZAPINE

Clozapine (Clozaril) is similar to other -apines in that it is highly sedating and causes weight gain. However, it is unique in that it is the **single most effective drug** for treating schizophrenia. Studies have shown that clozapine is better than all other antipsychotics for **treatment-resistant schizophrenia** that has not responded to multiple other antipsychotic trials. In addition, clozapine appears to be able to **improve negative symptoms** (rather than only treating positive symptoms).

Interestingly, clozapine does not have nearly as much activity at the D_2 receptor as other antipsychotics, yet it's still more effective. How can we explain this paradox? More than just reducing psychotic symptoms, clozapine targets mood and other cognitive symptoms associated with schizophrenia through its effects on **serotonin**. This may also explain why clozapine is one of two drugs in psychiatry that has been shown to reduce rates of suicide (the other being lithium, discussed in Chapter 5).

So if it's so great at treating psychosis and improving negative symptoms, why don't we use it all the time? Clozapine has a rare but potentially deadly side effect known as **agranulocytosis** where a patient's white blood cells become depleted, resulting in the risk of overwhelming infection and, death. Because of this, patients taking clozapine need regular blood draws to check their complete blood count (CBC) and in particular their absolute neutrophil count (ANC). All of this means that clozapine is not a first-line treatment for schizophrenia despite its peerless efficacy.

However, for patients who have failed two or more trials of other antipsychotics (one of which must be either olanzapine or risperidone), it is one of the best options we have. You can remember the association of clozapine and agranulocytosis by thinking that you have to watch **cloz**-apine **cloz**-ely to monitor for agranulocytosis.

Clozapine is the **most effective antipsychotic** but can cause **agranulocytosis**.

*You must watch **cloz**-apine **cloz**-ely to monitor for agranulocytosis!*

ASENAPINE

Asenapine (Saphris) is unlike the other -apines in that it doesn't appear to cause much sedation or weight gain, as it blocks histamine to a lesser extent. Instead, **S**-**N**-apine's strongest effects are at the **S**erotonin and α-1 **N**oradrenergic receptors, leading to additional efficacy in mood disorders (good!) as well as side effects like dizziness and orthostatic hypotension (bad...). The most notable thing about asenapine is that it must be taken sublingually, as bioavailability is quite low when absorbed through the gastrointestinal tract. Overall, though, asenapine is a fairly "**middle of the road**" antipsychotic and is not the best or worst on any particular outcome.

Asenapine antagonizes serotonin and α-1 receptors, leading to leading to efficacy in **mood disorders** and side effects like **dizziness and orthostatic hypotension**.

*S-N-apine's strongest effects are at the **S**erotonin and α-1 **N**oradrenergic receptors.*

SECOND GENERATION ANTIPSYCHOTICS: THE "-IDONES"

The -**idones** (such as risper<u>idone</u> and zipras<u>idone</u>) are SGAs that occupy a halfway point between traditional FGAs like haloperidol and other SGAs like olanzapine. Compared with the -apines, they are more "straight up" dopamine blockers without as many of the sedating and metabolic effects. The main thing that they have picked up from their SGA brethren is the involvement of **serotonin** which allows some -idones to have similar mood modulating effects. The downside of their resemblance to FGAs is that they have a **higher risk of EPS** and other dopamine-related side effects like hyperprolactinemia compared to the -apines. You can remember the larger dopamine involvement of the -i**done**s by focusing on the "**DoNe**" part and replacing it with "**Do**pamine **Ne**utralizer."

> **Antipsychotics** ending in -**idone** are less likely to cause **sedation** and **weight gain** but have **more EPS** and other dopamine-related side effects.
>
> Convert "**DoNe**" to "**Dopamine Neutralizer**" to link it with **stronger dopamine effects**!

RISPERIDONE

Risperidone (Risperdal) is one of the most popular -idones currently on the market. Like olanzapine, it is generally regarded as one of the "heavy-duty" options by most clinicians, with powerful antipsychotic effects that are often apparent within a few days of starting. Risperidone is on the **less sedating** side compared to most atypicals (though it is still sedating), which can be beneficial for patients who find themselves too fatigued when taking -apines. Think "**Ris**e and shine!" with **ris**peridone.

One of the more unfortunate features of risperidone is that, compared to other SGAs, it has a much higher rate of causing **hyperprolactinemia** and **gynecomastia**. This is an important fact for both boards and wards! Do your best to remember that **rise-pair**-idone can give **rise** to a **pair** of breasts.

> Risperidone is **less sedating** but can cause **hyperprolactinemia** and **gynecomastia**.
>
> "**Ris**e and shine!" with **ris**peridone.
> **Rise-pair**-idone can give **rise** to a **pair** (of breasts).

PALIPERIDONE

Paliperidone (Invega) is the primary active metabolite of the risperidone and acts in roughly the same way. Paliperidone is best known for having both one-month and three-month intramuscular injection forms (Invega Sustena and Invega Trinza) that can be helpful for patients who have difficulty taking a daily pill. The only other difference between risperidone and paliperidone is that it is **renally excreted** which requires dose adjustments in patients with kidney disease. In most other ways, however, you can think of **pal**iperidone as being basically identical to risperidone (it's risperidone's **pal**).

ZIPRASIDONE

Ziprasidone (Geodon) is like risperidone in that it has less weight gain and sedation compared to the -apines. It has strong serotonin modulating effects which has made it a helpful option for adjunctive treatment of mood disorders that aren't responding to conventional antidepressants. However, it has gained some notoriety for prolonging the QTc interval which is a frequently tested point. You'll recall from Chapter 3 that **seat**-alopram and es-**seat**-alopram can also cause QTc prolongation and require an electro-**car**-diogram. We can fit ziprasidone into this car mnemonic as well! When you see **zip**-rasidone, think of a **zip**py **car** to remind yourself to do an electro-**car**-diogram. An additional clinical pearl is that patients need to take ziprasidone with food, so make sure to remind patients of that as well!

> **Ziprasidone** can cause **QTc prolongation**.
>
> *Use a **zippy car** to remind you of **zip**-rasidone and electro-**car**-diograms.*

LURASIDONE

Lurasidone (Latuda) is not very sedating or weight-gaining, though it can cause more EPS compared to other atypicals. Like ziprasidone, lurasidone must be taken with food. In addition to reducing psychosis, lurasidone has strong serotonin modulating effects, making it helpful for treatment of bipolar disorder. In fact, it is one of the few medications that has been approved for treatment of bipolar depression! We will talk more about bipolar disorder in the next chapter, but for now you can remember that **low**-rasidone helps during the **low** phases of bipolar disorder.

> **Lurasidone** is an antipsychotic with efficacy against **bipolar depression**.
>
> *Low-rasidone helps during the **low** phases of bipolar disorder.*

ILOPERIDONE

Iloperidone (Fanapt) is the last -idone that we will talk about. To sum it up quickly: there isn't much reason to use iloperidone over other available options! Iloperidone has a reputation as a middling antipsychotic that is nowhere near as powerful as other options. In addition, it is a strong α-1 antagonist, leading to extremely high rates of **dizziness** and **orthostatic hypotension**. To avoid these side effects, you must start at a low dose and slowly go to the target dose. You can remember this by thinking of it as **high-low**-peridone: when you stand up **high**, your blood pressure drops down **low**!

> **Iloperidone** is only mildly effective and can cause **orthostatic hypotension**.
>
> *High-low-peridone = when you stand up **high**, your blood pressure drops down **low**.*

SECOND GENERATION ANTIPSYCHOTICS: THE "IPRs"

The final type of SGAs we will cover are the IPRs (so named because they tend to have "ipr" in their names, as in ari**pr**azole and cari**pr**azine). These are **partial agonists** at the dopamine receptor, allowing them to activate the receptor but to a lesser degree than dopamine in its free and unrestrained glory. This should theoretically lead to a more "balanced" profile of both positive and negative drug effects, and in some cases this is what we see! The IPRs tend to have less of the EPS associated with full-on dopamine blockade and in some cases may even help to mitigate these effects when combined with other antipsychotics (with a notable example being use of aripiprazole to decrease the risk of hyperprolactinemia when prescribing risperidone). That's not to say that IPRs are entirely without risk, however, and clinical experience tells us that these drugs can still cause EPS and weight gain, though often to a lesser degree than full antagonists. You can remember the unique effect of IPR antipsychotics by thinking that **IPR** stands for "**I P**artially **R**eactivate."

> **Antipsychotics** with "**ipr**" in the name are **dopamine partial agonists**.
>
> **IPR = I P**artially **R**eactivate *(dopamine receptors)*.

ARIPIPRAZOLE

Aripiprazole (Abilify) is the first of the dopamine partial agonists that was released. Aripiprazole locks in dopamine receptors at about 70% of maximum activation (compared to 100% from dopamine itself and 0% from a "heavy" dopamine blocker like haloperidol), meaning that it **blocks the receptor about 30%**. While the blocking effect is less than other antipsychotics, that doesn't mean that aripiprazole is necessarily a "weaker" drug, as studies have shown that it can be just as helpful for treatment of schizophrenia as more traditional antipsychotics. In terms of side effects, aripiprazole shares a risk of EPS like akathisia with -idones like risperidone. On the

plus side, it does not seem to cause as much hyperprolactinemia, is weight neutral, and is not as sedating as the -apines. Finally, as mentioned in Chapter 3, aripiprazole can be used as an adjunctive treatment of depression due to its activity at serotonin receptors. You can remember many of these properties into the drug name itself by thinking of it as "**light and airy**-piprazole" to link it with a "light" dopamine blockade, less weight gain, and a lightening of mood when used in depression!

> **Aripiprazole** is a **dopamine partial agonist** resulting in 30% activation.
>
> "**Light and airy**-piprazole" has a "light" dopamine blockade, has less weight gain, and lightens mood!

BREXPIPRAZOLE

Brexpiprazole (Rexulti) is similar to aripiprazole in many ways, as both are partial agonists at the dopamine receptor in addition to having effects at serotonin receptors, making them useful for treating both schizophrenia and depression. Compared to aripiprazole, brexpiprazole has a "heavier" dopamine blockade, with it **blocking receptors by about 50%**. This should theoretically make it less activating than aripiprazole (remember that **E**nergy is a key property of DOPAMIN**E**!). You can remember the heavier dopamine blockade associated with this drug by thinking of it as **bricks**-piprazole.

> **Brexpiprazole** is a **partial agonist** that blocks dopamine **more than aripiprazole**.
>
> **Bricks**-piprazole results in a **heavier** blockade than "light and airy-piprazole!"

CARIPRAZINE

Cariprazine (Vraylar) is another relatively new antipsychotic. Like brexpiprazole, it is a partial agonist at the dopamine receptor with a heavier blockade than aripiprazole. Unlike either aripiprazole or brexpiprazole (which are approved for use in *unipolar* depression), cariprazine has been approved for use in *bipolar* depression.

HOW TO USE ANTIPSYCHOTICS

Antipsychotics are most often used to treat **schizophrenia**. Cases of schizophrenia can be recognized by five core symptoms: **H**allucinations (typically auditory), **D**elusions (often paranoid in nature), disorganized **B**ehavior, disorganized **S**peech, and a variety of **N**egative symptoms such as a lack of emotional expression or motivation. These 5 key symptom domains can be remembered using the mnemonic **HD BS Network**. Per DSM-5 criteria, **at least 2** of these symptoms must be present for a period of at least **6 months** to qualify for the diagnosis of schizophrenia. You can remember this using the mnemonic **2-4-6**-ophrenia (**2** symptoms **for** at least **6** months).

For much of recorded history, people with schizophrenia were institutionalized, incarcerated, ignored, or abused, and this type of treatment continues today in both developed and developing parts of the world. When antipsychotics were discovered in the 1950s, it was hoped that these medications would allow patients to lead normal lives in the community. However, as the years passed, it became increasingly clear that antipsychotics did not live up to their initial promise. While they are effective at reducing some of the core **positive** symptoms of schizophrenia, they have proven to be much less effective at addressing the **negative** symptoms that are so impairing for these patients. Nevertheless, antipsychotics continue to be the mainstay of treatment for patients with psychotic disorders.

To make sure that we are wielding these powerful medications as responsibly as possible, let's distill what we have learned so far into a few key principles:

1. First and second generation antipsychotics are equally effective.
Despite initial excitement when they were first released that they would be more effective than existing antipsychotics, the reality is that studies have repeatedly failed to demonstrate that newer SGAs are any more effective than older FGAs. However, they do appear to be better tolerated by patients (including a lower risk of tardive dyskinesia), so it's generally reasonable to use them as first-line agents for treatment of schizophrenia. However, as with the antidepressants, you should generally...

2. Choose based on side effect profile.
Side effects differ much more between each antipsychotic than does the efficacy (the one exception to this rule being clozapine!). Therefore, you must consider the side effect profile and other features when deciding what medication to give. For example, if someone is already diabetic and overweight, olanzapine might not be the best choice. Conversely, if someone is very forgetful, it might be difficult for them to remember to take certain medications (like ziprasidone or lurasidone) with food. For patients in whom compliance is a significant issue, consider using an antipsychotic with a long-acting injectable form such as risperidone or aripiprazole.

3. Don't forget clozapine!
Clozapine has been shown to be more effective than other antipsychotics in cases of treatment-refractory schizophrenia. While we cannot underestimate the seriousness of agranulocytosis, we also cannot ignore the risk of allowing schizophrenia to be inadequately treated! When used responsibly (starting at a low dose, increasing slowly, getting regular blood draws to check the blood count, etc.), clozapine is one of the best options we have for allowing a patient to live free from the torment of untreated psychosis. For this reason, if a patient has failed multiple trials of other antipsychotics (including olanzapine and/or risperidone), consider clozapine unless otherwise contraindicated!

4. Don't forget long-acting injectables!
While long-acting injectable antipsychotics are not necessarily more effective at treating the symptoms of schizophrenia than oral forms, they *have* been shown to reduce rates of rehospitalization which can be just as meaningful of an outcome as symptom reduction! Consider offering patients a long-acting injectable, especially in cases with repeated hospitalizations.

5. Avoid polypharmacy whenever possible.
As with antidepressants, there is no evidence that using multiple antipsychotics at the same time results in better outcomes. However, the evidence is clear that multiple medications *are* associated with more side effects! Avoid polypharmacy whenever possible, although there may be some cases (such as using aripiprazole to reduce the risk of hyperprolactinemia from risperidone) when this is clinically appropriate.

6. Antipsychotics are not a cure-all.
Finally, it should be noted that antipsychotics are not a cure-all for schizophrenia! While they are effective at reducing positive symptoms such as auditory hallucinations and paranoia, they do much less for the negative symptoms like apathy, emotional

blunting, and cognitive deficits that contribute the most to dysfunction and disability. Because of this, antipsychotics are not necessarily associated with significant improvements in psychosocial functioning, and some have argued that the reductions in **A**ttention and **E**nergy associated with DOP**AMINE** blockers may actually *worsen* functional outcomes in some cases. Because of this, don't neglect to consider non-drug options for treatment schizophrenia, including psychosocial therapies such as case management, occupational rehabilitation, and CBT for psychosis.

PUTTING IT ALL TOGETHER

Antipsychotics are the very definition of a **double-edged sword**. They are incredibly powerful drugs with the potential to rapidly reverse psychotic symptoms like paranoia and auditory hallucinations (which can be very distressing for patients). However, they also run the risk of harming the patient through EPS, weight gain, sedation, or other side effects while globally reducing the patient's drive, motivation, and energy (all of which are often already compromised by schizophrenia itself). Be very familiar with **DOPAMINE**'s myriad effects as well as the mish-**MASH** of other receptors that antipsychotics tend to hit in order to choose the option with the highest chance of helping (and the lowest chance of hurting) this very vulnerable patient population!

Finally, here are a couple of quick mnemonics to help you remember which antipsychotics are available in an intramuscular form. To remember the **short-acting** IMs (which you will often be using in situations of chaos to help manage agitation), use the phrase "Into the **CHAOZ flew** an IM!" to remind you of **C**hlorpromazine, **H**aloperidol, **A**ripiprazole, **O**lanzapine, **Z**iprasidone, and **flu**phenazine.

Short-acting intramuscular antipsychotics can be helpful in
managing behavioral emergencies such as agitation.

*Into the **CHAOZ flew** an IM:*
Chlorpromazine, Haloperidol, Aripiprazole, Olanzapine, Ziprasidone, fluphenazine

For the **long-acting** IM depot antipsychotics, think of someone with a **long acting** career: Oprah Winfrey, who first starred in *The Color Purple* in 1985! Use the phrase "**OPRAH flew** through a long acting career" to help you remember that **O**lanzapine, **P**aliperidone, **R**isperidone, **A**ripiprazole, **H**aloperidol, and **flu**phenazine all have long-acting IM formulations available.

Long-acting intramuscular antipsychotics can help to **improve medication compliance** and **reduce rates of rehospitalization**.

OPRAH flew through a long acting career:
Olanzapine, Paliperidone, Risperidone, Aripiprazole, Haloperidol, fluphenazine

REVIEW QUESTIONS

1. A 24 y/o M is brought into the Emergency Department by police who found him running haphazardly into traffic while yelling and screaming. He is non-compliant with attempts at obtaining a history, performing an exam, or inserting an IV. He is agitated and attempts to assault staff several times, calling them "interlopers" and "agents of destruction." Which of the following forms of antipsychotic medication administration should be pursued?
   A. Oral
   B. Dissolvable oral
   C. Intravenous
   D. Intramuscular
   E. Intramuscular depot

2. (Continued from previous question.) The patient is admitted to the psychiatric unit. He continues to be agitated and requires additional doses of antipsychotics. His family arrives, having been looking for him for the past several days; they state that he has never had an episode like this before. Several hours later, the patient appears confused. Muscular rigidity is noted. Vital signs are HR 122, BP 172/140, RR 20, and T 105.2°F. All of the following steps should be taken *except*:
   A. Admit to the medical ICU
   B. Withdraw all antipsychotics
   C. Administer dantrolene
   D. Administer antipyretics
   E. Start aggressive cooling measures

3. A 33 y/o M comes into Urgent Care complaining of a sore throat and fevers. He states that this is "the most sick I've ever been." Vital signs are HR 104, BP 90/60, RR 16, and T 101.7°F. Lab studies reveal a low absolute neutrophil count of 0.4/μL. On further questioning, the patient says he moved across the country one month ago to "start again." What medication is most likely responsible for his fever?
   A. Haloperidol
   B. Chlorpromazine
   C. Clozapine
   D. Olanzapine
   E. Aripiprazole

4. A 33 y/o M is talking with his psychiatrist about starting a new antipsychotic. Which of the following statements is the psychiatrist *least* likely to make?
   A. "Olanzapine is associated with the potential for weight gain."
   B. "Ziprasidone can cause a wide QRS so we'll need to get an EKG first."
   C. "Risperidone comes with a risk of breast development, even in men."
   D. "Quetiapine can be highly sedating, so make sure to take it at night."
   E. "Haloperidol can cause a sudden onset of stiff muscles, particularly in the first few days after taking it."

5. A 41 y/o F with a history of schizophrenia beginning at age 20 has been treated with a long-acting injectable form of risperidone for many years. However, she has recently developed a prolactinoma which was confirmed on brain imaging as seen below:

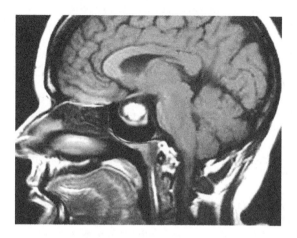

The patient has difficulty with taking oral medications. She is notably overweight with a BMI of 32, and her labs are notable for an elevated A1c suggestive of pre-diabetes. Which of the following medications is the best option for her at this time?
    A. Olanzapine
    B. Haloperidol
    C. Paliperidone
    D. Aripiprazole
    E. Ziprasidone

1. **The best answer is D.** Given the patient's agitation, oral forms (including dissolvable) will likely be ineffective (answers A and B). In addition, he is refusing blood draws, so intravenous access will likely prove impossible (answer C). Finally, IM depot forms should not be given before a medication has been trialed and would not be indicated in this circumstance (answer E). This leaves the short-acting IM form, which is often used in cases of agitation.

2. **The best answer is D.** This patient has neuroleptic malignant syndrome as evidenced by the presence of fever, confusion, muscular rigidity, and unstable vital signs. Treatment of neuroleptic malignant syndrome should include admission to the ICU for close monitoring and supportive care (answer A). Antipsychotics should be withdrawn (answer B), and either dantrolene or bromocriptine should be administered (answer C). Given the patient's high temperature, antipyretics may seem like a good choice, but they have not been shown in studies to be effective. Rather, physical cooling measures should be applied (answer E).

3. **The best answer is C.** This vignette illustrates a case of agranulocytosis, a feared side effect of clozapine. Agranulocytosis often presents as a sore throat, fever, and chills. On lab exam, WBC's will be low (often less than 3.5) despite an ongoing infection. While patients on clozapine are often closely monitored, this patient escaped that due to his recent move. None of the other options listed has agranulocytosis as a major side effect.

4. **The best answer is B.** Ziprasidone is indeed associated with abnormalities on EKG, but it is known for prolonging the QTc interval, not widening the QRS. As you may recall from the section on antidepressants, a wide QRS is associated with tricyclic overdose. All of the other statements correctly pair the drugs with the high-yield side effect that you should know them for.

5. **The best answer is D.** When choosing a long-acting antipsychotic, it is important to consider the long-term side effect profile. As this patient has developed high prolactin on risperidone, it wouldn't be appropriate to switch her to paliperidone as it is the active metabolite of risperidone and would likely have similar effects (answer C). Haloperidol is also a strong D_2 blocker and has an association with hyperprolactinemia (answer B). Given the patient's metabolic profile, a weight-gaining antipsychotic such as olanzapine would not be the best option (answer A). Ziprasidone does not have a long-acting injectable version (answer E). With all of these things in mind, aripiprazole is the best option and may even be helpful in cases of antipsychotic-induced hyperprolactinemia.

5 MOOD STABILIZERS

Mood stabilizers are psychiatric medications that are used to treat **bipolar disorder**. Unlike both depression and schizophrenia (where there is a single disease state that you are trying to treat), bipolar disorder is characterized by **two distinct phases of illness** (mania and depression) that must be treated using different approaches. This is the reason that these drugs are called mood *stabilizers*: your goal is to keep the patient's 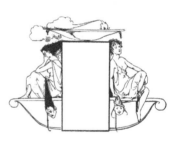 mood balanced between two extremes, rather than simply trying to reverse a single pathological state. In addition, when treating bipolar disorder, you will need to pay attention not only to treating symptoms when they are active but also to preventing symptoms even when the patient's mood is steady.

    Mood stabilizers are likely to be one of the most confusing classes of drugs you will ever study. Unlike antidepressants (which nicely showcased serotonin) and antipsychotics (which showcased dopamine), mood stabilizers showcase... well, not really much of anything. This is because they either have unknown mechanisms of action (like lithium) or do not work on neurotransmitters directly (like the anticonvulsants). Instead, mood stabilizers often exert their effects in multiple areas of the body with inconsistent and seemingly illogical results. This means that we can't simply apply all of those handy concepts we learned in Chapter 2 but will instead be memorizing brand new information. On the plus side, mood stabilizers are one of the smaller psychotropic drug classes, so even though each individual drug comes with a lot of new information, there are really only 4 or 5 new medications to study here. Let's venture forward in order to understand the treatment of a particularly difficult and debilitating disease!

MOOD STABILIZER EFFECTS

How do mood stabilizers work? The short answer is: we don't know! If you're just here for the high-yield stuff, you can probably skip the rest of this section, as there isn't much here beyond some attempts to make sense out of what little we have.

Still around? Great! Let's look at what we do and don't know about the effects of mood stabilizers. Unlike antidepressants and antipsychotics whose effects in the brain and body have been mapped out fairly well, mood stabilizers do not enjoy the same level of understanding. There is some evidence to suggest that lithium may interact with neurotransmitters in the brain, with the specific effect of increasing serotonin release and decreasing norepinephrine release. However, this can't be the whole story, as giving other drugs that do the same thing don't appear to have the same effects.

When a patient takes a mood stabilizer, they often report feeling **slowed, dull, or sedated**. Indeed, almost all of the mood stabilizers feature sedation as a prominent side effect. Is it possible that the anti-manic effects of mood stabilizers are due mostly to their general sedative properties? While this is an attractive hypothesis, it doesn't explain why benzodiazepines (drugs that work on GABA and are highly sedating) aren't as effective as mood stabilizers at treating mania, as would be the case if sedation was the only factor that mattered here.

Many mood stabilizers (particularly the anticonvulsants) appear to block the ion channels that are responsible for initiating and propagating an action potential, suggesting that **inhibition of neuronal firing** plays a key role. Some research suggests that lithium may work in a similar way by disrupting intracellular signaling processes that then lead to neuronal excitation. However, if this were the only mechanism at play, then *all* anticonvulsants would work as mood stabilizers, which (as we will find out shortly) is not the case.

On a psychological level, bipolar disorder is associated with errors of outcome appraisal. Specifically, people with bipolar disorder often *over*estimate the likelihood of success when embarking on any particular venture. This is particularly true during a manic episode, but studies have shown that this trait holds true when patients are at their baseline mood as well. In fact, **increased goal-directed activity** is now known to be a sensitive marker of bipolar disorder and is the one symptom that is most directly correlated with a diagnosis of this disorder. As you might recall, **E**nergy and **O**utcome appraisal are some of the core functions of D**O**PAMIN**E**, so it should come as no shock that dopamine blockers are also effective at treating mania. In fact, antipsychotics are even faster than mood stabilizers at reducing manic symptoms!

Overall, what can we take from this? As before, the best explanation we can give if someone asks exactly what a mood stabilizer is doing is, "We just don't know." While alteration of neurotransmitters, sedative effects, neuronal inhibition, and dopamine blockade all likely play a role to *some* extent, none of them are enough to hang your hat on (so to speak). What we *do* know, however, is that mood stabilizers just *work* and are some of the most effective medications we have in psychiatry!

With that in mind, let's look at each of the individual mood stabilizers, starting with lithium.

LITHIUM

The first mood stabilizer we will cover is the oldest drug in this class: lithium (brand names Eskalith or Lithobid, although everyone just calls it lithium at this point). Interestingly, we have known that lithium has effects on mood for quite some time (it was even part of the recipe for 7 Up in the early twentieth century, much like cocaine used to be an ingredient in Coca-Cola!). It wasn't until 1949, however, that it was shown to be effective for treating mania, and since that time it has been used widely and successfully for treating patients with bipolar disorder.

Despite various theories, the exact mechanism of action of lithium remains unknown. While the pharmacology isn't clear, we do know that lithium is the single best medication we have for bipolar disorder and is the only non-antipsychotic mood stabilizer that seems to have a robust effect at treating and preventing **both mania and depression**. Studies have shown that, for patients who fit the picture of "classic" bipolar disorder, there really is nothing like it. In addition, lithium is one of two medications in the entire world that has been shown to reduce rates of suicide (the other being clozapine). In fact, current research shows a 7-fold decrease in the risk of suicide for bipolar patients taking a therapeutic level of the drug. Interestingly, the anti-suicide effect is independent of its effects on mood (meaning that patients taking lithium are at a lower risk of suicide even if they still feel horribly depressed). Even at the level of populations, regions of the world with higher levels of naturally occurring lithium in their drinking water have lower suicide rates than places with lower levels.

Lithium is different from all of the drugs we have talked about so far in that you are not just titrating to clinical effect. Instead, the efficacy of lithium correlates with its **serum level**. The target level for lithium is 0.8-1.2 mmol/L for treating acute manic episodes, with incredibly high response rates between 70 and 80%! This dose roughly corresponds to a dose of 900-1,500 mg/day for most patients. Lithium should be taken as a **trough level** approximately **12 hours after** the last dose. Lithium reaches a steady state after **5 days**, so checking earlier than that can give incorrect results. For patients in a state of mania, there isn't much of a reason to go slowly, as using doses that are known to be subtherapeutic often only delays the patient getting to the needed serum level. (Of note, patients for whom you are prescribing lithium for its antidepressant effects can be managed on lower levels around 0.6-1.2 mmol/L.)

So if lithium is so great, why isn't it in everyone's drinking water (or at least in 7 Up still)? Once again, the Second Rule of Neurotransmission rears its head. Lithium pays for its incredible effectiveness with a **harsh side effect profile** that affects many organ systems in the body. We can use the mnemonic **LITHIUM SFX** to memorize all of the potential side effects of lithium:

L is for Low therapeutic index. We talked about monitoring lithium levels to ensure therapeutic effects, but we also need to worry about this in terms of toxic effects as well! Lithium has a low **therapeutic index**. This means that the level needed for its positive effect is uncomfortably close to the dose that will hurt or kill the patient, with a level of 2.0 or higher corresponding to lithium toxicity. For this reason, obtaining a lithium level is important, especially at the beginning when the stable dose is still being worked out. One of earliest and most consistent side effects of lithium toxicity is **tremor**, often of the hands. This is incredibly high-yield and will be an important clue both on boards and on wards! Treatment of lithium toxicity consists of fluid hydration and, sometimes, emergent hemodialysis for severely elevated lithium levels.

I is for Intestinal upset. Many patients experience nausea, vomiting, and diarrhea after starting lithium.

T is for Teratogenicity. Lithium is a known teratogen, especially during the first five weeks of pregnancy. Fetuses with *in utero* exposure to lithium have a higher chance of developing **Ebstein's anomaly**, a cardiac defect involving low implantation of the tricuspid valve, ventricularization of the right atria, and tricuspid atresia. Because of this, it's important to counsel any woman of reproductive age about the risks and benefits of taking lithium while pregnant. However, in many cases the risk of untreated bipolar disorder can be just as bad (if not worse) than the overall small risk of fetal abnormalities, so taking lithium during pregnancy is not contraindicated in all cases. You can remember the definition of Ebstein's anomaly by packing it into the first three letters of lithium: **L**ow **I**mplanted **T**ricuspid.

> **Lithium** exposure *in utero* can cause a cardiac defect known as **Ebstein's anomaly**.
>
> ***LIT**-hium can cause a **L**ow **I**mplanted **T**ricuspid.*

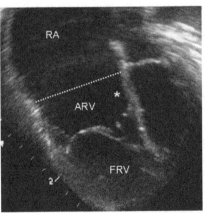

*Ultrasound of **Ebstein's anomaly** showing the right atrium (RA) and the low-implanted tricuspid valve leading to an atrialized right ventricle (ARV), with the functional right ventricle (FRV) below it.*

H is for Hypothyroidism. Hypothyroidism is the most common complication of long-term lithium use (occurring in up to 20% of patients who take lithium on an ongoing basis), so it's important to obtain a baseline TSH and follow the patient's symptoms and labs to monitor for emergence of thyroid abnormalities. Treatment is the same as for other cases of hypothyroidism and involves replacing thyroid hormone until the TSH has normalized. Discontinuation of lithium is generally not required as long as the hypothyroidism is treated adequately.

I is for Interactions. Lithium interacts badly with a number of other medications and medical conditions, particularly those involving the kidneys. While most psychotropic medications are metabolized in the liver, lithium is **renally metabolized**. This means that care must be taken to avoid prescribing lithium in patients with chronic kidney disease as well as to avoid concurrently prescribing NSAIDs, ACEIs, ARBs, diuretics, or other drugs that can lead to dehydration and/or kidney injury. Damage to the kidneys caused by lithium toxicity can resolve with hemodialysis and fluid hydration. However, in some cases it may become permanent, especially when the drug is taken over long periods of time.

U is for Urination. Patients taking lithium often report increased thirst (**polydipsia**) and frequent urination (**polyuria**). In some cases, this can be a sign of **nephrogenic diabetes insipidus**, although in other cases it is simply a side effect of the drug itself. If possible, aim for once daily dosing (as this can reduce the risk of this side effect) and encourage the patient to maintain fluid intake.

M is for Muscle weakness. Some patients will report feeling that their muscles are weaker while on lithium. For most people this is a transient finding, although for others it may persist.

S is for Skin. Lithium can affect the integumentary system including both **skin** and **hair**. Some patients see acne outbreaks after starting lithium, while others notice hair thinning or loss.

F is for Fatigue. Many patients who take lithium report feeling fatigue, sedation, and a lack of energy.

X is for Xtra pounds. Finally, weight gain can be seen while taking lithium in some patients, although typically not quite as much as is seen when taking metabolically active antipsychotics such as olanzapine.

Lithium has a wide ranging side effect profile involving multiple organ systems.

LITHIUM SFX:
Low therapeutic index
Intestinal upset
Teratogenicity
Hypothyroidism
Interactions
Urination
Muscle weakness
Skin
Fatigue
Xtra pounds (weight gain)

There is a set list of labs that should be checked in every patient before starting lithium as well as on a regular basis thereafter (including a lithium level, creatinine, TSH, and a pregnancy test). However, if you know the side effects of lithium, they should all be no-brainers. Take a moment to connect each lab to its side effect!

So where does that leave us on lithium? In essence, we have a drug that is incredibly effective at treating bipolar disorder and is one of the few in all of psychiatry that is proven to help prevent suicide, one of the most tragic outcomes of mental illness. Yet it also comes with no small amount of side effects (some of which can result in permanent illness or disability), so lithium must be monitored very closely. As always, with great power comes great responsibility!

ANTICONVULSANT MOOD STABILIZERS

The next several mood stabilizers we will cover are all **anticonvulsants**, meaning that they are used to treat seizure disorders as well. As mentioned earlier, slowing of neuronal firing in the brain may be one of the key drug effects that mood stabilizers have, and studies have shown that some anticonvulsants (though certainly not all) are effective mood stabilizers! We'll now go over each of these in more detail.

VALPROATE

Valproate (Depakote, Depakene), also known as valproic acid or divalproex depending on its formulation, was the first anticonvulsant to be used as a mood stabilizer. It is effective at treating mania, although it doesn't do much against bipolar depression. Valproate works by inhibiting voltage-gated **sodium channels** (which accounts for its anticonvulsant properties) while also increasing the amount of **GABA** (leading to its calming and sedative effects).

Like lithium, valproate's antimanic efficacy corresponds to its **serum level** and should be dosed accordingly. Like lithium, a valproate level should be taken as a **trough**, ideally about 30 minutes before the next dose. Valproate reaches a steady state in **2-3 days**. Your target level for valproate is approximately 50–150 mg/L, with some arguing for a narrower window of 80–120 mg/L both to ensure efficacy and to avoid toxicity. A handy rule of thumb to know what dose of valproate will likely correspond to a therapeutic level for any given patient is to take their weight in pounds and multiply it by 10 (or their weight in kilograms and multiply by 20). For example, a 150 pound patient is likely to reach their target level at a dose of 1500 mg/day while a 225 pound patient will probably need a dose closer to 2250 mg/day. Like with lithium, there is really no reason to start at a dose that you know to be subtherapeutic, as this only tends to delay the drug's benefits.

> A **therapeutic dose of valproate** is roughly **20 mg/kg/day**.
>
> *Take the patient's **weight in pounds** and **multiply by 10**!*

Valproate is associated with various side effects that span the range from "unpleasant but ultimately harmless" all the way to "severe and life-threatening." You can use the mnemonic **VALPROIC SFX** to remember these:

V is for Vomiting. Valproate can cause gastrointestinal side effects including diarrhea, nausea, and vomiting.

A is for Alopecia. Hair loss is common with valproate, although this is typically a short-term effect.

L is for Liver damage. Just like lithium is not only metabolized by but also potentially toxic to the kidneys, valproate is metabolized by the liver where it can similarly exert damaging effects. In some cases, this can even involve complete liver failure requiring an organ transplant.

P is for Pancreatitis. Inflammation of the pancreas is a rare but potentially fatal side effect of valproate. It tends to occur in first few months after starting the medication.

R is for Rebound seizures. If you take a patient off of valproate too quickly, you can precipitate rebound seizures, even in a patient with no seizure history! Make sure to gradually taper the dose rather than stopping all at once.

O is for Ovarian cysts. Use of valproate appears to increase the risk of polycystic ovary syndrome (PCOS) which can result in menstrual irregularity, masculinization of features, weight gain, and insulin resistance.

I is for Interactions. Valproate is a notoriously "dirty" drug that interacts with many other medications that are also metabolized by the liver.

C is for CBC abnormalities. While rare, both agranulocytosis (low white blood cells, like in clozapine) and thrombocytopenia (low platelets) appear to occur more often in patients taking valproate. These can be picked up by ordering a complete blood count (CBC) on a regular basis.

S is for Spina bifida. Valproate is absolutely **contraindicated in pregnancy**, as it is a known teratogen. Valproate exposure *in utero* is associated with multiple congenital malformations but is most famous for causing **neural tube defects** like spina bifida by interfering with folate metabolism.

F is for Fatigue. These last two side effects are exactly the same as lithium! Both of these mood stabilizers can cause fatigue, sedation, and low energy.

X is for Xtra pounds. Weight gain is another unfortunate side effect that valproate shares with lithium.

Valproate has a **wide ranging side effect profile** involving **multiple organ systems**.

> **VALPROIC SFX**:
> **V**omiting
> **A**lopecia
> **L**iver damage
> **P**ancreatitis
> **R**ebound seizures
> **O**varian cysts
> **I**nteractions
> **C**BC abnormalities
> **S**pina bifida
> **F**atigue
> **X**tra pounds (weight gain)

As with lithium, knowing these side effects can help you remember which labs to monitor with valproate (serum level, liver function tests, CBC, and a pregnancy test).

CARBAMAZEPINE
Carbamazepine (Tegretol) is another anticonvulsant that, like valproate, acts primarily by inhibiting voltage-gated **sodium channels** and augmenting **GABA** transmission. Also like valproate, it is good for treating mania but doesn't do much to help bipolar depression. In addition to being an anticonvulsant and a mood stabilizer, it can also be used to treat **trigeminal neuralgia** which is a form of neuropathic pain affecting the sensory nerves of the face. Carbamazepine is sometimes abbreviated CBZ, and we can pack its three main uses into that acronym: **C** for **C**ranial nerve pain (trigeminal neuralgia), **B** for **B**ipolar disorder, and **Z** for sei**Z**ures.

> **Carbamazepine** is used for **bipolar disorder, epilepsy**, and **trigeminal neuralgia**.
>
> **CBZ** treats **C**ranial nerve pain, **B**ipolar disorder, and sei**Z**ures.

Unlike lithium and valproate, carbamazepine does *not* depend on its serum levels for therapeutic effect! Instead, you are generally targeting a **specific dose** (800-1,200 mg/day for most adult patients). However, you can still order a carbamazepine level in your patients to ensure that it is not in a toxic range. (This is especially important given carbamazepine's drug interactions, as we will discuss shortly.) Like lithium and valproate, you should be checking a **trough** level about 30 minutes before the next dose. Carbamazepine reaches a steady state in **2-5 days**.

While effective for treating mania, carbamazepine is not a popular medication in bipolar disorder, largely due to its side effect profile. Like valproate, some of these side effects are obnoxious or uncomfortable (like nausea and blurry vision) while others are more severe or potentially life-threatening. You can remember the major side effects of carbamazepine using the mnemonic **CARB SFX**:

C is for CBC abnormalities. Like valproate, carbamazepine can cause abnormalities in blood cell count. Specifically, carbamazepine can cause **aplastic anaemia** leading to a deficiency of *all* blood cell types (including red cells, white cells, and platelets). There is a risk of agranulocytosis, though this risk is lower than with clozapine so the same intensive drug monitoring is not required.

A is for Adjustments. Carbamazepine is a notoriously "**dirty**" drug and wreaks havoc on multiple enzyme systems in the liver, requiring frequent dose adjustments to many of the other medications that the patient is taking. Ironically, carbamazepine even induces its own metabolism, so you'll have to adjust the dose of carbamazepine itself a week or two after starting it!

R is for Rash. Carbamazepine can cause **Stevens-Johnson syndrome**, a horrifying disease where the epidermis literally sloughs off of the dermis, as depicted below:

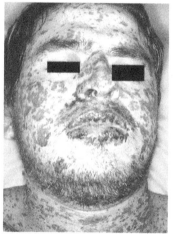

Stevens-Johnson syndrome.

Stevens-Johnson syndrome is a medical **emergency** and carries a mortality rate of around 5%. It is especially common when patients of **Asian** descent are prescribed carbamazepine due to the prevalence of a specific gene variant (HLA-B*1502). Because of this, **genetic screening** is recommended for all patients of Asian descent before starting carbam-**asia**-pine.

> People of **Asian descent** are at high risk for **Stevens-Johnson syndrome** from **carbamazepine** and should be **genetically screened** prior to starting.
>
> *Remember this association by thinking carbam-**asia**-pine.*

B is for Baby. Like valproate, carbamazepine carries a risk of neural tube defects in pregnant women (though the risk is overall less than with valproate).

S is for Sodium abnormalities. A unique effect of carbamazepine that is not seen with lithium or valproate is its interaction with sodium levels. Carbamazepine can cause hyponatremia and potentially syndrome of inappropriate antidiuretic hormone secretion (SIADH). For this reason, electrolyte levels should be monitored closely.

F is for Fatigue. Two friends (or more like enemies) return! Just like lithium and valproate, carbamazepine can cause sedation and fatigue.

X is for Xtra pounds. Finally, carbamazepine can cause weight gain, though generally to a lesser extent than valproate.

> **Carbamazepine** has a **wide ranging side effect profile** involving **multiple organ systems**.
>
> **CARB SFX:**
> **C**BC abnormalities
> **A**djustments
> **R**ash
> **B**aby (neural tube defects)
> **S**odium abnormalities
> **F**atigue
> **X**tra pounds (weight gain)

Just like lithium and valproate, carbamazepine requires monitoring of specific labs (CBC, electrolytes, serum level) that are all logical if you know the side effects! Overall, carbamazepine is generally not a first-line option for bipolar disorder given all of these potential concerns.

LAMOTRIGINE

Lamotrigine (Lamictal) is another anticonvulsant that also acts as a mood stabilizer. Unlike valproate and carbamazepine (which are primarily helpful for treating and preventing *manic* episodes), lamotrigine treats **bipolar depression** and has little, if any, effect on mania. This makes lamotrigine a particularly helpful drug, as it gives us  another tool to use against bipolar depression which can be stubbornly difficult to treat. (Indeed, while mania is the hallmark phase of the illness, the majority of patients with bipolar disorder spend most of their lives depressed, not manic.) You can remember this by thinking that **lam**-otrigine is helpful for when patients are feeling less **like a lion and more like a lamb.**

> Use **lamotrigine** for treating **bipolar depression**.
>
> Use **lam**-otrigine when your patients feel **less like a lion and more like a lamb**.

Like with carbamazepine, with lamotrigine you are targeting a **therapeutic dose** rather than a serum level. For most adult patients, your target dose is 100-200 mg/day. However, you can't just jump straight to that dose! Instead, you have to start lower and slowly work your way up. In general, lamotrigine is started at 25 mg/day for 2 weeks and then increased by 25 mg/day every 1–2 weeks until you hit the target dose.

Why do we have to move so slowly with lamotrigine? The main adverse effect to be aware of is that about 10% of patients will develop an itchy rash, which is uncomfortable but ultimately not too concerning. However, of these 10% an additional 10% (or 1% of the total) will go on to develop Stevens-Johnson syndrome, which *is* very concerning! The risk of causing either a benign rash or Stevens-Johnson syndrome can be reduced by doing the slow titration described above. Other than that, lamotrigine is generally **well tolerated**, with minimal side effects (which is why we don't need another long and involved mnemonic here!). To remember the association of lamotrigine with **itch**y rashes, think of it as lamotr-**itch**-gine.

Lamotrigine can cause **benign rashes** (10%) and **Stevens-Johnson syndrome** (1%).

*Lamotr-**itch**-gine can cause **itch**y rashes.*

One particular drug-drug interaction involving anticonvulsants that deserves special attention is the combination of valproate and lamotrigine. Given that valproate works for bipolar mania while lamotrigine works for bipolar depression, they are frequently combined to stabilize both ends of the mood spectrum. However, valproate can *increase* lamotrigine plasma levels by inhibiting the metabolism of lamotrigine in a dose-dependent fashion. Given that the risk of Stevens-Johnson syndrome is directly related to dose of lamotrigine, this interaction is potentially dangerous! Therefore, it is recommended to use *half* the dose of lamotrigine you normally would and to titrate the dose *half* as fast. You can remember this by thinking of **Valhalla**, the majestic hall located in the afterlife of Norse mythology. By thinking of

Valhalla, you can remember that when you use **val**-proate, you should use **hal**-f the dose of **la**-motrigine to avoid killing your patient and sending them to **Val-hal-la**!

Valproate inhibits the metabolism of **lamotrigine**. This requires a **slower titration** for lamotrigine in patients taking both drugs.

*When prescribing **val**-proate with lamotrigine, use **hal**-f the dose of **la**-motrigine to avoid killing your patient and sending them to **Val-hal-la**.*

THE "NOT MOOD STABILIZERS"

Finally, we'll cover the "not mood stabilizers" which are a group of anticonvulsants that *haven't* been found to be helpful for treating bipolar disorder. While it was initially hoped that these medications would be effective both as anticonvulsants and mood stabilizers, clinical trials showed that they were not better than placebo at treating bipolar disorder. So if they're not helpful, why are we covering them? Despite a lack of efficacy for treating the core symptoms of bipolar disorder, these medications can be helpful in other ways, so you are likely to encounter them on wards and in clinics. In addition, each one has some high-yield side effects that you will see on boards, so they're worth going over for general medical knowledge.

TOPIRAMATE

The first of the "not mood stabilizers" is topiramate (Topamax), an anticonvulsant that did not live up to hopes that it would be effective against bipolar disorder. While it is not a mood stabilizer, topiramate *does* appear to decrease impulsivity regardless of the patient's diagnosis, so it is sometimes used for that purpose! Despite the lack of efficacy in bipolar disorder, this drug can be popular with patients due to its "side effect" of **weight loss**, with patients losing anywhere from 5 to 15 pounds. On the other hand, many patients report general feelings of **mental dulling** (and word-finding difficulty in particular). You can remember the cognitive side effects of topiramate by thinking of it "**dope**-iramate."

> **Topiramate** is helpful for **reducing impulsivity** and **weight loss**, but it can also cause **cognitive dulling** and **word-finding difficulty**.
>
> *Dope-iramate can cause cognitive dulling!*

GABAPENTIN

The next "not mood stabilizer" is gabapentin (Neurontin), another anticonvulsant. While it is not helpful against bipolar disorder, you may see it being used for a variety of other purposes including treatment of **neuropathic pain** (like duloxetine and the tricyclics). In addition, there is some evidence that gabapentin is a decent **anxiolytic** without less risk of dependence and abuse than benzodiazepines. (More to come on both of these topics in Chapters 6 and 8!)

OXCARBAZEPINE

Finally we have oxcarbazepine (Trileptal) which is a close relative of carbamazepine. Oxcarbazepine is perhaps best classified as a *"maybe* mood stabilizer," as there are *some* studies that suggest that it has a similar efficacy in treating bipolar disorder as carbamazepine. However, these studies are very limited and are not considered to be high quality evidence. Nevertheless, it is a generally well tolerated medication without many side effects (it lacks the risk of agranulocytosis and all those nasty drug-drug interactions that carbamazepine has), so you may occasionally see it being used as a "why not?" drug for bipolar disorder when other options have been exhausted.

ANTIPSYCHOTICS

Antipsychotics are worth revisiting in the context of bipolar disorder, as they are known to have mood stabilizing properties and are useful for both **acute treatment** of bipolar mania and for **prevention** of future episodes. Antipsychotics even have an advantage over mood stabilizers in that they work much faster for an acute manic episode (showing effects within several hours compared to the 7-10 days it can take for mood stabilizers to kick in). Therefore, antipsychotics (*any* antipsychotic really, they all work!) should be your **first-line medication** for treatment of acute mania.

> **Initial treatment** of an **acute manic episode** is with an **antipsychotic**.
>
> *Antipsychotics come **earlier** in the alphabet than Mood stabilizers.*

While all antipsychotics are effective for treating mania, the idea that "any antipsychotic will do" unfortunately does *not* apply to bipolar depression as well. Only **four antipsychotics** (olanzapine, quetiapine, lurasidone, and cariprazine) have been shown to have efficacy in treating bipolar depression. Each of these antipsychotics interacts with serotonin more than most which may explain some of their actions here. However, as with many things in psychiatry, we don't know 100% of the reasons why these antipsychotics work for bipolar depression while the other ones don't. To 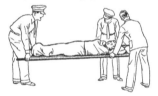 remember the four antipsychotics that can treat bipolar depression, use the phrase "**Carries the quiet, low, and old**" to remember that **Cari**-prazine, **Quiet**-apine, **Low**-rasidone, and **Old**-lanzapine can help when patients with bipolar disorder aren't feeling as robust as they would like.

> **All antipsychotics** can treat **mania**, but **only four** are helpful for **bipolar depression**.
>
> ***Carries** the **quiet**, **low**, and **old**:*
> *Cari-prazine, quiet-apine, low-rasidone, and old-lanzapine.*

ANTIDEPRESSANTS

One might wonder why antidepressants have not yet been mentioned in regards to bipolar disorder, especially since depressive episodes are part of bipolar disorder pathology. There are two things to consider here: do they work (**efficacy**) and do they have any negative effects (**harm**)?

Looking at the first question, the overall consensus seems to be that, while antidepressants are helpful for *unipolar* depression, they **aren't nearly as effective for bipolar depression**. In fact, most research suggests that there is little difference in rates of response or remission between patients on antidepressants versus those taking a placebo. However, the truth is probably more nuanced than simply saying "antidepressants don't work at all." Clinical experience and research have suggested that some patients with bipolar disorder *do* seem to respond well to antidepressants. The key here is that, for these patients, the antidepressant has been combined with a mood stabilizer or an antipsychotic. In fact, some combination medications such as olanzapine/fluoxetine (Symbyax) have been approved specifically for use in treating bipolar depression. So while antidepressants *on their own* don't seem to work, if you combine them with appropriate mood stabilizers, they *can* be helpful for at least some patients, although they probably shouldn't be a first-line option (try lithium, lamotrigine, or any of the four "Carries the quiet, low, and old" antipsychotics first!).

Looking at the question of harm, for a long time it was believed that if you prescribed an antidepressant to a patient with bipolar disorder, you could "switch" them into mania. However, later research failed to show a link between use of antidepressants and an increased risk of mania. So what's the truth? A closer look at the data suggests that *some*, but not *all*, antidepressants can potentially cause a switch into mania. The key factor here seems to be the extent to which **norepinephrine** is involved, with highly noradrenergic drugs like TCAs being the most likely to switch a patient while more serotonin-specific drugs are relatively blameless.

So where does that leave us on use of antidepressants in bipolar disorder? The key here is that a **nuanced approach** is best. Saying that antidepressants *never* work in bipolar disorder is probably just as wrong as saying that they *always* work. If you are going to use antidepressants in bipolar disorder, make sure that they are combined with an appropriate mood stabilizer, and try to avoid strongly noradrenergic drugs!

HOW TO USE MOOD STABILIZERS

Mood stabilizers are used to treat cases of bipolar disorder. As a reminder, you can use the mnemonic **DIG FAST** to remember the signs and symptoms of mania including **D**istractibility, **I**mpulsivity, **G**randiosity, **F**light of ideas, increased **A**ctivity, decreased need for **S**leep, and **T**alkativeness. Having at least 3-4 of these 7 symptoms for **1 or more weeks** qualifies the patient for a manic episode per DSM standards. Patients with a history of mania can be diagnosed with **bipolar I disorder**.

Bipolar depression is clinically indistinguishable from unipolar depression, so the same **SIGECAPS** and **"two blue weeks"** mnemonics we covered back in Chapter 3 apply here as well.

Some patients do not have "full blown" mania but instead experience periods of increased energy, activity, and elevated mood that don't quite reach the level of mania and are less functionally impairing. These episodes are known as **hypomania**, and patients who have a history of hypomania (but not mania) can be diagnosed with **bipolar II disorder**. These patients often experience depressive episodes as well.

Now that we have an understanding of the various forms of bipolar disorder, let's establish some basic principles for how best to use mood stabilizers:

Memorable Psychopharmacology

1. Choose based on phase of illness.
In contrast to antidepressants and antipsychotics (where you should choose based on side effects), your choice of medications should come down to the phase of the illness that you are trying to treat. For **mania**, use lithium, valproate, or carbamazepine as mood stabilizers; in addition, any antipsychotic (either alone or combined with a mood stabilizer) will do. For **depression**, use lithium, lamotrigine, cariprazine, quetiapine, olanzapine, or lurasidone. Once you've zeroed in on the phase of illness, then consider the side effect profile to select the specific drug to be used!

2. Think of future states as well.
Don't just think about what's immediately in front of you! When treating a manic patient, you should consider that they have a very high chance of developing a depressive episode in the future, so you should consider either starting a medications that has effects on both mania and depression or using two drugs to cover both ends of the mood spectrum. Which leads us to…

3. Polypharmacy is okay.
In contrast to antidepressants and antipsychotics (where polypharmacy is mostly associated with more side effects but not better outcomes), successful treatment of bipolar disorder often involves more than one medication to treat both depression and mania. Some medications (such as lithium or quetiapine) *do* cover both in a single drug, so you should always consider whether you can safely eliminate unnecessary medications in order to reduce the side effect burden. However, for some (if not most) patients with this disorder, a single drug just doesn't cut it, so you should not feel badly if your patient ends up needing multiple medications.

4. Know what your target is.
Each of the mood stabilizers has a specific target you're shooting for: either a **target dose** or a **target level**. Know what you're shooting for, and don't waste time (either the patient's or yours) with subtherapeutic doses. This is especially important because, while therapeutic effects aren't seen until the threshold is crossed, side effects *are*, so using suboptimal  doses only leaves the patient at risk of adverse outcomes without the promise of help. (This is especially true in the hospital where you can monitor closely for the emergence of side effects and adjust the dose if needed.)

5. Don't neglect psychosocial interventions.
Several forms of therapy, such as cognitive behavioral therapy, family-focused therapy, and psychoeducation, have been shown to improve outcomes for patients with bipolar disorder. While patients in an acute disorganized phase of manic illness are unlikely to benefit, nearly all other patients should be referred to some form of therapy as appropriate. In general, therapy on its own is not considered to be enough treatment for most patients with bipolar disorder, but as an add-on to medications, therapy can be a huge help for our patients.

6. Get the diagnosis right.
We've just taken a tour of some the incredibly scary and even potentially life-threatening side effects that mood stabilizers can have (such as permanent kidney damage, liver failure, pancreatitis, or Stevens-Johnson syndrome). Now imagine that you have just given one of these side effects to a patient who didn't need the drug in the first place. Those are the stakes that are involved when treating bipolar disorder. These are powerful drugs that are often needed to combat one of the most devastating illnesses in psychiatry. However, "With great power comes great responsibility," and it is our job to make sure that we are only using these medications when they are absolutely needed.

This job is complicated by the fact that bipolar disorder is difficult to diagnose. One of the most important distinctions to make is between bipolar disorder and **borderline personality disorder**. For bipolar disorder, the mainstay of treatment is medications, although therapy can help as well. However, for borderline personality disorder, no drugs have shown to be effective at treating the disorder (although drugs may be used to target specific symptoms). Instead, specific forms of treatment such as dialectical behavior therapy (DBT) or good psychiatric management (GPM) are much more effective. So if you misdiagnose a patient, you could spend years trying to help but failing because you are using the wrong treatments.

So how can we distinguish the two? There are a few key differences. First, in bipolar disorder, changes in mood tend to happen over weeks and months, whereas borderline patients can switch between their highs and lows in minutes or hours. Second, mood episodes in bipolar disorder tend to occur independently of life events, whereas the mood of patients with borderline personality disorder is often *highly* dependent on events (especially interpersonal relationships). Finally, the frequency of the disorders is different, with bipolar disorder being more rare (as low as 1% of the population), whereas borderline personality disorder is up to ten times more common. Use this table as a quick reminder on how to differentiate between these two diagnoses:

	Bipolar Mood Disorder	**Borderline Personality Disorder**
Mood changes	Over weeks or months	Over minutes or hours
Mood reactivity	Often independent of life events	Highly dependent on life events
Frequency	Rare (1-3%)	More common (6-10%)
Treatment	Primarily medications (therapy helps too)	Primarily therapy (drugs don't really help)

While borderline personality disorder is the most notable example, it is not the only one, with other diagnoses (such as substance use disorders) often being confused as well. At the end of the day, take the time to improve your diagnostic skills so that you can target treatments appropriately and avoid harming patients for no reason.

PUTTING IT ALL TOGETHER

Congratulations! You made it through one of the most difficult chapters in the book. Mood stabilizers are insanely complicated due to the their wide-ranging side effects, the need for monitoring, the different therapeutic targets, and the various phases of bipolar disorder. Review the **LITHIUM SFX**, **VALPROIC SFX**, **CARB SFX**, and lamotr-itch-gine mnemonics to help simplify the incredible complexity of these drugs!

To help sum up what we've learned, let's review for each of the mood stabilizers what your therapeutic target is. For lithium and valproate, you are targeting a specific serum level, as their efficacy as a mood stabilizer correlates to the serum level (as does their toxicity). For carbamazepine and lamotrigine, you are targeting a specific dose range. For carbamazepine, psychiatric efficacy does not correlate to the serum level, but toxicity does so it's still worth checking. You can obtain a lamotrigine level as well, but there is no good evidence that the level correlates with either efficacy or toxicity, so there's not much of a point. You can remember the target serum level for each of these mood stabilizers easily using the "**1-10-100 Rule**":

Medication	Target	Level	Correlates To	Steady State
Lithium	Level	1 (0.8 – 1.2)	Efficacy and toxicity	5 days
Carbamazepine	Dose (800-1200 mg/d)	10 (8 – 12)	Toxicity only	2-5 days
Valproate	Level	100 (80 – 120)	Efficacy and toxicity	2-3 days
Lamotrigine	Dose (100-200 mg/d)	n/a	n/a	n/a

Serum levels of **lithium**, **valproate**, and **carbamazepine** can be monitored to assess for both **efficacy and toxicity**.

Use the **1-10-100 Rule** to dose mood stabilizers:
Lithium = **1**
Carbamazepine = **10**
Valproate = **100**

REVIEW QUESTIONS

1. A 23 y/o F is brought into the ED by worried family members who report that she has been "flying around the house" and has not slept in several days. During the interview, the patient talks incessantly and frequently refers to her plan to run for political office to "save the children from pesticides!" Which medication would be expected to most rapidly reverse her psychiatric symptoms?
   A. Lithium
   B. Valproate
   C. Venlafaxine
   D. Lamotrigine
   E. Olanzapine

2. A 21 y/o M with a history of known bipolar I disorder on valproate comes to see his psychiatrist. He states that he is "as depressed as I have ever been" and is unable to work due to neurovegetative symptoms. His psychiatrist suggests attempting a trial of lamotrigine. What of the following side effects should the patient be counseled on?
   A. Dermatologic reactions
   B. EKG abnormalities
   C. Urinary retention
   D. Rapid cycling mood
   E. Neuropathic pain

3. A 24 y/o G2P1A1 F with a 5-year history of bipolar I disorder has just given birth to a newborn boy. Several hours after birth, the newborn becomes agitated and appears to be in respiratory distress. On exam, his nail beds are observed to have a bluish tinge, as below:

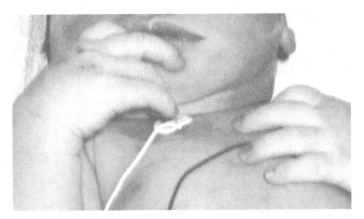

Transthoracic echocardiogram reveals significant structural abnormalities. What is the most likely cause of this presentation?
A. Aspiration of foreign object
B. Congenital malformation
C. Medication withdrawal
D. TORCH infections
E. Smoking during pregnancy

4. A 37 y/o F is talking with a psychiatrist about switching to a new medication to treat her bipolar disorder after she experienced significant side effects from her previous mood stabilizer. Which of the following is *least* likely to accurately describe her side effects?
A. Weight gain, cold intolerance, and constipation while taking lithium
B. A sudden drop in white blood cell count while taking oxcarbazepine
C. Mental dulling and difficulty finding words while taking topiramate
D. Yellow skin, excessive bleeding, and altered mental status while taking valproate
E. Blistering and peeling of the skin while taking lamotrigine

5. (Continued from previous question.) During the discussion, the patient says that she wants to take the "lowest number of medications possible." She has a history of both manic episodes requiring hospitalization and severe depressive episodes leading to significant dysfunction. Which of the following medications is most likely to be successful at preventing both manic and depressive episodes?
A. Valproate
B. Lamotrigine
C. Haloperidol
D. Aripiprazole
E. Lurasidone

6. A 29 y/o M who weighs 200 lbs (90 kg) is admitted to the hospital after he begins staying up all night for several weeks trying to write screenplays for a trilogy of movies that he describes as "science-fiction fantasy romance horror historical survival dramas." He is pressured in his speech and interrupts people around him constantly. His treatment team starts him on quetiapine 200 mg and valproate 2000 mg, both taken at night. A valproate level taken the next morning shows a level of 45 mg/L. Since this is below the target range of 80-120 mg/L, the team increases the dose to 3000 mg. Several days later, the patient appears confused and lethargic. He has difficulty walking upright and is slurring his words. A repeat valproate level is 170 mg/L, and his liver function tests are both elevated. Which of the following could have prevented this outcome?
A. Starting only one medication at a time
B. Having a different target range for valproate
C. Taking the valproate level at a different time
D. Starting lamotrigine concurrently
E. Nothing could have prevented this outcome

1. **The best answer is E.** The most important immediate treatment for a patient in an acute manic episode is antipsychotics. Mood stabilizers such as lithium or valproate (answers A and B) should be ordered as well, but they work too slowly for acute management. Lamotrigine is a mood stabilizer, but it only has efficacy in bipolar depression and is not expected to help with mania (answer D). Strongly noradrenergic antidepressants such as venlafaxine (answer C) should be avoided.

2. **The best answer is A.** Lamotrigine has a high rate of skin reactions, occurring in up to 10% of patients started on the drug. However, there is an association with Stevens-Johnson syndrome which can be life-threatening, so patients should be counseled to seek emergency services immediately if they experience a rash, fever, and/or mucous membrane changes. None of the other side effects are associated with lamotrigine.

3. **The best answer is B.** The newborn likely has Ebstein's anomaly, a congenital heart defect in which the tricuspid valve leaflets are displaced towards the apex of the right ventricle. Ebstein's anomaly is related to maternal lithium use during the first trimester of pregnancy. The other options are unlikely given the significant risk factors for lithium exposure.

4. **The best answer is B.** Agranulocytosis is associated with carbamazepine, not oxcarbazepine. Hypothyroidism is associated with lithium (answer A), cognitive dulling is associated with topiramate (answer C), hepatic failure is associated with valproate (answer D), and Stevens–Johnson syndrome is associated with lamotrigine (answer E).

5. **The best answer is E.** Olanzapine, quetiapine, cariprazine, and lurasidone are the only four antipsychotics that can treat both manic and depressive episodes related to bipolar disorder. Aripiprazole would only be expected to treat unipolar depression, not bipolar depression (answer D). Haloperidol does not appear to have antidepressant effects in either unipolar depression or bipolar disorder (answer C). Valproate can only treat manic episodes (answer A), while lamotrigine can only treat bipolar depression (answer B).

6. **The best answer is C.** Valproate reaches a steady state approximately 2-3 days after being started, so taking a level earlier than that will reveal a falsely low serum level. The team's target range for valproate was appropriate (answer B). Starting only one medication at a time is a good goal in many cases, although when treating mania it is often appropriate as antipsychotics work faster than mood stabilizers (answer A). Starting lamotrigine alongside valproate results in elevated levels of *lamotrigine* and would not be expected to alter levels of valproate (answer D).

6 ANXIOLYTICS AND HYPNOTICS

Anxiolytics are drugs which break (or "lyse") a mental state of anxiety. They are prescribed for many conditions within the category of anxiety disorders, including both **acute** episodes like panic attacks as well as more **chronic** states like general anxiety disorder. Anxiety can affect someone's life without necessarily being part of an anxiety *disorder* per se, whether that happens in relation to another mental condition (such as depression, OCD, PTSD, and various personality disorders) or as a completely normal and adaptive response to various stresses in life.
Anxiolytics can work in these situations as well, although caution must be taken to avoid either "medicating normalcy" or missing the underlying cause of the anxiety.

In this chapter, we will also talk about **hypnotics** which are drugs used to treat insomnia by helping someone fall asleep more easily. While anxiolytics and hypnotics are in some ways separate things, there is so much overlap between the two drug classes (both in terms of the mechanisms involved as well as which drugs can be used) that we will functionally lump them into the same category here.

Anxiolytics and hypnotics can generally be divided into a few discrete classes: **GABAergics**, **serotonergics/noradrenergics**, and a mixed bag of **other anxiolytics and hypnotics** that feature a variety of mechanisms. When discussing anxiolytics and hypnotics, it's important to point out that these classes are ultimately **more different than they are alike**. (This is in contrast to both antidepressants and antipsychotics where we made a major point about these drugs ultimately being more similar than different!) It would be a grave error to lump all drugs that are used to treat anxiety together into a single category due to the major differences in efficacy, indications, and side effect profile associated with each.

ANXIOLYTIC EFFECTS

Let's first talk about GABAergic anxiolytics which work on the **GABA receptor**. Recall that GABA is the major *inhibitory* neurotransmitter in the brain which causes neurons to fire less often and makes you feel sleepy and relaxed (like a lecturer who **gab**s on and on). There are two main types of GABAergic anxiolytics: **benzodiazepines** and **barbiturates**. While both drug classes enhance GABA's inhibitory effects in the brain, the way they go about this differs somewhat. Benzodiazepines increase the frequency at which the GABA channel opens, while barbiturates increase the length of time that the channel stays open. You can remember this by thinking of these medications as **fre**nzodiazepines (for **fre**quency of channel opening) and barbi**durate**s (for **duration** of channel opening).

> **Benzodiazepines** increase GABA channel opening **frequency**, while **barbiturates** increase GABA channel opening **duration**.
>
> *Fre*-nzodiazepines increase *fre*-quency, barbi-*durate*-s increase *duration*.

While having this mechanistic understanding of barbiturates can be helpful for learning, it won't come into play very often these days, as barbiturates have largely fallen out of favor in modern psychiatry. While effective for anxiety, barbiturates have a high potential for dependence and a tendency to cause serious injury or death in overdose. Barbiturates were directly responsible for the deaths of Marilyn Monroe, Judy Garland, and Jimi Hendrix, and their use today in the United States includes physician-assisted suicide and lethal injections as capital punishment. These are not playful drugs and, as a general rule of thumb, should almost never be prescribed for psychiatric purposes! Moving forward, we'll focus solely on benzodiazepines.

Clinically, benzodiazepines (or just "benzos") are some of the most helpful drugs ever discovered when used on a short-term basis, as they result in immediate and drastic relief of anxiety symptoms. People in a state of anxiety often describe both **physical sensations** (such as a pounding heart, difficulty breathing, and sweating) as well as **psychological symptoms** (such as racing thoughts, a sense of losing control, or a fear of dying), and benzos help to bring a quick end to both. A helpful analogy can be drawn between benzos and a water hose being used to fight a fire: they are both great emergency response systems that can help to bring a crisis to an end once it has already started. (In a similar vein, benzos can be used even before anxiety has started to help prevent an episode, like covering a patch of land with water to make it less likely to catch fire.)

However, just like it doesn't make sense to use a water hose to fight a fire for weeks or months on end, there are limits to how helpful benzos are when used on a long-term basis. For one, benzos cause both psychological and physiologic **tolerance**. This can lead to issues of abuse and dependence, as patients need to take larger and larger amounts of the drug to achieve the same effect. In addition, while benzos are helpful for anxiety in the short-term, they have significant **side effects** such as sedation, memory impairment, and cognitive dulling which can interfere with your patient's ability to function on a daily basis as well as prevent them from being able to engage in the therapies that will help them most in the long run. (For further evidence of their memory-impairing qualities, consider that many benzos also double as date rape drugs!) Finally, for elderly patients the risk of **dizziness** and **falls** is high, leading to benzos being included on the Beers List of drugs which are not recommended for patients over 65.

From a psychiatric standpoint, what is most troubling about benzos is the fact that they have actually been shown to make anxiety *worse* in the long run, exacerbating the very problem they were meant to solve! To understand why, we need to return to the First Rule of Neurotransmission: "What goes up must come down." In the case of benzodiazepines, however, it may be more fair to say that **what goes down must come back up**, as all of the sedating and anxiolytic effects of these drugs get reversed during the withdrawal phase. In the short term, this leads to rebound anxiety, restlessness, insomnia, and even seizures when withdrawing from a benzo. In the long-term, as the brain becomes sensitized to the presence of benzos and stops being as sensitive to the GABA that it creates on its own, anxiety can go through the roof, creating levels of anxiety that are even worse than what prompted the patient to seek treatment in the first place. This is why some people refer to a "benzo trap" that is hard to get out of, as these drugs offer short-term relief while creating a brain that is **more susceptible to anxiety** in the long-term. (Benzos are known to make depression worse in the long-term as well, which makes sense as they inherently worsen the low energy and poor concentration that are core symptoms of the disorder.)

So if relying too heavily on GABA isn't great in the long-term, what other options are there? This is where **serotonergic** medications come into play. (Of note, drugs that inhibit the reuptake of norepinephrine, either instead of or in addition to serotonin, can also be helpful for anxiety! Revisit the "noradrenergic paradox" from Chapter 3 if this feels unfamiliar.) Serotonergic drugs don't do anything to stop anxiety in the moment once it has already started. Instead, they help to **bring down anxiety in the long-term**. People taking serotonergic medications for anxiety often report that the frequency and intensity of anxiety episodes goes down over time or that the effects of chronic anxiety are less debilitating than they once were. In this way, serotonergics are more like brush clearing and other fire prevention techniques: not as helpful in the *immediate* sense, but much more helpful in the long run!

Besides just GABA and serotonin, a few other neurotransmitters will pop up in this chapter. Blocking **histamine** can result in sedation which, while it doesn't treat anxiety directly, can still help prevent a person from feeling it as much. In addition, a few **anticonvulsants** will appear! Recall that most mood stabilizers have fatigue and sedation as a side effect, and (just like with antihistamines) we can use that property here as well. Finally, blocking specific **norepinephrine** receptors can help to stop some of the *physical* symptoms of anxiety like increases in heart rate and sweating.

BENZODIAZEPINES

Compared to barbiturates, benzodiazepines remain very commonly used in medicine today, as they offer a cleaner neurotransmitter profile and lower toxicity in overdose. More than just the anxiolytic and sedating properties that we have discussed already, benzos have found uses throughout the medical field, including as anti-seizure drugs.

Unlike the antidepressants, antipsychotics, and mood stabilizers where a strong foundation in each individual drug is essential, with benzodiazepines you can largely treat them as a group. You can recognize the majority of benzos from the letters **A-Z-E** within the name, with many ending in -**azepam**. One quick look at any of the benzodi-**aze**-pines (such as lor-**aze**-pam, di-**aze**-pam, and tem-**aze**-pam) should convince you of that (although occasionally there will be slight variations, as in alpr-**azo**-lam). Overall, this should be an A-Z-E thing to remember!

> You can recognize **benzodiazepines** by the "**aze**" in their name.
>
> *This is an **A-Z-E** thing to remember!*

We will not be covering each benzodiazepine individually, as there are too many of them and they are all fairly similar. However, it can be useful to group the benzos into several groups based on their **half-life**, as this has clinical importance. (As a brief aside, remember that half-life and onset of action are two different concepts! Onset refers to how quickly the drug's effects are achieved, whereas half-life refers to how long the drug stays in the system. These two concepts are easily confused, but try to keep them separate in your mind! As an example, diazepam has a long half-life *but* a rapid onset.)

SHORT-ACTING BENZODIAZPINES

The short-acting benzos, including **triazolam** (Halcyon), **oxazepam** (Serax), and **midazolam** (Versed), have both a rapid onset and a short half-life between 1-12 hours. Because of this, they are often used as hypnotics to induce sleep without causing too much "hangover" sedation the next morning. However, their rapid clearance can be advantageous in other ways. As one example, midazolam is often used in the ICU for prolonged sedation, as the sedation can rapidly be withdrawn when it is no longer needed (as opposed to a longer-acting benzodiazepine, which would hang around in the system for several hours after stopping it). The three most common short-acting benzodiazepines can be abbreviated **TOM** (**T**riazolam, **O**xazepam, and **M**idazolam).

LONG-ACTING BENZODIAZEPINES

The long-acting benzos have a half-life of over 24 hours and include **diazepam** (Valium) and **chlordiazepoxide** (Librium). In contrast to the short-acting benzos, you would not want to use these for sleep, as they would cause sedation far into the next day. Rather, their long half-life has proven useful for detoxing someone off of alcohol as this results in fewer swings between activation and sedation. To remember which benzodiazepines have a long half-life of several **días** ("days" in Spanish), just look for the ones with **diaz** in their names: chlor-**diaz**-epoxide and **diaz**-epam.

INTERMEDIATE-ACTING BENZODIAZEPINES

Finally, the intermediate-acting benzos (with a half-life between 12 and 24 hours) are the most common of the bunch and include **lorazepam** (Ativan), **clonazepam** (Klonopin), **alprazolam** (Xanax), and **temazepam** (Restoril). As you might expect, these drugs combine the best (and worst) of the short and long-acting groups. As hypnotics, they are effective (but often have some residual "hangover" effects in the morning). As detox agents, they are helpful (but have to be dosed more frequently). To remember the intermediate-acting benzodiazepines, think of using them to **lure** a **CAT** (**lor**azepam, **C**lonazepam, **A**lprazolam, and **T**emazepam).

To keep track of which commonly used benzos belong to which class, we can combine these mnemonics into a new *super*mnemonic which goes, "**TOM** moved **fast**, to **lure** the **CAT**, but still took several **días**." **TOM** and **fast** are together, "**lure** the **CAT**" is in the **middle** of the other two, and **días** helps remind you that the long-acting benzos have a half-life of several **days**.

> **Benzodiazepines** can be categorized as **short**, **intermediate**, and **long-acting** based on their **elimination half-life**.
>
> *TOM moved fast, to lure the CAT, but still took several días.*

As a final note, it is helpful to remember that benzos are generally **metabolized by the liver**. For patients with hepatic dysfunction, three benzos are safe to give: Oxazepam, Temazepam, and Lorazepam. The classic mnemonic for this is to remember that they are metabolized **O**utside **T**he **L**iver. However, this mnemonic isn't exactly accurate, as these three benzos are all actually metabolized *in* the liver. The difference is that they are metabolized by conjugation, meaning that *they don't have active metabolites* which makes their half-lives the same as always even in advanced liver disease. So if you're going to use the "**O**utside **T**he **L**iver" mnemonic (and it *is* handy!), also remember that it is not entirely accurate!

> **Oxazepam, temazepam**, and **lorazepam** are safe to use even in **liver dysfunction**.
>
> *Oxazepam, Temazepam, and Lorazepam are (practically) metabolized Outside The Liver.*

SEROTONERGIC AND NORADRENERGIC ANXIOLYTICS

In contrast to benzodiazepines, serotonergic and noradrenergic anxiolytics have much less potential for dependence and abuse. In addition, they don't impair cognition or cause a worsening of anxiety and depression (and may even *help* with the latter to boot!). However, they also don't result in the immediate relief that many people seek, which is important to talk to patients about before starting these medications, especially if they have taken benzos before and are expecting these drugs to work the same way. Nevertheless, if you can set the right expectations prior to treatment, these are among the most helpful drugs we have for treating anxiety!

ANTIDEPRESSANTS
As discussed earlier, most antidepressants help with anxiety as well (remember that these are "broad-spectrum antineurotics"). While they are not side effect free (indeed, all the same caveats that we went over in Chapter 3 apply here as well), in general they have a favorable side effect profile and should be considered **first-line agents** for treating anxiety. Of note, some antidepressants can also be used as hypnotics, particularly those that are known to be sedating such as trazodone and mirtazapine.

BUSPIRONE
Buspirone (Buspar) is a **serotonin partial agonist** (at the 5-HT$_{1A}$ receptor in particular) that it is most often used to treat **generalized anxiety disorder**. Importantly, GABA is *not* involved, meaning that buspirone does not cause sedation, has no withdrawal effects, and displays very little dependence potential. Like the antidepressants, its therapeutic effect can take a few weeks to kick in. Nevertheless, if patients have been properly counseled not to expect immediate relief, buspirone can be a helpful drug. To remember the indication for **buspirone**, to think of someone who is always **anxious** about every little thing like missing the **bus**. This anxiety about missing the **bus** de-**part**-ure can be managed with **bus**-pirone, a **part**-ial agonist. (Another clinical pearl: for patients with sexual side effects from antidepressants, adding buspirone and its partial agonist effects can help to improve sexual function, similar to how aripiprazole's partial agonism can reduce the prolactin-related side effects of antipsychotics like risperidone!)

Buspirone is a **serotonin partial agonist** that is helpful for long-term management of **generalized anxiety disorder**.

Anxious about missing the **bus** de-**part**-ure again?
Take **bus**-pirone, a serotonin **part**-ial agonist.

ANTIHISTAMINES

As you may recall from the **H₁S+A**-mine mnemonic, antihistamines have profound **sedating** properties and are therefore useful for treating both anxiety and insomnia. Unlike other sleeping aids, many are also available over-the-counter, making them both cheap and easily available. On the other hand, antihistamines can mess with the sleep cycle, so while they can help someone *get* to sleep, they do not provide a good *quality* of sleep. Antihistamines are also prone to tolerance, and after a few days of continued use they are no better than placebo for inducing sleep. Overall, their accessibility makes them a good option for *occasional* use.

DIPHENHYDRAMINE

Diphenhydramine (which almost always goes by its trade name Benadryl) is an older antihistamine which is not only a **strong H₁ receptor antagonist** but also a potent **anticholinergic** drug as well. While it is commonly used for allergies, it has found use as a hypnotic due to its sedating properties. It's not as helpful during the daytime, however, as its anticholinergic effects can lead to high levels of cognitive impairment (with even a normal therapeutic dose having the ability to cause unsafe driving similar to someone drinking alcohol!). In psychiatry, diphenhydramine is often used as well for its **antiparkinsonian** effects, as it can help to offset the EPS caused by strong dopamine blockers like haloperidol (remember di-**bend**-hydramine from Chapter 4!).

> **Diphenhydramine** is an **antihistamine** with strong **anticholinergic** effects.
>
> *Diphen-**H₁**-dramine hits the **H₁** receptor.*

HYDROXYZINE

Hydroxyzine (Vistaril, Atarax) is another **first-generation antihistamine**. Compared to diphenhydramine, hydroxyzine is **selective for the H₁ receptor** and is only weakly anticholinergic. This makes it sedating but without as much cognitive impairment, allowing patients to take it for daytime anxiety and still be (relatively) functional in the time afterwards. You can remember the selectivity of hydroxyzine for the H₁ receptor and resultant drowsiness by thinking of it as **H₁-drowsy**-zine.

> **Hydroxyzine** is an **antihistamine** that is selective for the **H₁ histamine receptor**.
> It is used as an as-needed medication for **anxiety**.
>
> ***H₁-drowsy**-zine selectively hits the **H₁** receptor to make you **drowsy**.*

DOXYLAMINE

The last antihistamine we will talk about is doxylamine (Unisom) which is found in many over-the-counter sleep aids like NyQuil. In contrast to diphenhydramine (which has *strong* anticholinergic effects) and hydroxyzine (which has *weak* anticholinergic effects), doxylamine has *moderate* anticholinergic effects. Still, the anticholinergic load is big enough that you will generally want to avoid daytime usage of doxylamine.

OTHER ANXIOLYTICS AND HYPNOTICS

Finally, let's round out this chapter with a few other drugs that can be used to treat anxiety and insomnia in various ways. Some will be familiar, while others will be new!

GABAPENTIN

You may remember gabapentin (Neurontin) as one of the "not mood stabilizers" we discussed in Chapter 5. While it's not so great at stabilizing mood, gabapentin *does* appear to have some benefit in treating anxiety (as well as efficacy at treating various forms of pain, as will discuss in Chapter 8). While it's easy to be tricked into thinking that this is due to the drug's effects at the GABA receptor (since "gaba" is right there in the name of the drug), don't be fooled! Despite its name, gabapentin has **nothing to do with GABA receptors**! Instead, it works as an inhibitor at voltage-gated **calcium channels**, leading to decreased neuronal firing via other mechanisms. Because the "gaba" part of gabapentin is such a sham, let's focus instead on the "PEN" part to remember the main reasons to use this drug: to treat various forms of **P**ain, to treat focal **E**pileptic seizures, and to treat **N**ervousness on an as-needed basis.

> **Gabapentin** is an **anticonvulsant** that can be used to treat **anxiety** and **pain**.
>
> *Gaba-**PEN**-tin can treat **P**ain, **E**pileptic seizures, and **N**ervousness.*

When used for anxiety, gabapentin can be considered a "**benzo-lite**," as it works quickly to induce a sense of calm shortly after someone takes it (though not nearly to the same extent as taking a benzo). The upside of gabapentin's weaker effects on anxiety is that it is not as prone to abuse or dependence as benzos (as with *less* power comes *less* responsibility!). Overall, gabapentin can be a great option for patients who require an as-needed medication for anxiety without the same risks as benzos, though antidepressants and therapy should still be your first-line options.

PREGABALIN

Pregabalin (Lyrica) was developed to be similar to gabapentin, and in many ways this goal was achieved! They both inhibit calcium channels without touching the GABA receptor (making the "gaba" in pregabalin just as much of a sham as before!), and they both have the same indications (seizures, pain, and anxiety). In fact, the main differences between the two drugs are that pregabalin is absorbed more easily across the gut and **reaches peak levels faster** (within 1 hour versus the 3 hours it takes for gabapentin). Pregabalin also has a **better bioavailability**, meaning that most of the drug is absorbed (versus gabapentin which sees a lower and lower percentage of the drug actually getting into the system with higher and higher doses). Overall, you can think of pregaba-**lean** as the **lean**-er, faster version of gabapentin!

> **Pregabalin** is **similar to gabapentin** in most ways but has a **faster onset**.
>
> *Pregaba-**lean** is the **lean**-er, faster version of gabapentin!*

PROPRANOLOL

Propranolol (Inderal) is a non-specific **beta-blocker** meaning that it blocks the activation of both β-1 and β-2 noradrenergic receptors. While it has multiple uses in the medical field (such as treating hypertension, irregular heart rate, and migraines), within psychiatry it has found a niche for itself in the treatment of anxiety disorders. Propranolol seems to be particularly helpful for **blocking the physical symptoms of anxiety** like heart racing and palpitations due to its antagonism of the β-1 receptors in the cardiovascular system. (Notably, its antagonism of β-2 receptors makes it a bad choice for people with asthma, as it can prevent relaxation of bronchioles.)

In addition to its effect on peripheral norepinephrine receptors, propranolol also has effects in the brain as well, as it is able to easily cross the blood-brain barrier. Clinically, propranolol is often used for **performance anxiety**, as it can be helpful if taken by a public speaker an hour before giving a large speech or by a violinist an hour before their recital. To remember the mechanism of propranolol, you can remember that **pro**s take it to **ban all** β receptors (both β-1 and β-2).

Propranolol is a **beta-blocker** that is useful for **performance anxiety**.

Pro-ban-it-all is taken by pros to ban all beta receptors.

PRAZOSIN

Prazosin (Minipress) is another drug that blocks norepinephrine receptors that has found a specialized use in psychiatry. Specifically, prazosin appears to reduce both the frequency and severity of **nightmares** in patients with **PTSD**. Pr-**a**-zos-**in** works as an α-1 **in**-hibitor and blocks the overactive sympathetic nervous system response that is likely involved in the pathogenesis of PTSD-related nightmares. By interfering with the sympathetic nervous system, however, you also inhibit the ability of peripheral vessels

to constrict, leading to an increased risk of **orthostatic hypotension**. As long as your patients are counseled on this, however, pra**zzz**osin remains a very helpful drug for when your patients with a history of trauma need to catch some **zzz**'s at night.

Prazosin is an **α-1 inhibitor** that reduces the frequency of **nightmares** in **PTSD**.

Pr-a-zos-in works as an α-1 in-hibitor.
Consider prazzzosin when your patients need to catch some zzz's at night.

Z-DRUGS

The "**Z-drugs**" (known formally as "non-benzodiazepines") are a class of medications which usually start with the letter Z, as in **Z**olpidem (Ambien), **Z**aleplon (Sonata), and **Z**opiclone (which is only available in its S-enantiomer form as Lunesta). Like benzos, Z-drugs interact with the GABA receptor, but they are more selective for the $GABA_A$ receptor subtype (which is involved in sleep) and have less of an effect at the $GABA_B$ receptor subtype (which is involved  more in the anxiolytic and anticonvulsant effects of benzos). Because of this, the Z-drugs have a reduced (though certainly not absent!) risk of dependence and tolerance compared to benzos. In addition, they tend to preserve sleep architecture better than either benzos or antihistamines, resulting in a better quality sleep.

One adverse effect of Z-drugs is **amnesia**, meaning you may forget everything that happens in the hours after you take them. Another significant side effect to be aware of is **somnambulism** which includes sleepwalking and other behaviors during a state of sleep. There are reports of people taking a Z-drug and then walking around their house, making a sandwich, or even driving their car. Given their potential for bad outcomes, it is important to counsel patients on these potential effects and to advise strict parameters on their use (taking as infrequently as possible, at the lowest dose possible, and only when going to bed immediately).

The three main Z-drugs differ from each other primarily in terms of half-life. Zaleplon has the shortest half-life (about 1 hour) and can be taken even when there are only 4 hours of sleep time remaining. Zolpidem is in the middle and can be taken with 6 hours of sleep remaining. Finally, zopiclone is the longest at 8 hours. You can remember the relative order of the Z-drugs by putting them **alphabetically**: zaleplon (4 hours), **zol**pidem (6 hours), and **zop**iclone (8 hours).

Z-drugs are are used for treating **insomnia**. They differ primarily in terms of **half-life**.

*To remember the order of Z-drug half-life, put them **alphabetically**:*
*Z**a**leplon (4 hours) → Z**ol**pidem (6 hours) → Z**op**iclone (8 hours)*

SUVOREXANT

Suvorexant (Belsomra) is a newer hypnotic that works as an **orexin receptor antagonist**. Since **go**-rexin normally helps you be awake and on-the-**go**, it makes sense that *blocking* its effects with suvorexant would reduce wakefulness and promote sleep. Despite its new mechanism, there isn't much evidence that suvorexant works any better than other hypnotics, and it is associated with potential side effects including next day impairment. You can remember the effect of suvorexant by naming it **soothe**-orexant to link it to its soothing, sleep-inducing effects.

Suvorexant is an **orexin receptor antagonist** that is used for treating **insomnia**.

***Soothe**-orexant has **soothing** effects.*

MELATONIN

Melatonin is a **naturally occurring hormone** that is involved in circadian rhythms. Mela-**turn-in** is normally released at night in response to low light levels which signals the brain to think, "I should probably **turn in** for the night." For people who have trouble falling asleep, taking additional melatonin may help to bolster this effect. Melatonin is available as an over-the-counter supplement in the United States. (Notably, the doses that melatonin supplements are sold in are often way higher than they need to be! While melatonin is usually packaged in 3, 5, or even 10 mg pills, evidence suggests that as little as 0.3 mg is enough to attain maximum benefits.) When used at appropriate doses, melatonin supplements have few side effects and can be a helpful option for sleep.

> **Melatonin** is a **naturally occurring hormone** that is **released at night** and helps to induce feelings of **tiredness**. It is available as an **over-the-counter supplement**.
>
> *Mela-**turn-in** signals the brain to think, "I should **turn in** for the night."*

In addition to melatonin itself, there are a variety of prescription drugs that also act at the melatonin receptor, with ramelteon (Rozerem) and tasimelteon (Hetlioz) being notable examples. These drugs have a similar mechanism to melatonin (they both bind to melatonin receptors), although certain details such as strength of binding and drug half-life differ. Overall, it's unclear how much additional benefit these drugs have over just "straight up" melatonin.

HOW TO USE ANXIOLYTICS AND HYPNOTICS

Learning to use anxiolytics and hypnotics can be a messy affair. Unlike depression, bipolar disorder, and schizophrenia, there isn't a single prototype anxiety disorder to learn about and treat. Unlike antidepressants and antipsychotics, there are no core mechanistic similarities shared by most or even all of the drugs in this class. Instead, anxiolytics and hypnotics are a hodge-podge of different drugs from different classes, which turns the process of making sense out of treatment into a harder task than we've had so far. Nevertheless, for some patients medications can play a major role in treating anxiety, so use the following principles to guide your clinical decision making:

1. Therapy should be the first-line treatment for anxiety and insomnia.
Psychotherapy is more effective and produces longer-lasting results than medications when treating anxiety disorders. (This is true not only for benzos but also for more "benign" drugs like antidepressants as well.) For this reason, therapy should be the first-line treatment for anxiety disorders in most cases.

The superior efficacy of therapy over drugs applies to insomnia as well. Many of the drugs that are used to treat insomnia (such as benzos and antihistamines) tend to disrupt sleep architecture. Z-drugs preserve sleep quality but are associated with tolerance and somnambulism, limiting their utility. Even seemingly harmless drugs like melatonin can ultimately impair sleep if the patient starts to believe that they need to take drugs to do what is ultimately a natural process. This process of **psychological dependence** can make sleep worse in the long run even for drugs that do not cause *physical* dependence. Because of these limitations, consider educating your patients on sleep hygiene and referring them to therapies (like CBT for insomnia) which are more effective than drugs and don't come with the same downsides.

2. Avoid the benzo trap.
The best clinicians understand that knowing when to use a drug is just as important as knowing when *not* to use it. Benzos are an excellent example of this. There is no question that they are effective for anxiety when used acutely, but over the long-term a host of troubling issues arise, including the fact that these drugs make one's brain less sensitive to internally produced GABA and often end up *increasing* the baseline state of anxiety. As weird as it is to say after having devoted so much time and energy into studying them, with benzos the best thing you can do in many cases is to simply not use them! Ultimately, every patient is different, so try your best to avoid taking a rigid approach. Instead, you should always discuss the risks and benefits of starting any medication with patients, with a clear focus on longer-term outcomes over short-term benefits.

3. Go for "brush clearing" over "water hoses."
When medication treatment of anxiety is warranted, always aim for "brush clearing" drugs like antidepressants and buspirone over "water hose" drugs like benzos, antihistamines, or gabapentin, as they are much more sustainable in the long run and come with fewer side effects. If a "water hose" drug is needed, aim for the lowest possible dose for the shortest amount of time.

4. Pay attention to unique features.
Certain parts of a patient's history, such as trauma-related nightmares or anxiety around public performances, should make specific medications shoot up to the top of your list!

PUTTING IT ALL TOGETHER

Anxiolytics and hypnotics are a large and diverse group of medications without a lot of unifying concepts or principles. Luckily, if you internalized most of what we learned in Chapter 2, most of the details here should come easily! Take some time to review the **gab**ber, H_1S+Amine, **SPAROW**-tonin, and "$\alpha 1 1$ over the place" mnemonics as all are in play when it comes to treating anxiety!

REVIEW QUESTIONS

1. A 42 y/o M was brought to the Emergency Department by police officers who found him wandering the streets intoxicated with alcohol. He is well-known by ED staff members who have seen him several times for alcohol related incidents. During rounds, the attending states, "We will have to monitor him closely for alcohol withdrawal. We should start a benzodiazepine with a long half-life." Which of the following options should be prescribed?
   A. Chlordiazepoxide
   B. Triazolam
   C. Alprazolam
   D. Lorazepam
   E. Midazolam

2. A 60 y/o M veteran comes to the primary care clinic requesting zolpidem for sleep. Upon taking a further history, the doctor discovers that the patient's problem is not difficulty falling asleep but rather difficulty staying asleep. The patient describes vivid nightmares about his time in combat that wake up him several times per night. The doctor prescribes a medication that she says will help with this. What should the patient be cautioned about when taking this medication in particular?
   A. "Make sure not to stand up too fast."
   B. "You may notice that it becomes more difficult to urinate."
   C. "Call me if you develop a rash."
   D. "Avoid alcohol while taking this medication."
   E. "Don't drive for 8 hours after taking this."

3. A 33 y/o F presents to a free county clinic for patients without health insurance. She states that she is concerned because 3 or 4 times per month she will lie awake in bed for hours unable to fall asleep. She denies feeling depressed or anxious. She lacks health insurance or any form of identification and has been told by several pharmacies that she is unable to pick up prescription medications. What would be the best pharmacologic option for this patient?
   A. Zolpidem
   B. Suvorexant
   C. Melatonin
   D. Lorazepam
   E. Alprazolam

1. **The best answer is A.** Of all the options listed, only chlordiazepoxide is considered to have a long half-life, which makes it an excellent choice for a benzodiazepine taper in a patient withdrawing from alcohol. Triazolam and midazolam (answers B and E) are both considered short half-life benzodiazepines, while alprazolam and lorazepam (answers C and D) are medium half-life. Lorazepam is often used for alcohol withdrawal, so using it here would not be inherently incorrect except that the attending requested a benzodiazepine with a long half-life.

2. **The best answer is A.** The doctor most likely prescribed prazosin which can reduce the frequency and severity of nightmares for patients with PTSD. Prazosin inhibits the sympathetic nervous system, including its ability to vasoconstrict upon standing. Therefore, orthostatic hypotension is a concern, and patients should be counseled to avoid standing up too quickly. None of the other answers apply to prazosin (and answer B is particularly incorrect, as prazosin actually makes it easier to urinate!).

3. **The best answer is C.** Melatonin is an effective sleeping aid for patients without significant side effects. In particular, its low cost and over-the-counter status make it a good recommendation in this setting. For patients without the ability to receive prescription medications, options such as zolpidem and suvorexant would be unrealistic (answers A and B). Benzodiazepines should not be first-line agents for insomnia (answers D and E).

7 STIMULANTS

Stimulants are a class of psychoactive substances that have a net **activating effect** on the central nervous system. In contrast to the sleepy sedation caused by GABAergic drugs like benzodiazepines, stimulants instead cause someone to feel more awake, alert, energetic, and active. Stimulants have found uses in psychiatry where they are used to treat cases of attention deficit hyperactivity disorder (ADHD). They can also be taken recreationally to make  people feel giddy, euphoric, and productive. We will talk about recreational stimulant use more in Chapter 10, but in this chapter we will focus our discussion primarily on the use of stimulants in a clinical setting.

As a class, prescription stimulants can be divided into two broad categories: **amphetamines** and **methylphenidates**. Both types work by boosting the effect of **dopamine** and **norepinephrine** in the brain. This makes sense mechanistically, as **A**ttention is a function of DOPAMINE while norepinephrine is known to increase **F**ocus. There are some potentially negative side effects of stimulants, and these all stem from the involvement of dopamine and norepinephrine as well. In some cases, these side effects have been turned into selling points, with stimulants being used at times to increase blood pressure in people who are hypotensive (remember that α-1 receptors are found **α1**1 over the place, including in blood vessels) or as appetite suppressants for people trying to lose weight (since **F**asting is another function of norepinephrine). However, for this chapter we will primarily focus on the use of stimulants to treat ADHD and other psychiatric conditions.

In addition to stimulants, there are a variety of non-stimulants that play a role in treatment of ADHD which we'll cover in this chapter as well.

STIMULANT EFFECTS

Stimulants have distinct and noticeable effects on both **cognition** and **motor activity**. This makes them perfectly suited to treat ADHD given that its core symptom domains are an inability to focus ("attention deficit") and difficulty sitting still ("hyperactivity"). Unlike antidepressants and mood stabilizers (which often take days or even weeks to kick in), the effects of stimulants are noticeable within minutes and last only for the time that they are in one's system (making them more like benzos in terms of timing).

People taking stimulants often report an **improved ability to concentrate** and **increased motivation** to finish tasks. Whereas someone with ADHD may struggle to complete a 30-minute task due to constantly being distracted by all the things in their  environment, when taking a stimulant they would be much more able to direct their mental energies to the given task at hand. Many patients with ADHD describe a mental calmness and a decrease in "thought noise" when taking stimulants which helps them to block out irrelevant external and internal stimuli. (Notably, this increase in concentration is seen even when people *without* ADHD take stimulants!)

While the effect of stimulants on attention makes intuitive sense, their role in reducing hyperactivity can be a more confusing. After all, doesn't DOPAMINE make **M**ovement *more* likely to happen? And wouldn't norepinephrine make you feel **F**ired up? Shouldn't these be *bad* to use in a disorder that features hyperactivity as a core symptom? This highlights a difference between the effect of stimulants on attention and their effects on activity. While giving a stimulant to a random person on the street will likely make them more energetic, when giving stimulants to people *with* ADHD results in a **paradoxical reaction** of *reduced* hyperactivity. This surprising finding has been consistently seen since stimulants were first used to treat ADHD in the 1950s, and in some cases it can be considered diagnostic. The exact reasons why stimulants work differently in people with ADHD is still under investigation, with some research suggesting that specific subtypes of dopamine receptors may be involved.

Stimulants are incredibly effective at what they do, with an overall response rate of about 80% (which is one of the highest of any treatment in psychiatry!). However, it's worth pointing out that the effectiveness of stimulants is defined in terms of **symptom response** rather than functional outcomes. Contrary to a commonly held belief, there is no evidence that stimulants will inherently take a C- student and turn them into an A+ student. Instead, stimulants can only remove the obstacles to success, with the rest coming from the patients themselves!

Like all of the drugs we have talked about so far, the side effects of stimulants are directly tied to their therapeutic effects. Let's use the mnemonic **RACING** to tie together all the potential side effects of stimulants:

R is for Restlessness. Some patients describe feelings of increased energy, jitteriness, restlessness, or irritability while taking stimulants.

A is for Appetite suppression. Stimulants can suppress appetite, likely due to norepinephrine's promotion of **F**asting.

C is for Cardiovascular effects. There was concern that stimulants would increase the risk of cardiovascular disease given that norepinephrine hits α-1 receptors in the blood vessels and β-1 receptors in the heart. However, multiple studies have failed to reveal any association between stimulant use and clinically significant changes in heart conduction or blood pressure. At most, some patients will experience small and transient increases in heart rate or blood pressure that do not appear to be associated with any immediate or long-term harm.

I is for Insomnia. Because stimulants are a time-limited drug (with the effect lasting only as long as the drug is in the body), there can be a "**come down**" period as the medication exits the body. This can cause insomnia and difficulty sleeping, although this is usually a sign that the medication was taken too late in the day and should be dosed earlier.

N is for Narcotic potential. Some patients report a "buzz" or "high" while on stimulants, typically in the first hour or two after ingestion. This means that stimulants have **abuse potential**, especially when taken at high doses or in unusual ways such as snorting. (This makes sense given **D**OPAMINE's role in **D**rug addiction.)

G is for Growth restriction. When taken by children and adolescents, stimulants may shorten final adult height by as much as an inch (although people will generally make up the difference once the stimulant is stopped). It's unclear whether or not this is related to appetite suppression or represents a separate effect.

Of note, stimulants do have the potential to cause **P**sychotic symptoms due to the involvement of DOPAMINE. However, this rarely occurs at normal therapeutic doses and is primarily seen in cases of prescription stimulant abuse.

Stimulants both **increase attention** and **reduce hyperactivity** in people with ADHD but can also cause **physical and psychological side effects**.

RACING:
Restlessness
Appetite suppression
Cardiovascular effects
Insomnia
Narcotic potential
Growth restriction

STIMULANTS

As mentioned previously, stimulants can be divided into two main categories: **methylphenidates** (based on Ritalin) and **amphetamines** (based on Adderall). Both are considered to be equally effective at treating ADHD, making either one a reasonable choice in clinical settings. (Some have described the choice between amphetamines and methylphenidates as a "Coke or Pepsi?" situation, although in reality the class differences are probably a little bigger than that!) In fact, the choice of drug class probably matters *less* than the choice between **short, medium, and long-acting formulations**. While the base drugs in both classes are immediate release,  each class also has a variety of sustained or extended release versions lasting up to 12 hours. Getting the formulation and timing can help the patient to function optimally in settings where they need the help (such as at work and at school) without having too many side effects at other times (like when trying to fall asleep at night).

METHYLPHENIDATES

Methylphenidates are **norepinephrine-dopamine reuptake inhibitors** (NDRIs) which prevent the pumping of these two neurotransmitters out of the synapse. (You can remember the neurotransmitter profile by putting it into the name itself: methylphe-**N**-i-**DA**-tel) Methylphenidates are considered the **milder** of the two stimulant classes, although they still work and are very effective for this purpose! Methylphenidate is still prescribed in its original form as Ritalin. Derivatives include long-acting formulations (Concerta), a transdermal patch (Daytrana), and dexmethylphenidate (Focalin).

> **Methylphenidates** are **norepinephrine-dopamine reuptake inhibitors** that are considered the **milder stimulant option**.
>
> *Methylphe-**N**-i-**DA**-te boosts **N**orepinephrine and **D**op**A**mine!*

AMPHETAMINES

Wait, amphetamines? Like *meth*-amphetamines?! Indeed, the amphetamines used to treat ADHD are structurally related to the methamphetamines used recreationally. In contrast to methylphenidates, amphetamines not only block the reuptake of *existing* norepinephrine and dopamine out of the synapse but also force the release of *new* neurotransmitters out of neuronal cells! They do this by activating a protein known as trace amine-associated receptor 1 (TAAR1) as well as inhibiting another protein known as vesicular monoamine transporter 2 (VMAT2). This leads to higher levels of norepinephrine and dopamine in the synapse compared to methylphenidate, and accordingly amphetamines are considered to be the more potent of the two. This potency can be seen clinically, as patients taking amphetamines will often report more of a "high" than patients taking methylphenidate. Amphetamines also appear to be more liable to abuse and psychosis than methylphenidates by virtue of their sledgehammer-like approach.

Derivatives of the original amphetamine salt (which goes by the name Adderall) include long-acting formulations like Adderall XR, dextroamphetamine (Dexedrine), and lisdexamfetamine (Vyvanse). A few amphetamine derivatives are used outside the context of ADHD as well, such as ephedrine (which is used as an appetite suppressant through norepinephrine's **F**asting effects) and pseudoephedrine (which is used as a decongestant through its vasoconstrictive effects through α-1 receptors). You can remember the more stimulating effects of this drug class by thinking of them as **amp**-phetamines (as they amp people up more than methylphenidates!).

> **Amphetamines** are **norepinephrine and dopamine releasing agents** that are more **stimulating** than methylphenidates.
>
> *Amp-phetamines amp people up more than methylphenidates!*

NON-STIMULANTS

There are several non-stimulant medications that are available for treating ADHD. While non-stimulants are significantly **less effective** than stimulants (with a response rate of about 40% compared to 80% for stimulants), they can be helpful in cases where the patient is not able to tolerate any of the **RACING** side effects of stimulants or when there is concern about drug abuse.

ATOMOXETINE
Atomoxetine (Strattera) is a **norepinephrine reuptake inhibitor**, with minimal effects on either serotonin or dopamine. It is usually well tolerated, with appetite suppression and hypertension being the main side effects to watch out for (due to norepinephrine's **F**asting and **F**ull body effects). While it has basically non-existent **D**rug abuse potential due to the lack of **D**OPAMINE involvement, it is also less effective than stimulants (as the increased **F**ocus from norepinephrine alone just isn't as good as the combination with better **A**ttention from DOPAMINE!). Overall, you can remember **atom**-oxetine's **smaller** effects compared to stimulants by thinking of an **atom**, the **small**est unit of matter!

> **Atomoxetine** is a **norepinephrine reuptake inhibitor** that is used to treat **ADHD**.
>
> *Atom-oxetine has smaller effects compared to stimulants.*

CLONIDINE AND GUANFACINE

Clonidine (Catapres, Kapvay) and guanfacine (Tenex, Intuniv) are both **α-2A receptor agonists** that are used to treat ADHD. You'll recall from Chapter 2 that α-2 is unique among noradrenergic receptors in that it *inhibits* sympathetic nervous system output. So why would α-2 agonists be helpful in treating ADHD, especially considering that other treatments for the disorder work by *increasing* dopamine and norepinephrine? The key to understanding guanfacine and clonidine is that they work best to inhibit the **hyperactivity** and **impulsivity** found in the disorder. That's not to say that they have *no* effect on attention, although it's likely that any improvements in attention are secondary to their behavioral effects (after all, it's hard to focus on work when you're running around all the time!).

Due to their unique mechanism of action, clonidine and guanfacine end up having almost the exact *opposite* side effect compared to stimulants. Instead of insomnia and restlessness, these drugs cause **sedation**. Rather than tachycardia and hypertension, they can cause **bradycardia** and **hypotension**. In lieu of appetite suppression, they can **stimulate appetite** and even lead to small amounts of weight gain. This makes them good for combining with stimulants, as their side effects largely cancel each other out while their therapeutic effects are additive (although the goal is always to use as few medications as possible!). You can remember the side effect profile of these drugs by focusing on the "awn" sound to remember that cl-**awn**-idine and gu-**awn**-facine make you **yawn** and put **weight on**.

> **Clonidine** and **guanfacine** are **α-2 receptor agonists** that are **less effective than stimulants** but have the **opposite side effect profile**.
>
> Cl-***awn***-idine and gu-***awn***-facine make you **yawn** and put **weight on**.

BUPROPION

An old friend from Chapter 3! You may remember from the "**budane**" mnemonic that **bu**propion inhibits the reuptake of both **D**op**A**mine and **N**or**E**pinephrine which is the exact same mechanism as methylphenidate. However, the effect of bupropion on these two neurotransmitters is considerably **weaker** than stimulants, so ultimately bupropion is *not* considered to be sufficient treatment for ADHD. While it was hoped that bupropion could be a "one stop shop" for folks with both depression and ADHD, evidence suggests that a "real" stimulant is needed for all but the mildest symptoms of ADHD.

MODAFINIL

Unlike the rest of the drugs in this chapter, modafinil (Provigil) and its R-enantiomer armodafinil (Nuvigil) are not often used to treat ADHD! Instead, what makes these drugs unique is their profound effect on increasing **wakefulness**, as people taking modafinil report that they simply don't feel sleepy regardless of how little sleep they've gotten. Because of this, modafinil has been approved for various conditions in which wakefulness is needed, including people who do overnight shift work, patients with narcolepsy, and those with fatigue related to sleep apnea. (The United States military even uses modafinil off-label during air force missions, as they've found that it can keep pilots alert and at their usual levels of accuracy for up to 40 consecutive hours without sleep – an impressive feat!) The precise mechanism of modafinil is cloudy, but research suggests  that it inhibits the reuptake of dopamine which leads to downstream release of both **orexin** and **histamine** (which makes sense given the effects of **go**-rexin and H_1**S**+Amine). It is generally well tolerated, with minimal side effects. Abuse potential appears to be lower than with stimulants, and there is little evidence of tolerance even when the drug is taken for months or even years at a time! To remember the association of modafinil and wakefulness, think about taking **modafinil** if you need **mo'** time to study for **da final** exam.

> **Modafinil** is a **wakefulness-promoting agent** that is useful for treatment of **narcolepsy** and **shift work disorder**.
>
> Need **mo'** time to study for **da final**? Take **modafinil**.

HOW TO USE STIMULANTS

Stimulants are often used to treat ADHD. You can remember the diagnostic criteria for ADHD using the word **FIDGETY** to remember that it involves **F**unctionally impairing patterns of **I**nattention and **D**isinhibition that are **G**reater than normal for one's age, are **E**xclusive of similar symptoms seen in other psychiatric conditions (like the poor concentration that can be seen in cases of depression), are seen in **T**wo or more settings (such as both at home and at school), and have been seen from a **Y**oung age (beginning before the age of 12).

Treating ADHD in children can be tricky due to the power structures involved. While some children with ADHD are bothered by their inability to pay attention, in many cases it is instead the parents and teachers who are bringing the child in for evaluation. While medications should be used cautiously in all patients, it is necessary to be a little more vigilant than usual when treatment is intended for a person other than the ones with the concern. Use the following principles to guide your clinical decision making around stimulants.

1. Get the diagnosis right.
Some safeguards against overdiagnosis are built into the criteria for the disorder itself (such as the requirement that signs and symptoms must be observed in two or more settings to prevent environmental problems from being mislabeled as ADHD). This serves as an important reminder to take a complete view of the patient's life and look for other problems that could be masquerading as ADHD prior to starting treatment.

For example, a child with disruptive behavior at school and difficulty focusing on work at home *may* have ADHD. However, these symptoms may also stem from chronic sleep deprivation owing to food insecurity, an unstable home environment, or undiagnosed learning disabilities such as dyslexia or hearing impairment. To avoid overmedicating cases like these, make a **full psychosocial history** a part of every assessment before offering a stimulant prescription.

2. Remember to use non-pharmacologic treatments.
While medications are effective, they are not the only treatment for ADHD! For most patients, behavioral strategies (such as rewarding positive behavior, ignoring negative behavior, keeping a daily schedule, and setting attainable goals) should be used as well. As in depression, the best outcomes are seen with a combination of therapy and medications, so use these therapies to maximize your patients' chances of success.

3. Stimulants are more effective than non-stimulants.
While stimulants are the most effective drugs for treating ADHD, they come with the potential for various side effects (as captured in the RACING mnemonic). On the other hand, non-stimulants are less effective but come with fewer side effects and minimal abuse potential. Once again, remember the Second Rule of Neurotransmission: "With great power comes great responsibility!" The more powerful drugs come with more side effects to consider but can be very helpful for helping these patients achieve their goals when used correctly.

4. Stimulants are more alike than they are different.
Because the efficacy of methylphenidates and amphetamines is largely the same, the choice largely comes down to patient and provider preference. Some patients do better with amphetamines, while others find that they can better tolerate the side effects of methylphenidates. Choose one, and if it works for the patient, stick with it!

5. Dose, timing, and duration often matter more than the choice of drug!
Unlike other chapters in this book where we have labored over specific differences between drugs in each class, with stimulants the exact drug choice matters less than the dose and timing, as there is often a "sweet spot" at which therapeutic effects are at their max and side effects are minimal. The exact timing of the drug matters as well, as having the medication wear off too soon can be problematic at work or school while having it linger in the system for too long can result in irritability, anxiousness, and insomnia when the patient should be winding down for the evening. Choosing between short, medium, and long-acting formulations of each drug can also help to fine tune the medication's effects. At the end of the day, finding the right regimen often comes down to trial-and-error which can require some patience on both sides.

PUTTING IT ALL TOGETHER

ADHD is a common disorder, and being able to treat it knowledgeably is an important skill for any physician, particular those who work with children. Luckily for learning, stimulants have been used clinically for decades now and have neatly worked out neurotransmitter effects. This means that if you understand the functions of both dopamine and norepinephrine through the **DOPAMINE** and "Oh **FFFFFF**" mnemonics, both the therapeutic and adverse effects of stimulants should be easy to grasp.

When stimulants aren't an option, you can turn to non-stimulants for additional support without the same side effects. To remember which medications can be used as non-stimulants, recall that **A**tomoxetine, **G**uanfacine, and **C**lonidine are **A G**ood **C**ompromise for treating ADHD!

> **Atomoxetine, guanfacine**, and **clonidine** are **less effective** than stimulants, but are helpful in cases of **intolerable side effects** or **substance abuse**.
>
> *Atomoxetine, Guanfacine, and Clonidine are **A G**ood **C**ompromise.*

REVIEW QUESTIONS

1. A 14 y/o F with a history of ADHD presents to her psychiatrist's office. She recently started high school and has been having difficulty with the longer school days and increased amount of homework. She no longer feels that her current medication regimen is working for her. She has been taking methylphenidate for 5 years with previously good effects. Which of the following is the best response regarding pharmacologic management?
    A. "You need to continue taking this medication."
    B. "Okay, we can stop the drug."
    C. "As long as your parents are okay with it, we can stop it."
    D. "Let's try switching to a non-stimulant."
    E. "Let's try switching to a different medication known as Adderall."
    F. "Let's try changing to an extended release formulation."

2. A 9 y/o boy is brought into the pediatrician's office by his mother. She is concerned because a recent parent-teacher conference did not go well, with the teacher saying that the patient is unable to sit still in class, often cuts in line, and is failing his classes. His mother has noticed similar symptoms at home for several years. She balks at the idea of medication treatment, saying that prescription stimulants are "no different than street drugs." What feature of prescription stimulants separates them from recreational stimulants?
    A. Long half-life
    B. Involvement of serotonin
    C. Once-daily dosing
    D. Weaker ability to release monoamines
    E. Antagonism of neurotransmitter receptors

3. A 45 y/o M with a history of obesity and hyperlipidemia presents to his intake appointment with a psychiatrist reporting difficulty concentrating. He wonders if he has "adult ADHD" as he denies having symptoms as a child. His primary complaints are severe and persistent fatigue throughout the day, lack of motivation, and poor concentration. He denies changes in appetite. He does not have trouble falling asleep at night and denies early morning awakenings. He denies thoughts of guilt, hopelessness, or suicide. He states that his fatigue has been persistent for the past several years. He denies sleeping on more than one pillow, although he notes that his wife has slept in another room for the past five years. He also endorses severe headaches in the morning. He says that it is very difficult for him to function at his job. What would be the best initial treatment for this patient?
    A. Bupropion
    B. Modafinil
    C. Methylphenidate
    D. Amphetamines
    E. Atomoxetine
    F. None of the above

4. An 8 y/o M is brought to see a psychiatrist by his foster mother after he hit another child at his group home. His foster mother describes him as impatient, irritable, impulsive, and inattentive, saying that he "never finishes the tasks that he's given." On interview with the patient, he is very withdrawn and gives short, mostly one-word responses to most questions asked. A repeat appointment is scheduled, and the foster mother is asked to bring in report cards and statements from his teachers. At the next appointment, the records are reviewed. While his grades are average, his teachers do not note any impulsive or disruptive behavior. The mother asks about starting a medication, as "most of the kids I have in my home have ADHD so it's nothing new for me." Which of the following would be the most appropriate initial treatment?
   A. Methylphenidate
   B. Atomoxetine
   C. Amphetamine salts
   D. Modafinil
   E. Clonidine
   F. None of the above

1. **The best answer is F.** It is not uncommon for a patient who has tolerated a stimulant with good effect to have difficulty when their life circumstances change. The best pharmacologic strategy is to change the amount prescribed, the time of the dosing, and/or the formulation such as switching to an extended release form. In addition, non-pharmacologic options should be explored as well. Switching to a different stimulant (answer E) is not wrong, but it would not be the next best step for a patient who has previously had a good response to her first stimulant when no other strategies have been attempted. Switching to a non-stimulant (answer D) is associated with lower rates of response and should be avoided in the absence of specific contraindications. Either leaving the medication as is (answer A) or stopping it entirely (answers B and C) would not be appropriate.

2. **The best answer is D.** Amphetamine salts such as Ritalin have the same mechanism of action as recreational stimulants like methamphetamine but are differentiated by a lower potency which allows them to increase patients' level of functioning rather than decrease it. None of the other options contribute as strongly to the difference in clinical uses.

3. **The best answer is B.** Signs and symptoms of ADHD are generally present during childhood, so a lack of history consistent with this argues against ADHD as the diagnosis. Instead, the patient's history of severe daytime fatigue accompanied by obesity is highly suggestive of obstructive sleep apnea. This should be evaluated further with a sleep study and, if present, treated with a machine that provides continuous positive airway pressure (known as a CPAP). In the meantime, however, there is no harm in prescribing a symptomatic treatment for daytime fatigue associated with sleep apnea, and modafinil is indicated for this purpose. If obstructive sleep apnea is diagnosed and treated, a trial can be attempted off modafinil to see if it is still necessary. None of the other options are indicated for daytime sleepiness secondary to obstructive sleep apnea.

4. **The best answer is F.** While this patient has some symptoms of ADHD (such as inattentiveness and impulsivity), they are very non-specific and are limited to a single setting, which makes a diagnosis of ADHD less likely. Therefore, more diagnostic clarification is necessary before starting a treatment for ADHD.

8 ANALGESICS

Analgesics are a group of drugs that help to **relieve pain** (they are commonly called "painkillers" for this reason). Pain is a complex phenomenon that straddles the line between the **physical** and the **psychological**. While mechanical injuries (like hitting your thumb with a hammer) usually lead to direct and immediate pain, the brain is not a passive observer in this process. Indeed, due to various psychological factors, different people will experience pain from the same injury differently. Because there are both physical and psychological aspects of pain to intervene on, analgesics end up being a very broad category of drugs! Some of the medications we will cover work on the physical and inflammatory mechanisms of pain (including common over-the-counter medications  like aspirin and acetaminophen) while others interface with the brain more directly by modulating neurotransmitters (like heroin and oxycodone). Indeed, this chapter will largely be a showcase of the effects that opioids have in the brain (although a few old friends from the chapters on antidepressants and mood stabilizers will also make an appearance here!).

Like with benzodiazepines, it is more helpful to understand these medications in terms of classes rather than learning them individually (as we did for antidepressants, antipsychotics, and mood stabilizers). To keep the review focused, aspects of these drugs not related to pain relief (like aspirin's effects on heart disease or the use of indomethacin to treat gout) will not be covered here.

ANALGESIC EFFECTS

While all analgesics help to reduce the sensation of pain, the way they go about this leads to some pretty big differences in both therapeutic and side effects.

Let's start with the opioids. You should be familiar with the effects of opioids by way of our **ARMED C**olonialist mnemonic. The **A**nalgesia experienced with opioids is often immediate and dramatic. People who take opioids for severe pain often report that their pain simply *disappears*. How wonderful is that! If that were the end of the story, then we could safely conclude that opioids are one of the best classes of drugs that we have in medicine.

However, we also have the rest of the ARMED Colonialist mnemonic to contend with. Let's start with **E**uphoria and **D**rowsiness. Rather than simply removing pain, opioids provide a feeling of intense pleasure, satisfaction, and relaxation. Many people taking opioids also report feeling tired, but it's not a *stressed out* kind of tired but rather a pleasant sedation. This can lead to a dulled but enjoyable vacancy of thought, with no cares, no worries, and no self-criticism. Opioids affect not only the brain but the entire body as well, with constriction of the pupils (**M**iosis) and **C**onstipation both being common. Opioids also lead to **R**espiratory depression, particularly in those who have never taken the drug before and are not tolerant to its effects.

If what goes up must come down, then we would expect that all of these things would be reversed in a state of opioid withdrawal. Indeed, as seen in the following table, withdrawal from opioids is associated with the opposite of everything that is seen during intoxication!

Opioid Intoxication		Opioid Withdrawal
Analgesia	→	Hyperalgesia
Respiratory depression	→	Tachycardia and hypertension
Miosis	→	Mydriasis
Euphoria	→	Dysphoria
Drowsiness	→	Restlessness, anxiety, and irritability
Constipation	→	Diarrhea and abdominal cramping

If you can tie each of these findings to its equivalent in the **ARMED C**olonialist mnemonic, then no additional mnemonic is needed here! It's worth noting that, in addition to these findings, opioid withdrawal can cause other signs and symptoms as well, including nausea, sweating, tremors, yawning, body aches, runny nose, and lacrimation. **Piloerection** (commonly called "goose bumps") is fairly specific to opioid withdrawal and is the basis for the phrase "quitting cold turkey."

Like benzodiazepines, opioids have a bad habit of creating more problems than they solve when used for long periods of time. As you might expect from any drug that can cause **Euphoria**, opioid **addiction** is common. **Tolerance** is another issue, and many people taking opioids for more than a few days find themselves needing to use higher and higher doses to achieve the same level of pain control (or euphoria). Owing to its tendency to cause respiratory depression, opioids can be incredibly **deadly in overdose**, with recent decades seeing a significant rise in opioid-related deaths in the United States. For these reasons, many are calling for reductions in use of opioids, with exceptions being made primarily for conditions that are largely self-limited in nature (such as recovering from a surgery) or involve conditions where palliation is the primary goal (as in terminal cancers).

However, simply avoiding opioids does not make pain go away! For this reason, having additional non-opioid options for pain management is essential. There are three main categories to be aware of: NSAIDs, analgesic adjuvants, and cannabinoids.

NSAIDs (short for **N**on-**S**teroidal **A**nti-**I**nflammatory **D**rugs) are among the most common drugs in the world. While they do have some significant side effects, many are available over-the-counter in the United States. Mechanistically, NSAIDs work by inhibiting **cyclooxygenase** (COX) enzymes which produce molecules known as prostaglandins and thromboxanes. These molecules help to promote inflammation, fever, and pain, so *blocking* their production results in the anti-inflammatory, antipyretic, and analgesic effects seen with NSAIDs. Notably, neurotransmitters are *not* directly involved, so there are no clear or obvious psychological effects associated with NSAIDs. Instead, the main side effects of NSAIDs use are physical in nature (as we will talk about shortly).

Adjuvants are medications that are typically prescribed for things *other* than pain but have also been shown to have analgesic effects as well. Many adjuvants are **antidepressants**, with those involving **norepinephrine** appearing to have stronger pain-relieving effects than those that are strictly serotonin! To understand why norepinephrine is involved here, remember that **F**eedback pain inhibition is one of the components of the "fight of flight" state. After all, an organism in a life-threatening situation will often benefit from ignoring pain signals from any injuries they might have and instead acting quickly to face down the threat or get away. This is why people in highly stressful circumstances are sometimes said to have "superhuman" powers: they are simply more able to suppress the pain signals that hold most people back in normal situations! Other adjuvants include specific **anticonvulsants** that are known to have pain-relieving properties as well (which likely work by slowing down neuronal firing and thus inhibiting pain signals traveling to the brain).

Finally, **cannabinoids** (the psychoactive compounds in cannabis or marijuana) have been shown to alleviate multiple forms of pain and are used both clinically and recreationally for this purpose. We haven't talked much about cannabinoids yet, but there will be more to come on these in Chapter 13!

OPIOIDS

Let's talk about the individual opioids! There are many opioids that are available in various formulations, but we will focus on those that are most commonly used. Just as we classified benzos according to their half-life, we will also classify opioids by their **potency** compared to morphine (with the strength of other opioids defined in terms of "morphine equivalents" or how much you would need to equal 1 mg of morphine).

LOW-POTENCY OPIOIDS
Common **low-potency** opioids include codeine, tramadol (Ultram), and meperidine (also known as pethidine and sold as the brand name Demerol). While it may be tempting to think that "low potency" means less addictive, this isn't the case! People just have to take more of it to achieve the same effect.

Codeine (or **low**-deine) is a simple opioid that has about one-tenth the strength of morphine. Because of this, it is generally used for milder applications (such as being mixed with antihistamines and then sold as cough syrup).

> **Codeine** is a **low-potency opioid** that is used in cough syrups.
>
> *Low*-deine is *low* potency.

In contrast, tramadol and meperidine work not only on opioid receptors but also on other receptors as well. Tramadol can be thought of as a combined opioid and SNRI which makes it slightly better at managing chronic pain issues such as arthritis or fibromyalgia (although it is still not a first-line option for this indication!). The mnemonic "**tram it all**" can remind you that tramadol attempts to "tram it all in" with lots of different neurotransmitters. Meperidine hits even more receptors and is known to be dopaminergic, noradrenergic, serotonergic, and anticholinergic as well. You can remember this by thinking that me-**pair**-idine **pair**s its opioid effects with other neurotransmitters!

> **Tramadol** and **meperidine** are **low-potency opioids** with **complex neurotransmitter profiles** involving serotonin, norepinephrine, and more.
>
> *Tramadol* will *tram it all* in, while me-*pair*-idine *pairs* with other neurotransmitters.

MEDIUM-POTENCY OPIOIDS
The most common **medium-potency** opioids are morphine (MS Contin), hydrocodone (Norco, Vicodin), and oxycodone (OxyContin, Percocet). Morphine is the prototypical opioid that is derived from the opium poppy. It has been used throughout history for its pain-relieving properties and is still routinely used in modern medicine! In contrast, hydrocodone and oxycodone are both synthetic opioids that are roughly equivalent to morphine in power. The latter two are often combined with acetaminophen and sold under new trade names. Mixing two analgesics with different mechanisms of action appears to have a synergistic effect, leading to more pain relief than with either alone.

HIGH-POTENCY OPIOIDS

We'll round out this list with a couple of **high-potency** opioids you should be familiar with. Hydromorphone (Dilaudid) is a powerful opioid that is about 5 times stronger than morphine. You will likely become familiar with hydromorphone after working in emergency settings, as its high potency results in a particularly intense effect, making it especially useful when patients have developed some tolerance to other opioids but still need pain relief. In general, hydromorphone should not be a first-line agent for pain except in severe cases. While it can be tempting to focus on the "high" of high-dromorphone to remember its high potency nature, that would be an error as you could easily confuse hydrocodone for a high potency opioid as well! Instead, focus on the "**morphone**" part and think of the "Mighty **Morphone** Power Rangers," a popular 1990s children's TV series. This will help you link "mighty" and "morphone"!

> **Hydromorphone** is a **high-potency opioid** that is often used in emergency settings.
>
> *"Mighty Morphone Power Rangers!"*

Finally, fentanyl (Duragesic, Sublimaze) is the **most potent** opioid that is used in clinical practice, being about 50 to 100 times stronger than morphine. It is not an exaggeration to say that a light sprinkle of this stuff can kill you. In fact, the amount shown in the following image represents a lethal dose for most people! You can remember the highly lethal nature of fentanyl by thinking that even a little bit of **vent**-anyl can make you need a **vent**-ilator to survive.

A lethal dose of fentanyl.

In clinical settings, fentanyl is commonly used today as a transdermal patch, which not only allows for a slower release and longer-term pain control than pills but also helps to prevents abuse and overdose. In terminal conditions like cancer, the patch is often prescribed along with an additional oral opioid for breakthrough pain.

> **Fentanyl** is the **most potent opioid** used clinically. It is **highly lethal in overdose**.
>
> *Even a little bit of **vent**-anyl can make you need a **vent**-ilator.*

There are some additional opioids that are more commonly prescribed to treat opioid addiction than pain such as buprenorphine. We will hold off on talking about those here, but stay tuned for more on those in Chapter 11!

NON-OPIOID ANALGESICS

As mentioned before, there are many non-opioid options for treating pain! Let's explore a few of those here, with an eye towards understanding general concepts rather than memorizing each individual drug (since there are so many!).

NON-STEROIDAL ANTI-INFLAMMATORY DRUGS

NSAIDs are helpful pain relievers that, while not as potent as opioids, are generally less harmful and have no potential for addiction. Many are available over-the-counter and have become household names, such as acetylsalicylic acid (Aspirin), ibuprofen (Advil, Motrin), and naproxen (Aleve, Naprosyn). Others, like meloxicam (Mobic) and ketorolac (Toradol), are less well-known as they are only available with a prescription.

As mentioned earlier, NSAIDs work by inhibiting COX enzymes and thereby reducing the production of pro-inflammatory compounds. It's worth noting that there are two different COX enzymes (COX-1 and COX-2) that have distinct functions in the body! While this is an oversimplification, for the purposes of learning we'll say that COX-1 is primarily responsible for protecting the stomach from its own acidic environment while COX-2 is the one causing all the inflammation and pain. You can remember this distinction by thinking of someone with stomach pain: they **1** (want) **food** but it's **2 painful**.

> **COX-1** protects the **stomach**, while **COX-2** is involved in **inflammation** and **pain**.
>
> *Someone with stomach pain may 1 (want) food but it's 2 (too) painful.*

Most NSAIDs inhibit both COX-1 and COX-2. While inhibition of COX-2 results in the positive effects of NSAIDs, the simultaneous inhibition of COX-1 causes irritation of the stomach and can lead to various side effects ranging from uncomfortable (stomach upset) to life-threatening (ulceration and bleeding). For this reason, it is important to counsel your patients to take NSAIDs with food, and in cases of long-term use, adding a proton pump inhibitor can help to reduce the risk of bleeding!

Later on, scientists developed what are now known as **selective** NSAIDs which inhibit *only* COX-2. As you might expect, selectively inhibiting COX-2 resulted in lower rates of gastrointestinal side effects. However, it didn't get rid of all the problems and even introduced some of its own, as selective NSAIDs are now known to be associated with an increased risk of major vascular events such as myocardial infarction and stroke when compared to nonselective NSAIDs. The most common of the **selective** NSAIDs is **celecoxib** (Celebrex) which you can think of as **select**-coxib to remind you of its **select**-ivity for COX-2.

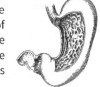

> **Celecoxib** is a **reversible NSAID** which **selectively** inhibits **COX-2** over COX-1. It has a lower risk of stomach damage but an increased risk of **vascular events**.
>
> *Select-coxib is select-ive for COX-2.*

NSAIDs also differ in terms of how they interact with the COX enzymes. Most NSAIDs are **reversible** COX inhibitors, meaning that their effect will stop once the drug is withdrawn. However, aspirin is unique in that it is an **irreversible** COX inhibitor, and some hypothesize that this is the reason why aspirin is the only NSAID that is considered to be **cardioprotective**. You can remember this unique feature of aspirin by thinking that **ass-pair-en** is an **ass** to a **pair** of **en**-zymes (*both* COX-1 and COX-2) as it continues to harass them even after it's gone.

Aspirin is an **irreversible nonselective NSAID** which inhibits both COX-1 and COX-2.

Ass-pair-en is an ass to a pair of en-zymes (both COX-1 and COX-2).

In addition to their effect on the gut and the vascular system, there is increasing evidence that NSAIDs cause injury to the kidneys as well, especially when used regularly for long periods of time. Keep this in mind when working with patients who are taking NSAIDs daily, and make sure to check the occasional creatinine. (Recall that lithium, from Chapter 5, is similarly nephrotoxic, so NSAIDs should generally be avoided in patients taking lithium!)

NSAIDs can **damage** both the **kidneys** and the **gastrointestinal tract**.

NSAID = Nephrons and Stomach Are Incidentally Damaged.

Despite these side effects, NSAIDs remain incredibly useful drugs and should be a first-line treatment for pain in the majority of cases (along with acetaminophen, which we'll talk about next).

ACETAMINOPHEN

While often lumped in with the NSAIDs, acetaminophen (which is sold as Tylenol in the United States and is also known as paracetamol or APAP in other places) is actually *not* an NSAID. While acetaminophen shares with the NSAIDs an ability to decrease pain and reduce fevers, it has little effect on inflammation, so it's not a non-steroidal *anti-inflammatory* drug. This is because acetaminophen works by blocking COX-2 in the **central nervous system** primarily (where fever and pain are generated) but not as much in the peripheral organs where inflammation takes place. Nevertheless, its effect on the brain makes acetaminophen an excellent analgesic.

Because it is not an NSAID, acetaminophen does not share the same risks of gastrointestinal effects, nephrotoxicity, and vascular events. However, it comes with its own set of adverse effects, including **liver damage**. As long as you don't exceed a certain dose per day, acetaminophen is a very safe drug, but its propensity to cause liver damage in a dose-dependent fashion makes it highly toxic in overdose. Given the risk of hepatotoxicity, special care should be taken around acetaminophen in patients with thoughts of suicide or a history of suicide attempts (although given that it is widely available over-the-counter, there is not much you can do to prevent someone from getting their hands on it).

You can remember the link between **acet**-aminophen and the **liver** by imagining a butler setting a plate of **liver** on the table and asking you to "Have **acet** (a seat)!"

Acetaminophen is an effective **non-opioid analgesic** but is **hepatotoxic** in overdose.

*Picture a butler putting down a plate of **liver** and telling you to "Have **acet**!"*

You can treat **acet**aminophen overdose with N-**acet**ylcysteine, which is most helpful when given in the first 24 hours post-ingestion. This association is easy to remember as they both have **acet** in their names.

Acetaminophen overdose is treated with **N-acetylcysteine**.

*Use N-**acet**ylcysteine for **acet**aminophen overdose.*

ANTIDEPRESSANTS
Do you remember **dual**-oxetine and its **dual** mechanism? You should also remember that **dull**-oxetine works to **dull** chronic pain conditions like fibromyalgia and diabetic neuropathy. However, beyond just memorizing that specific drug, the core concept here is that most antidepressants that boost **norepinephrine** will be effective, including venlafaxine, levomilnacipran, and the tricyclics.

ANTICONVULSANTS
Recall that **P**ain is one of the clinical uses of gaba-**P**EN-tin! Indeed, gabapentin and its close relative pregaba-lean are both effective at treating a specific type of pain known as **neuropathic pain** which occurs when nerve endings are damaged due to injury, infection, diabetes, or other causes. Neuropathic pain is experienced as "burning," "tingling," or "pins and needles" in the fingers or other affected areas.

CANNABINOIDS
While high-quality studies on the use of cannabinoids to treat pain are lacking, there is some evidence to suggest that cannabis can reduce pain and spasticity for patients who use it. While there are some side effects associated with cannabinoids (which we will discuss in Chapter 13), they are less severe than opioids, so cannabinoids can be considered a reasonable option for patients, particularly those with chronic pain!

HOW TO USE ANALGESICS

When discussing the pharmacotherapy of pain management, we are reminded yet again of the Second Rule of Neurotransmission: "With great power comes great responsibility." Opioids are a formidable tool in our fight against suffering, and no modern healthcare system could operate without them. However, they are also associated with a risk of addiction and are potentially lethal in overdose. Therefore, they must be used judiciously to avoid creating more problems for our patients, and other options should be tried first for cases of chronic pain. Consider the following treatment strategies to inform your clinical decision making.

1. Use the pain ladder.
The idea of using the least powerful option that still yields good results is reflected in the idea of a "pain ladder." This suggests starting with non-opioids such as NSAIDs before adding weaker opioids and only using stronger opioids after other options have failed. No healthcare provider wants to stand in front of a patient who is clearly suffering and not be able to offer anything to relieve their agony. On the other hand, aggressive management of pain over the past few decades has resulting in ever-increasing rates of opioid dependence and overdose. The task of being prudent in our prescribing practices falls to us, and the pain ladder represents a rational way of going about it.

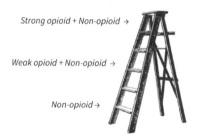

Strong opioid + Non-opioid →

Weak opioid + Non-opioid →

Non-opioid →

2. Consider non-opioid options.
It's easy to think that "non-opioid" is synonymous with NSAIDs and acetaminophen. However, there are other options for controlling pain in addition to these, including antidepressants, anticonvulsants, and cannabinoids. Keep these in your toolkit!

3. Focus on the type of pain.
While opioids are effective at reducing all types of pain, non-opioid analgesics can often target one kind of pain or another. In particular, neuropathic pain opens up a lot of options like gabapentin that are potentially less risky to use long-term than opioids.

4. Consider non-pharmacologic options.
Pain relief isn't limited to the medications we have discussed here. There are a variety of tools and techniques (including acupuncture, massage, mindfulness, physical therapy, ice, rest, and TENS units, among others) that are very helpful for alleviating pain without the side effects of medications. Always consider if these would be helpful for your patients, either alone or in combination with medications.

PUTTING IT ALL TOGETHER

Pharmacologic management of pain may remind you of treating anxiety in some ways. Both involve treating a symptom that is experienced subjectively rather than objectively (no matter how many "1–10" pain rating scales you try to throw at it), and both involve finding a balance between the "big guns" (benzos for anxiety, opioids for pain) and the "little guys." In both cases, the "big guns" are effective in the short-term but have potentially disastrous long-term consequences, while the "little guys" are less immediately effective but are more sustainable for the long haul.

To keep all of the options for treating pain in mind, use the mnemonic **C N AGONY** (pronounced "see in agony") to remind you of your options when you see a patient of yours in agony, including **C**annabinoids, **N**SAIDs, **A**cetaminophen, **G**abapentin (and its relative pregabalin), **O**pioids, **N**oradrenergic antidepressants, and **E**verything else (non-pharmacologic options like acupuncture and TENS units).

> There are a **large variety** of both **pharmacologic** and **non-pharmacologic** options for **treating pain**.
>
> **C N AGON-E** *("see in agony")*:
> **C**annabinoids
> **N**SAIDs
> **A**cetaminophen
> **G**abapentin/pregabalin
> **O**pioids
> **N**oradrenergic antidepressants
> **E**verything else (non-pharmacologic options)

REVIEW QUESTIONS

1. A 42 y/o F presents with complaints of pain due to long-standing severe rheumatoid arthritis. She states that she has tried all of the over-the-counter options but has not been able to find relief from the pain in her joints. Looking through her chart, her doctor notices that she donated her right kidney when she was younger. What is a reasonable analgesic to try in this patient?
    A. Ibuprofen
    B. Acetaminophen
    C. Hydrocodone/Acetaminophen
    D. Oxycodone
    E. Hydromorphone
    F. Gabapentin

2. A 59 y/o M with a history of prostate cancer metastatic to the vertebrae presents to his oncologist's office for pain relief. He has a poor prognosis and has been given only three more months to live. During their discussion, he states, "I wake up constantly throughout the night with this gnawing pain in my back." Previous attempts at pain control "lasted only an hour or two but then stopped working." What is the most reasonable pain control strategy?
    A. Naproxen
    B. Morphine
    C. Hydromorphone
    D. Fentanyl
    E. Amitriptyline
    F. A combination of two drugs

3. A 53 y/o F who was recently widowed when her husband died in a car crash presents to her primary care doctor's office complaining of widespread pain "all over my body" and states that "it hurts all the time." She reports feeling like "there is a cloud hanging over me" and says that she does not find pleasure in her usual activities. Her sleep is disrupted, and she has been eating only a few bites of food during the day. On physical exam, there is diffuse tenderness to palpation, particularly over the back, shoulders, buttocks, and knee. What is the most reasonable pain control strategy?
    A. Morphine
    B. Celecoxib
    C. Duloxetine
    D. Hydrocodone/acetaminophen
    E. Pregabalin
    F. Aspirin

1. **The best answer is C.** Patients who have failed to find relief using over-the-counter medications should be started on a low-potency opioid in combination with an NSAID or acetaminophen. Both ibuprofen and acetaminophen (answers A and B) are over-the-counter options which have not been sufficiently powerful for pain relief in this patient. In addition, this patient's history of a nephrectomy makes ibuprofen, with its renal side effects, particularly contraindicated. Both oxycodone and hydromorphone (answers D and E) should be avoided until lower potency opioids have been tried. Gabapentin (answer F) is most effective for neuropathic pain and would not be expected to help with rheumatoid arthritis.

2. **The best answer is F.** Fentanyl (answer D) is a powerful opioid that is available as a transdermal patch, which provides a slow release of the drug for analgesia throughout the day and night. However, it should be combined with another agent, such as morphine or hydromorphone, to manage breakthrough pain. Morphine and hydromorphone on their own (answers B and C) wear off too quickly to provide relief throughout the night. Naproxen (answer A) is not sufficiently powerful to manage severe metastatic bone pain. Tricyclic antidepressants (answer E) would not be effective for palliative pain control.

3. **The best answer is C.** This patient's history and physical exam findings are highly suggestive of a diagnosis of fibromyalgia, with complaints of diffuse pain and tenderness to palpation on the classical fibromyalgia tender points. In addition, the patient was recently bereaved, which may have resulted in depression also contributing to her pain. Therefore, the best choice would be an antidepressant that also provides pain relief such as duloxetine. Opioids like morphine and hydrocodone/acetaminophen (answers A and D) would provide relief from pain but are associated with the potential for significant adverse outcomes that limit their use. NSAIDs such as celecoxib and aspirin (answers B and F) would likely prove ineffective at managing the patient's pain. Pregabalin (answer E) is indicated for neuropathic pain, not chronic pain, and would not be expected to relieve depressive symptoms.

9 ANTIDEMENTIA

The final category of prescription psychotropics that we will cover are the **antidementia** drugs. These are used in patients who have developed dementia for the purpose of producing mild transient improvements in cognitive abilities. While there are many forms of dementia, Alzheimer's disease is by far the most common form, accounting for 60-70% of all cases. The pathophysiologic hallmark of Alzheimer's disease is a **loss of cholinergic neurons** in the brain. As you may recall from Chapter 2, acetylcholine's effects at nicotinic receptors play a large role in learning and memory. You can remember this association by thinking that **A**lzheimer's **D**isease is caused when **A**cetylcholine is **D**own. (This should remind you of a similar mnemonic we used in Chapter 4 for **Pa**rkinson's **D**isease, which happens when do**Pa**mine is **D**own.)

> **Alzheimer's disease** is associated with a **loss of cholinergic neurons** in the brain.
>
> *Alzheimer's Disease happens when Acetylcholine is Down.*

Given the loss of cholinergic neurons seen in Alzheimer's disease, it would make sense that *boosting* acetylcholine would help to offset certain symptoms, resulting in improved memory and cognition. Indeed, all but one of the antidementia drugs are **acetylcholinesterase inhibitors** (sometimes called just "cholinesterase inhibitors") that work by inhibiting the enzyme that breaks down acetylcholine, resulting in a higher amount of this neurotransmitter being active in the synapse. For this reason, this chapter will be a showcase of the effects of **acetylcholine** in the body and the brain! We will also talk memantine, an antidementia drug that works via a separate mechanism, as well as a few other treatment strategies for dementia.

ANTIDEMENTIA DRUG EFFECTS

Recall from Chapter 2 that acetylcholine interacts with both muscarinic and nicotinic receptors, each of which are associated with vastly different effects (remember "I see two cholines"!). Muscarinic receptors are found throughout the body and carry out the "feed and breed, then rest and digest" functions of the parasympathetic nervous system, resulting in the **SLUDG-E BM** signs and symptoms. In contrast, nicotinic receptors are found in the brain (where they are involved in learning and memory) and at the neuromuscular junction (where they lead to muscle contraction), as **Nic** and his **muscle memory** will remind you. With these principles in mind, we can more easily understand the effects that acetylcholinesterase inhibitors have in the brain and body.

By increasing the amount of acetylcholine in the synapse, acetylcholinesterase inhibitors help to offset the effects that the widespread death of cholinergic neurons in the brain have on learning and memory. This results in a temporary improvement in cognitive function, leading to the patient having "more lights on more often." Patients with dementia (or, more often, their families) will often notice that their recall of past events, their awareness of their surroundings, their recognition of other people, their ability to concentrate, and their capacity to accomplish tasks are all improved when taking acetylcholinesterase inhibitors.

However, the effect of these drugs tends to be transient, lasting only **about 6-12 months** before the normal course of the illness resumes. This is because, as the disease progresses, the brain stops producing any acetylcholine at all so there is nothing left in the synapses for these drugs to boost in the first place. For this reason, we cannot and should not promise anyone that these drugs will result in any significant changes to the course of Alzheimer's dementia. Indeed, **no medication** has been shown to halt or reverse the progression of Alzheimer's disease at this time.

While the intended targets of these drugs are the acetylcholinesterase inhibitors in the *brain*, these medications also increase levels of acetylcholine throughout the *body* as well, resulting in side effects consistent with increased parasympathetic tone. The most common side effects of these drugs include nausea, diarrhea, bradycardia, and muscle cramping (each of which can be connected to the SLUDG-E BM and "Nic's muscle memory" mnemonics from earlier). Unlike the transient nature of these drugs' therapeutic effects, their side effects tend to persist. For this reason, the utility of continuing these medications should be reassessed regularly to ensure that they are not simply causing side effects with no benefit on cognition.

While most antidementia drugs work on acetylcholine, there is one drug that is an exception to this! Recall from our discussion of glutamate in Chapter 2 that NMDA receptor antagonists can be used as **M**emory enhancers. While the exact mechanism by which blocking of NMDA receptors leads to improved memory is still debated, there is clinical evidence that this approach works. Because NMDA receptors are located primarily in the brain rather than being spread out all over the body, the side effects of NMDA antagonists are generally psychological rather than physical (including headaches, dizziness, drowsiness, and insomnia). While the side effects differ between these two drug types, the overall course is unfortunately quite similar: the benefits are transient, with no ability to halt or reverse the progression of the disease.

ANTIDEMENTIA DRUGS

There are four antidementia drugs that we will cover here: donepezil, rivastigmine, galantamine, and memantine. The first three work as acetylcholinesterase inhibitors, while the last is an NMDA receptor antagonist.

When discussing these medications, it's worth pointing out that while most antidementia drugs are acetylcholinesterase inhibitors, not all acetylcholinesterase inhibitors are antidementia drugs! Some acetylcholinesterase inhibitors are known to have stronger effects on muscle contraction than cognition and are therefore used to treat neuromuscular diseases like myasthenia gravis. Others are too short-acting or have an unfavorable risk-to-benefit ratio for routine clinical use. Once these are weeded out, only the following three acetylcholinesterase inhibitors are still used clinically as antidementia drugs in modern medicine. We'll go over a few of the differentiating factors between them now.

DONEPEZIL

Donepezil (Aricept) is a selective reversible acetylcholinesterase inhibitor which can be used to treat Alzheimer's disease. It has a notably **long half-life** of around 70 hours (and possibly even longer in elderly patients given their slower metabolism!). This means that it can be taken once per day, which you can remember by thinking of it as "**one and done**-epezil." Donepezil seems to be somewhat better tolerated than either rivastigmine or galantamine, likely due to its longer half-life.

> **Donepezil** is an **acetylcholinesterase inhibitor** with a **long half-life**, allowing for **once daily dosing**.
>
> *"One and done-epezil!"*

RIVASTIGMINE

Rivastigmine (Exelon) is another acetylcholinesterase inhibitor that, in contrast to donepezil, has a very **short half-life** of under 2 hours. This short half-life means that it has to be dosed multiple times per day and has more noticeable side effects than donepezil. You can remember the rapid nature of **river**-stigmine by thinking of a fast-flowing **river**. Luckily, rivastigmine is also available as a slow-release transdermal patch that negates both of these downsides (it can be applied once per day and is associated with fewer side effects than the immediate release oral form).

> **Rivastigmine** is an **acetylcholinesterase inhibitor** with a **short half-life** and **higher side effects**, although these are both improved by using a **slow-release patch**.
>
> *River-stigmine should have you thinking of a fast-flowing river.*

GALANTAMINE

Galantamine (Razadyne) is the last acetylcholinesterase inhibitor we will talk about. Interestingly, galantamine can be isolated from flowering plants known as snowdrop, and due to this natural availability it is classified in the United States as both a prescription drug and an over-the-counter supplement! Compared to donepezil's long half-life and rivastigmine's short half-life, galantamine has a **medium half-life** (about 7 hours) which requires twice a day dosing, although there is a once daily extended release version available as well.

MEMANTINE

The fourth and final antidementia drug, and the only one that does *not* work as an acetylcholinesterase inhibitor, is memantine (Namenda). Memantine has a rather complicated neurotransmitter profile, but it primarily works as an **NMDA receptor antagonist**.

Memantine appears to be most helpful for moderate to severe cases of Alzheimer's disease, with less efficacy in mild cases. As noted before, it has fewer physical side effects compared to acetylcholinesterase inhibitors, with most of the side effects being psychological such as confusion, headache, insomnia, agitation, or even hallucinations. You can recognize the function of **mem**-antine by connecting it to **mem**-ories.

> **Memantine** is an **NMDA receptor antagonist** that works as an **antidementia** agent.
>
> ***Mem**-antine allows you to better retain **mem**-ories.*

OTHER DRUGS USED IN DEMENTIA

While donepezil, rivastigmine, galantamine, and memantine are the only drugs that are used clinically to improve cognition in Alzheimer's disease, there are a variety of other medications that are often used in cases of dementia to address non-cognitive symptoms like agitation. In addition, there are non-Alzheimer's forms of dementia that require different treatment considerations than Alzheimer's disease.

ANTIPSYCHOTICS

Antipsychotics are commonly used to treat **behavioral dysregulation** in Alzheimer's disease. Some patients in advanced stages of the illness can become agitated and combative, striking out at their caregivers or refusing necessary medical care. Even when appropriate non-pharmacologic strategies for managing agitation have been tried, patients can still be confused to the extent that they become violent towards themselves or others. Unfortunately, there are no treatment options for agitation in dementia that are both safe and effective. Antipsychotics are routinely used because they are at least **partially effective** at reducing agitation. Olanzapine, risperidone, quetiapine, and haloperidol are commonly used, though any of them are likely to be effective.

However, use of these drugs for patients with Alzheimer's disease is associated with an **increased risk of mortality** (particularly in stroke and myocardial infarction), leading the FDA to put out a warning against using them in this patient population. Nevertheless, few other options are currently available for severe agitation associated with dementia, and the downsides of not treating are significant, leaving both the patient and their caregivers at risk of violence. Therefore, it seems likely that use of antipsychotics will continue until something better comes along.

As a final note, there is a specific subtype of dementia known as **dementia with Lewy bodies** (DLB) that characterized by a rapid cognitive decline and recurrent **visual hallucinations**. Patients with this form of dementia are known to be exquisitely **sensitive to antipsychotics** (especially those that are strong dopamine blockers) and are at higher risk of severe EPS, confusion, catatonia, or even neuroleptic malignant syndrome. While antipsychotics should be used with caution in dementia generally, with DLB they should be avoided completely. If an antipsychotic must be used, then quetiapine (a weak dopamine blocker) is usually the best tolerated.

ANTIDEPRESSANTS

In general, antidepressants have not been found to be very helpful in dementia. The main exception to this is (es)citalopram and possibly sertraline which can potentially help to **reduce agitation** in patients with severe dementia.

Of note, some of the core SIG**EC**APS symptoms of depression (such as low **E**nergy and poor **C**oncentration) can resemble dementia, especially in elderly patients. These patients may even score poorly on cognitive tests, although further testing usually reveals that this is the result of poor effort rather than any true cognitive deficits. Clinicians have used the term "**pseudodementia**" to describe these cases. If pseudodementia is identified, it should be treated like any other case of depression!

Finally, a specific type of dementia known as **frontotemporal dementia** (FTD) involves inappropriate behavior and a lack of impulse control in addition to cognitive deficits. Acetylcholinesterase inhibitors will generally *not* have any positive effect in frontotemporal dementia, as the disease does not involve loss of cholinergic neurons. Instead, medication management typically involves an SSRI, with antipsychotics used as a last resort.

ANTICONVULSANTS

While some have attempted to use anticonvulsants such as valproate to treat agitation in dementia, there is no evidence that they work (and plenty of evidence that they don't!) so they should generally **not be used** in this population.

STROKE PREVENTION

Vascular dementia is a form of dementia that is related to repeated strokes doing damage to the brain, each leading to further cognitive impairment. Its progression is characterized by **stepwise decreases** in cognition, with each drop representing another ischemic event. From a treatment standpoint, addressing the underlying risk factors for the strokes (such as using ACE inhibitors for hypertension or statins for hyperlipidemia) is the most important thing! Once cognitive deficits become severe enough, acetylcholinesterase inhibitors and memantine may be used as well.

HOW TO USE ANTIDEMENTIA DRUGS

Before antidementia drugs can be used, you must first diagnose dementia (also known more formally as a major neurocognitive disorder). Cases of dementia can be diagnosed using the mnemonic **DIRE**, as they will involve a clear **D**ecline in cognition leading to functional **I**mpairment, with the requirement to both **R**ule out delirium and **E**xclude other psychiatric conditions such as depression as possible causes. While memory loss is seen in nearly all cases, other cognitive domains such as language and execution function are often involved as well. Clinically, diagnosis often involves tests such as the Mini-Mental State Examination (MMSE) or Montreal Cognitive Assessment (MoCA) which can provide a numerical estimate of the severity of the disease.

Once dementia has been diagnosed, use the following points to decide on the best treatment for a patient with dementia:

1. No medication can slow or reverse dementia at this time.
To reiterate an important point brought up earlier, there is no medication that has been shown to halt or reverse the progression of Alzheimer's disease or any other form of dementia (with the exception of vascular dementia). Therefore, the goal of these drugs is **symptomatic treatment**. Memantine and acetylcholinesterase inhibitors can provide mild improvement in memory for a few months, while antidepressants and antipsychotics can lower caregiver burden by reducing levels of agitation.

2. Carefully consider goals of care before initiating treatment.
While goals of care should be a key consideration when treating any illness, it is especially important with dementia. Because the benefit of these medications is often quite limited while the risk of adverse effects (such as increased mortality with antipsychotics) is quite high, the goals of care should be clearly defined from the start of treatment. Medications should be used when they are in line with those goals and avoided when they are not. For someone in the early stages of Alzheimer's disease, something like donepezil can be helpful in allowing for a few more "good months." In other cases where the illness is more advanced, medications may do little more than make an already confused patient feel sick to their stomach. It's possible that in the future more effective treatments will become available, but for now we are stuck with these limited options, making it important to always keep goals of care in mind.

3. Consider non-pharmacologic options.
While therapies and behavioral interventions also are unable to halt or reverse the progression of dementia, they can still be effective at treating specific symptoms and behaviors like incontinence or time disorientation.

4. Helping the family can be as important as treating the patient.
Having a family member with dementia can make a major impact on one's life. For this reason, working with the family can often be just as important as treating the patient. Becoming well-versed in issues like residential care, conservatorship, and driving privileges will help you to guide patients' families through these complex decisions. In addition, encouraging family members to engage in self-care and educating them on the signs of caregiver fatigue can help to reduce burnout.

PUTTING IT ALL TOGETHER

Dementia is among the most tragic and disabling conditions that we encounter in the medical field. The tragedy is compounded further by the fact that our ability to treat these conditions is so limited. In many cases, the treatment for dementia probably shouldn't involve psychopharmacology at all but instead be focused on non-drug options and goals of care discussions. Nevertheless, for some patients there may be a role for the specific drugs that we have talked about in this chapter. Take yet another moment to review what you know about acetylcholine, as this will tie together most of what we have learned in this chapter! For the specific acetylcholinesterase inhibitors, the half-life is the most important consideration, although both rivastigmine and galantamine have extended release options available to bridge this gap. Finally, if you want to avoid cholinergic side effects completely, consider using memantine which works through an entirely separate mechanism! You can remember these four drugs using the mnemonic **R**elatively **G**ood **D**ementia **M**eds (for **R**ivastigmine, **G**alantamine, **D**onepezil, and **M**emantine).

There are **only a few medications** available to **treat dementia**.
They have **limited utility** and do not alter the trajectory of the disease.

*R*elatively *G*ood *D*ementia *M*eds:
*R*ivastigmine
*G*alantamine
*D*onepezil
*M*emantine

REVIEW QUESTIONS

1. A 79 y/o M is brought in by his wife who reports that over the past several months he has been increasingly forgetful. One year ago, he was independent and handled many aspects of his life including finances, but he now forgets to engage in these activities despite constant reminders. No hallucinations are reported. A Mini-Mental State Examination score is 17/30. A recent visit with the primary care physician revealed no major metabolic or endocrine abnormalities outside of elevated lipid levels. What pharmacologic therapy is most likely to halt the progression of this disease?
    A. Rivastigmine
    B. Memantine
    C. Donepezil
    D. Haloperidol
    E. Citalopram
    F. None of the above

2. (Continued from previous question.) The patient is started on an antidementia medication after discussing goals of care with the patient and his wife. Several years pass, during which time the patient has begun staying in a skilled nursing facility. One evening, he is brought to the hospital by staff at his facility saying that he has been increasingly angry and hostile towards staff, attempting to hit them when they approach him to change his diaper. He is admitted to the hospital for behavioral management. He is started on an antipsychotic. Which of the following statements should be made to his wife?
    A. "This may help to reduce his agitation."
    B. "This medication is safe and generally well tolerated."
    C. "There are no other options."
    D. "We aren't really sure how this medication works."
    E. "This will help with his memory deficits."

3. (Continued from the previous question.) The patient is discharged from the hospital. Several weeks later, he suffers a stroke and is admitted again. His hospital course is complicated by healthcare-acquired pneumonia, and he is transferred to the ICU. In line with his goals of care, a decision is made to switch to comfort care only. He dies several days later. Autopsy would most likely reveal damage to which area of the brain?
    A. Nigrostriatal pathway
    B. Nucleus basalis of Meynert
    C. Raphe nuclei
    D. Locus ceruleus
    E. Mesocortical pathway

4. A 58 y/o F is brought to the hospital after she was found wandering around in traffic. On interview, she denies suicidal intent and has poor recollection of the event. She is notably confused and asks where she is several times. She makes reference to "the little people" while pointing towards an empty corner of the room repeatedly. Her husband arrives and explains that over the past two months the patient has had increasing difficulties remembering things, although the severity of her memory problems appears to fluctuate throughout the day. Which medication should be avoided for this patient?
   A. Rivastigmine
   B. Memantine
   C. Donepezil
   D. Haloperidol
   E. Citalopram
   F. None of the above

5. A 75 y/o F with a diagnosis of Alzheimer's disease is prescribed donepezil. In the weeks after starting this new medication, she appears more upset and irritable to her caregivers. Rather than sleeping through the night, she awakens frequently. She has more frequent episodes of diarrhea, though she resists help from her caregivers when they try to clean her up afterwards. She is noted to be constantly "twitching" throughout the day. Which of the following would changes be most likely to help reduce her side effect burden?
   A. Switching to rivastigmine
   B. Switching to a long-acting form of donepezil
   C. Switching to memantine
   D. Adding an antidepressant
   E. Adding an opioid

1. **The best answer is F.** No drugs have been shown to halt the steady progression of Alzheimer's disease. Antidementia agents can only provide temporary boosts to cognition and minor symptomatic benefits.

2. **The best answer is A.** It is possible that an antipsychotic will reduce the patient's level of agitation, although the evidence shows that the effect is generally weak. Antipsychotic use in dementia is associated with an increased risk of death (answer B). Other options such as SSRIS, behavioral strategies, or even no treatment could be considered (answer C). The dopamine blocking mechanism of action of antipsychotics is well established (answer D). Antipsychotics do not improve memory and may even make cognitive deficits worse (answer E).

3. **The best answer is B.** Recall from Chapter 2 that Alzheimer's disease is caused by damage to cholinergic neurons in the brain which are predominantly found in the acetylcholine-rich area of the brain known as the nucleus basalis of Meynert. The nigrostriatal pathway and the mesocortical pathway are involved in dopamine transmission (answers A and E). The raphe nuclei are the site of serotonin production (answer C), while the locus ceruleus is the site of norepinephrine production (answer D).

4. **The best answer is D.** This patient is likely suffering from dementia with Lewy bodies as evidenced by her visual hallucinations, rapid decline, and fluctuation in cognitive symptoms. Given this, antipsychotics should be avoided, as they are associated with many more adverse effects compared to other types of dementia. While none of the other medications are likely to be helpful, there is not the same need to avoid them as with an antipsychotic.

5. **The best answer is C.** Acetylcholinesterase inhibitors are associated with both physical and psychological side effects such as irritability, insomnia, diarrhea, and muscle cramping. Side effects are reduced when using a drug with a longer half-life. However, donepezil itself already has a long half-life, so a long-acting form is not needed (answer B). Rivastigmine is faster-acting than donepezil, so switching to it would likely result in *worse* side effects (answer A). Memantine has less chance of causing physical side effects like diarrhea, so switching to it would be a reasonable next step (answer C). Antidepressants would not be expected to mitigate the side effects of acetylcholinesterase inhibitors and, if anything, could potentially make gastrointestinal side effects worse (answer D). Opioids are often constipation and could potentially help to improve her diarrhea, although given their other side effects this would not be a good option (answer E).

10 RECREATIONAL STIMULANTS

For the second half of this book, we will switch from prescription medications to **recreational drugs** that are used outside of medical contexts. Recreational drugs can be divided into three major categories: **stimulants** ("uppers" which induce feelings of alertness and energy), **depressants** ("downers" which give a sense of relaxation  and drowsiness), and **hallucinogens** ("trippers" that cause perceptual disturbances and altered sensation). We'll also cover a few other drugs that don't fit neatly into any of these categories, including cannabis, inhalants, and steroids, in Chapter 13.

When discussing recreational substances, it can be helpful to try and understand why people use them. With most drugs, there is often an element of **pleasure**, such as cocaine inducing a feeling of giddy energy or opioids giving a sense of euphoria. In addition to providing *positive* feelings, many drugs also provide **relief** from *negative* ones, such as combating fatigue with caffeine or reducing anxiety with alcohol. Other drugs (such as hallucinogens) don't necessarily provide immediate pleasure or relief; instead, the goal in taking them is to **alter one's experience** for enjoyment or novelty.

As we go through these next few chapters, try to recognize each substance by the characteristic set of signs and symptoms that they produce during a state of **intoxication** (known as its **toxidrome**). You should also be able to recognize the signs and symptoms of **withdrawal** (which, following the First Rule of Neurotransmission, are often the opposite of those seen during intoxication). For any drugs that are prone to abuse, make of note of what options are available for treating **addiction**. Addiction is a disorder characterized by repeatedly engaging in a specific activity (specifically those that are pleasurable, or at least were at some point) despite suffering negative consequences as a result. Addiction involving drugs is known as a **substance use disorder**. While the concepts of intoxication, withdrawal, and addiction are related, they are ultimately separate things (as someone can be intoxicated without being addicted and someone can be addicted without being intoxicated).

Dependence potential of various psychoactive substances plotted against their lethality in overdose.

While we have portrayed the transition from prescription to recreational drugs as a major shift, the reality is that there is **considerable overlap** between these two groups, both in terms of specific drugs as well as mechanisms of action! Heroin and morphine share the exact same mechanism of action, yet one is illegal and the other is prescribed in the United States. Ketamine is used clinically as an anesthetic and for treatment of depression, but it is also available on the street as a dissociative hallucinogen. Cannabis is a widely used recreational drug that is also available in prescription form as an antiemetic and appetite stimulant. Rather than treating these as separate groups, we can gain clearer insights into how each type of drug works by studying prescription and recreational drugs together.

In addition, there is **no correlation** between the legality of a drug and the harm it can cause. Consider the graph at the top of this page which plots the dependence potential of various drugs against their lethality in overdose. At the top of the scale are famous "bad boys" like heroin and cocaine which are both highly addictive and highly dangerous. However, you'll also see drugs like alcohol and nicotine here which *are* completely legal. At the other end of the spectrum are hallucinogens which are neither particularly dangerous nor prone to dependence, yet they are illegal in most places. The majority of other drugs fall somewhere in the middle!

With these principles in mind, let's focus now on recreational stimulants, including both legal drugs like caffeine and nicotine as well as illicit drugs like cocaine and methamphetamine. What ties all of these drugs together is that they have an overall net **activating** effect on the central nervous system, increasing mental awareness, motor activity, and autonomic arousal. However, the extent to which they do this accounts for some pretty major differences in their effects, as we will soon see!

CAFFEINE

Caffeine is the single most widely used drug in the world. In fact, on any given day, 90% of people in the United States will have consumed caffeine in some form! Caffeine is so ubiquitous that many people don't even think of it as a drug, yet one glance at its neurotransmitter profile (with boosting effects on dopamine, serotonin, norepinephrine, and acetylcholine and a minor inhibitory effect on GABA) will remind you that caffeine does in fact qualify as a psychoactive substance.

Caffeine works by **inhibiting adenosine** which is a breakdown product of metabolism in the central nervous system. When the brain is working hard, lots of adenosine is produced. Adenosine itself has an inhibitory effect on neuronal activity and produces a subjective sense of fatigue when it builds up. By *inhibiting an inhibitor*, caffeine exerts its excitatory and defatiguing effects, effectively tricking the brain into thinking that it's not as tired as it is. You can remember the tiring effect of a-**den**-osine by thinking that it makes you want to crawl into a **den** to sleep.

> **Caffeine inhibits adenosine** which helps to reverse a sense of fatigue.
>
> *Caffeine will wake you up and bring you out of a-**den**(osine).*

Inhibiting adenosine leads to downstream effects as well. Specifically, it potentiates the big three **monoamines** (dopamine, serotonin, and norepinephrine) and kicks the sympathetic nervous system into higher gear. This results in increased **F**ocus, **A**ttention, and **E**nergy (remember DOPAMIN**E** and "Oh **FFFFFF**!") as well as a mild transient elevation in mood. The monoamines are also responsible for some of the physiologic effects of caffeine such as increased blood pressure and tachycardia.

Caffeine also potentiates **acetylcholine** which you'll recall is involved in learning and memory. (This explains the large numbers of people you see studying in coffee shops!) In addition, caffeine also appears to inhibit **GABA** at high doses which explains some of the additional stimulatory effects (such as severe anxiety, insomnia, and panic-like symptoms) that are seen at high doses.

Caffeine's effects usually last a **few hours** at most. Withdrawal from caffeine can be uncomfortable, especially for regular users, with headaches, irritability, and fatigue being common. However, it is not associated with any clinically significant outcomes.

Clinically, you probably won't encounter caffeine "addiction" per se, but it is still important to ask about caffeine intake. Several of the problems we see in psychiatry can be directly caused by caffeine use or as a downstream effect of its use. For example, while caffeine does have some antidepressant properties, it can potentially worsen or prolong depression in the long-term by disrupting sleep. People are often unaware of exactly how much caffeine they are taking in every day, so for patients presenting with insomnia or depression, it can help to recommend a **caffeine log** to see if they are related. Don't neglect to inquire about caffeine usage, especially in patients presenting with insomnia, anxiety, or mood disorders.

NICOTINE

Nicotine is behind only caffeine and alcohol as the world's third most commonly used psychoactive substance. It is found in cigarettes, cigars, pipes, vaporizers, hookah, snuff, chewing tobacco, and many other forms. Nicotine hits **nicotinic** receptors (naturally), leading to mild stimulatory effects in the central nervous system. Nicotine also has downstream effects on the big three monoamines which can lead to increased alertness as well as mild hypertension and tachycardia through the sympathetic nervous system. Like many stimulants, nicotine also works to suppress the appetite. However, compared to some of the other drugs we will study in this chapter, the overall stimulating effects of nicotine are slight.

In addition to its stimulant effects, nicotine also has slight **sedative** effects through the opioid receptor, making it a mild painkiller as well. The opioid receptor is increasingly affected with higher doses and prolonged use, so long-time smokers will often smoke more to relax than for any kind of mental stimulation.

Through its interaction with both dopamine and opioids, nicotine is one of the **most physiologically addictive** substances known to man. What contributes to this? A big part of the equation is the speed at which nicotine reaches the brain. After you inhale a cigarette, your brain's chemistry is altered within about 7 seconds, and the immediacy of reinforcement is well-known to increase how addictive something is.

Nicotine's effects usually last **about an hour** or so. Withdrawal from nicotine is associated with irritability, anxiety, and cravings. In addition, appetite is often increased when abstaining from nicotine, so some smokers resist the idea of quitting because they are worried that they will gain weight.

As you are doubtless aware, smoking is associated with numerous poor health outcomes, including heart disease, stroke, and various types of cancer. Because of this, smoking cessation remains the **single best lifestyle intervention** to improve health and reduce the risk of death for nearly all patients who smoke.

> **Smoking cessation** is the **single best lifestyle intervention** for improving health and reducing the risk of death.
>
> *Smo-**king** cessation is the **king** of lifestyle interventions!*

Because of the enormous health benefits associated with quitting, smoking cessation should be included as a part of **every healthcare visit** regardless of specialty. There are a variety of methods available, including the classic "cold turkey" approach, counseling, support networks, medications, or a combination of these. While the cold turkey method remains popular, the data are clear: less than 10% of people are able to quit smoking without medication or other forms of assistance, while using medication is associated with quit rates between 25 and 33% provided that appropriate psychosocial support is provided.

Regardless of the method used, quitting smoking is hard, and most of your patients will need more than one try to quit smoking. You may often get frustrated in these attempts, but keep in mind that it takes on average **5 to 7 tries** to successfully quit smoking. So hang in there, and encourage your patients to do the same!

VARENICLINE

Varenicline (Chantix) is a **partial agonist** at the nicotinic receptor, binding to it without activating it strongly. By doing this, it blocks the effects of nicotine and reduces the chemical reinforcement while also stabilizing the withdrawal state. Of all the pharmacologic options, varenicline is the **most effective**, with quit rates above both bupropion and nicotine replacement. When it was first released, there were concerns that varenicline could worsen suicidal thoughts or psychotic symptoms in some patients, and for this reason it was recommended that all patients should undergo psychiatric screening before starting varenicline. However, recent research suggests that it can be used safely even in patients with a psychiatric history, so this is no longer required. Remember to use **very**-**nic**-**clean** when your patients need to get **very clean** from **nic**otine!

Varenicline is the single best medication for smoking cessation.

Use **very-nic-clean** to get **very clean** from **nic**otine!

NICOTINE REPLACEMENT

One of the best options for helping patients to quit smoking is nicotine itself! Because the negative effects of smoking don't come from nicotine *per se* but from the tars, toxins, and carcinogens found in tobacco smoke, nicotine replacement can manage cravings for tobacco without the negative effects. Nicotine replacement comes in many forms including gums, patches, and inhalers. Evidence suggests that, as long as at least **two forms** are used (such as gums *and* patches), nicotine replacement can be as effective as varenicline!

Nicotine replacement is an effective strategy for **smoking cessation** provided that **at least two forms** of replacement are used.

To quit smoking using nicotine, you'll need a nico-**team** (more than one form).

BUPROPION

A familiar friend is back! Bupropion (which goes by the brand name Zyban when used for smoking cessation) is another medication option for smoking cessation (remember our visual of using "budane" to light a cigarette). It is likely that the dopaminergic effect of bupropion can help to mitigate the cravings, while its antidepressant effect can help to stabilize the withdrawal state. While it is not as effective as either varenicline or nicotine replacement, it can be a good choice for patients with comorbid depression.

PRESCRIPTION STIMULANTS

As we move up the potency scale, we next hit prescription stimulants. We'll talk about these only very briefly, as they were discussed in more detail back in Chapter 7. As a quick reminder, methylphe-**N**-i-**DA**-tes are **N**orepinephrine and **D**op**A**mine reuptake inhibitors while **amp**-phetamines are norepinephrine and dopamine releasing agents that are more potent and more likely to **amp** people up than methylphenidates.

Abuse of prescription stimulants is not uncommon, with up to 5% of high school students and 10% of college students having taken stimulants that were not prescribed to them. Most school-aged users of diverted stimulants take them in hopes of improving their academic performance, although some will abuse stimulants for their psychological effects by snorting, injecting, or taking them at supratherapeutic doses. High doses are associated with all of the **RACING** side effects (**R**estlessness, **A**ppetite suppression, **C**ardiovascular effects, **I**nsomnia, **N**arcotic potential, and **G**rowth restriction) but at a higher "volume" than at normal doses. At very high doses, psychosis can occur.

MDMA

MDMA (or 3,4-**M**ethylene**D**ioxy**M**eth**A**mphetamine) is known colloquially as ecstasy, E, X, XTC, or molly. MDMA is like other stimulants in that it increases synaptic levels of the big three monoamines, leading to sympathetic activation and increased energy, activity, heart rate, and blood pressure. However, MDMA differs from most stimulants in that it hits **serotonin** a little harder and increases levels of **oxytocin** as well. As you'll recall from the **BLOC**-ytocin mnemonic, oxytocin plays a key role in feelings of social **C**onnection, and this likely accounts for MDMA's association with feelings of "connection" and "oneness" reported by people taking the drug. Use the **X** in **X**TC to remind you of o**X**ytocin!

When taken orally, MDMA's effects are noticeable in around 45 minutes and lasts anywhere from **4 to 8 hours**. Withdrawal from MDMA is your classic post-stimulant crash with feelings of lethargy and depression (known as "suicide Tuesday" as it usually occurs a few days after a weekend of partying). One high-yield symptom that is unique to MDMA is that users often experience **bruxism** (or intense grinding of 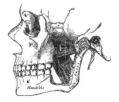 the teeth) during withdrawal, which can help you to distinguish MDMA withdrawal from other types of stimulants. Use the **X** in **X**TC to remind you of bru**X**ism!.

Addiction to MDMA is relatively rare, likely due to the greater effect on serotonin than dopamine and the exhausting crash that happens afterwards. MDMA is currently being explored as a pharmacologic aid for certain types of psychotherapy.

> **MDMA** is a **stimulant** that involves **oxytocin**, leading to feelings of **connection**.
>
> *X*TC *(ecstasy) is associated with both o**X**ytocin and Bru**X**ism.*

COCAINE

Moving further up the potency scale, we hit cocaine (also known as coke, coco, crack, or blow). Cocaine acts by **inhibiting the reuptake** of the big three monoamines, resulting in a powerful stimulating effect via the sympathetic nervous system. This causes the high levels of energy, activity, euphoria, and excitement for which cocaine is famous. However, it is not uncommon for unpleasant psychological symptoms such as anxiety, paranoia, and hallucinations to occur as well. On a physiologic basis, cocaine causes exactly what you'd expect from activation of the sympathetic nervous system, including tachycardia, hypertension, sweating, and pupillary dilation.

Cocaine can be ingested in various forms including swallowing, chewing, rubbing on the gums, injecting, or inhaling. The classic image of cocaine, however, comes from when it is arranged in a line (stereotypically with a razor or credit card) and insufflated or "snorted." All forms of cocaine are not created equal, with inhaling, injecting, and insufflating each being significantly more addictive than ingesting orally due to the faster onset.

Cocaine's effects last only around **one hour**, making it a fairly "quick" stimulant (especially compared to methamphetamines, which we will discuss shortly). As expected from the First Rule of Neurotransmission, the signs of cocaine withdrawal are the opposite of what is seen during intoxication, with sedation and lethargy being common. While uncomfortable, withdrawal from stimulants such as cocaine is generally not life-threatening (unlike depressant withdrawal, which we will talk about in Chapter 11).

Medically, it is important to be aware of cocaine's cardiac effects. Cocaine's effects on the heart are widespread and, sometimes, deadly. Not only does cocaine raise the heart's oxygen demands by increasing both contractility and afterload, it also limits the heart's ability to obtain oxygen by causing vasospasm of coronary arteries. For most, the ischemic effects of cocaine are short-lived and cause only mild chest pain. In other cases, however, myocardial infarction can occur, leading to loss of cardiac tissue and even death. For this reason, you need to be aware of **co**caine's **co**nstricting effects on **co**ronary arteries.

Cocaine can cause **coronary vasospasm**, leading to **myocardial ischemia**.

Cocaine constricts coronaries.

Unfortunately, evidence-based treatment for cocaine addiction is limited. At this time, **no medications** have been shown to be helpful in reducing risk of relapse. The best options appears to be cognitive behavioral therapy combined with motivational therapy, although various other strategies are currently being studied.

METHAMPHETAMINES

Methamphetamines (also known as speed, crystal, meth, or crystal meth) are among the most potent stimulants that are commonly used. Methamphetamines are in many way the "Adderall" to the "Ritalin" of cocaine, with a stronger potency, longer-lasting effects, and a higher addictive potential. This analogy applies to the mechanism of action as well: while cocaine merely inhibits the reuptake of monoamines, methamphetamine actually forces the release of monoamines from the presynaptic neuron, damaging the cell in the process. This accounts for why the rush of  euphoria experienced with methamphetamine is so much more immediate and intense as well as why chronic use is associated with death of brain tissue.

During intoxication, meth-**amp**-phetamine generally resembles an **amp**ed up version of cocaine, with increased mood, energy, and activity. In addition, meth seems to have a greater effect on libido and sexual desire, with some people saying that it makes them able to have sex continuously for hours or days on end. This brings up another significant difference from cocaine: while cocaine has a relatively short duration (about one hour) that requires multiple hits over a single night of partying, meth lasts much longer (upwards of 24 hours) on a single dose!

At high doses, a state of confusion, paranoia, and hallucinations known as **methamphetamine psychosis** can occur. This can resemble a primary psychosis, although there are generally higher levels of agitation and confusion than would be seen in schizophrenia. Owing to its long half-life, the effects of taking too much meth can last for over a day, and these patients will sometimes end up in emergency rooms for agitated or threatening behavior. Treatment involves giving an **antipsychotic** (sometimes with a benzodiazepine for additional sedative effect) and allowing the patient time to "crash out." For most patients, the psychotic symptoms will stop once the drug clears from their system, although for chronic users residual psychotic symptoms are not uncommon. At extreme doses, meth can result in cardiogenic shock, renal failure, seizures, and/or cerebral hemorrhage, so monitoring physical condition and vital signs for these patients is crucial.

> **Methamphetamines** are **powerful stimulants** that act as **monoamine releasing agents**. They can be associated with **psychosis**.
>
> *Just like **amp**-phetamine is an **amp**ed up version of methylphenidate, meth-**amp**-phetamine is an **amp**ed up version of cocaine.*

The comedown from meth resembles cocaine withdrawal and leads to depressed mood, anxiety, anhedonia, and lethargy. Just as the effects of meth intoxication last longer than cocaine, meth withdrawal often lasts longer as well.

Like cocaine, there are **no medications** that have been shown to be effective for treating methamphetamine addiction, with therapy and psychosocial support being the best options available.

CATHINONES

Cathinones are recreational stimulants, which are relatively rare in the Western world but are much more commonly used in parts of Africa and the Middle East. It is often ingested in the form of **khat**, a leafy plant that releases cathinone when it is chewed. In its countries of origin, khat is not illegal and is often used socially (just as coffee, tea, or cigarettes would be in the United States).

Khat can be thought of as either a strong version of coffee or a weak version of cocaine. Like other stimulants, khat increases synaptic levels of serotonin, norepinephrine, and dopamine. In the first hour or two after ingestion, this produces feelings of euphoria as well as increased energy and alertness. Withdrawal happens several hours after that and is characterized by lethargy and mild depression.

While khat use is rare in the United States and therefore unlikely to be seen either on boards or on wards, you may hear about **synthetic cathinones** (also known as "bath salts" due to their appearance). Unlike khat where the potential for abuse, dependence, and both personal and societal harm is relatively low, synthetic cathinones have unpredictable effects and can be much more potent and dangerous. In addition, they are not picked up on most urine toxicology screens, making detection difficult. Given their increasing use, you should keep synthetic cathinones on your differential when evaluating a patient with a **negative urine drug screen** that you nevertheless suspect of having substance-induced psychosis.

ARECOLINE

The final recreational stimulant we will talk about is **arecoline** which, like khat, is uncommon in the Western world but is found elsewhere (in this case, in Southeast Asia and some Pacific islands). It is found in the **betel nut** (also known as the areca nut) which is chewed and spat out. Arecoline acts as an agonist at nicotine receptors, giving it mild stimulant effects similar to smoking. However, it is also a muscarinic partial agonist which leads to vasoconstriction and increased gastrointestinal motility, among other effects. Like tobacco, use of arecoline is associated with an increased risk of multiple cancers (most notably those of the mouth and throat) as well as other diseases such as heart abnormalities, hypertension, and diabetes, making arecoline use a major public health matter in places where it is used commonly.

Khat leaves.

Bath salts.

Woman selling betel nuts.

PUTTING IT ALL TOGETHER

While the line between from prescription and recreational drugs is thin (if not non-existent), the fact that these drugs are treated differently in society means that our approach must necessarily change as well. With prescription medications, you are the "**decider**." While you can counsel patients on what to expect with any given medication and hopefully provide information so that the patient agrees with your choice, ultimately you are the one making the decision on what to prescribe (or not prescribe). In contrast, with recreational substances, your role is more as a "**guider**," as you cannot directly control what recreational drugs your patients use. In your role as a healthcare provider, all you can do is to provide information on what is known about the risks and benefits of each type of drug.

Rather than coming up with the best treatment, your goal here is to be able to **knowledgeably converse** about the drugs your patient is taking. By being able to speak knowledgeably and reasonably with your patients about substance use, you can build up trust and become a better guide to helping your patients make the best choices for themselves. With this in mind, here are a few key points to consider when talking about recreational stimulants in a clinical setting:

1. Stimulants are more alike than they are different.
As a general rule, stimulants are more alike than they are different. You'll notice that many of their effects (euphoria, energy, activity, tachycardia, hypertension, and mydriasis) are consistent between the different drugs owing to their shared effects on the big three monoamines and the sympathetic nervous system. What primarily sets one stimulant apart from another is its **potency**. This is why some stimulants (like methylphenidate) are helpful for ADHD and can improve quality of life, whereas others (like methamphetamine) can end up destroying lives. This is a theme we'll see again and again when studying psychopharmacology, especially when talking about recreational substances. Even though the overall structure and neurobiological effect of two drugs may be similar, the details (such as potency, onset of action, and half-life) account for the large differences in clinical effect.

2. Smoking cessation is the best thing your patients can do for their health.
This is true in almost all cases, with few exceptions! It can be difficult to talk about smoking cessation with your patients, especially when the time allotted for healthcare appointments seems to be getting shorter and shorter. Nevertheless, asking your patients about nicotine use and gently encouraging them to consider quitting (using the principles of motivational interviewing, discussed more in Chapter 15) should be a part of every outpatient visit.

3. Treatment options for stimulant abuse are limited.
With the exception of nicotine, there is a general lack of treatments available for stimulant abuse. No medications have been found to be effective for either cocaine or methamphetamine abuse. Psychosocial therapies are the best treatments available, although the evidence base supporting them is small. Nevertheless, referring to these services can make a world of difference for patients dealing with stimulant abuse.

Memorable Psychopharmacology

REVIEW QUESTIONS

1. A 22 y/o M college student comes into the student health office saying he feels "on edge." He says that he is constantly anxious and is unable to fall sleep until 3:00 or 4:00 in the morning. He says that he goes to the bathroom frequently and wonders if he is developing diabetes. When asked about his anxiety, he denies any specific stressors and states that he is doing well in school. He denies suicidal ideation. He does report a single panic attack last week which is what convinced him to seek treatment. What is the most appropriate next step?
    A. Start sertraline
    B. Start alprazolam
    C. Start buspirone
    D. Refer for cognitive behavioral therapy
    E. Recommend a diet and drink log

2. A 44 y/o F comes to her primary care physician for management of chronic cough. She has a 60 pack-year smoking history and was recently diagnosed with chronic obstructive pulmonary disease. She verbalizes her need to quit smoking but appears frustrated, stating, "I've tried five times before but have never been able to quit for more than a month." She denies having used smoking cessation medications before. History reveals no significant psychiatric history and no suicidal ideation. What is best option to recommend for this patient?
    A. Nicotine replacement therapy
    B. Varenicline
    C. Bupropion
    D. Nicotine replacement therapy + support
    E. Varenicline + support
    F. Bupropion + support

3. Which drug is *incorrectly* paired with its description?
    A. Caffeine – Most frequently used psychoactive substance in the world
    B. Nicotine – Increases risk of lung cancer and heart disease
    C. Cocaine – Mechanism of action is inhibiting monoamine reuptake
    D. MDMA – Causes bruxism in withdrawal states
    E. Cathinones – Has a short time of effect lasting only a few hours

4. A 53 y/o M Vietnam War veteran is seen in a smoking cessation clinic. He reports a history of 10 attempts to quit smoking, but none of them have resulted in lasting change. During the interview, he complains, "It's so hard! This is the hardest thing I've ever had to do. Why can't I let it go?" What feature of nicotine's pharmacology most contributes to its addictive potential?
    A. Agonism at acetylcholine receptors
    B. Potentiation of monoamines
    C. Involvement of multiple neurotransmitters
    D. Speed at which nicotine reaches the brain
    E. Social cues that reinforce smoking behaviors

5. A 21 y/o M ingests a substance at the urging of his friend before going out to a party on a Saturday night. He initially thinks that he must have taken a "dud" pill because he does not notice any effects immediately. One hour later, he notes that he wants to be around people and particularly likes touching skin and hugging others. His blood pressure and heart rate are both elevated above baseline. Pupil size is 7 mm bilaterally. He attempts to have sex with someone he meets at the party but finds he is unable to keep an erection long enough to reach orgasm. His erectile dysfunction and anorgasmia is most likely related to this drug's effects on which of the following neurotransmitters?
    A. Opioids
    B. Serotonin
    C. Dopamine
    D. Glutamate
    E. Norepinephrine
    F. Oxytocin

1. **The best answer is E.** This patient may be suffering from a psychiatric disorder such as generalized anxiety disorder or panic disorder, at which point pharmacologic treatment strategies could be discussed (answers A and C), although benzodiazepines should likely be avoided (answer B). However, given the high likelihood of caffeine overuse (as evidenced by polyuria and insomnia), substance-induced anxiety disorder must be ruled out first. Cognitive behavioral therapy (answer D) may be a helpful adjunct after caffeine overuse has been ruled out.

2. **The best answer is E.** Research indicates that a combination of drug therapy and support (whether that involves support groups, online support, or telephone support) results in better outcomes than drug therapy alone (answers A–C). Of the remaining options, varenicline (answer E) has the best evidence base for efficacy. Nicotine replacement therapy (answer D) and bupropion (answer F) could be considered in the future if varenicline therapy is insufficient.

3. **The best answer is B.** While smoking is associated with risk factors including lung cancer and heart disease, this effect is secondary to the tars and carcinogens found in cigarette smoke and is not linked to nicotine itself. All of the other answer choices are correctly paired.

4. **The best answer is D.** While all of the listed properties of smoking play a significant role in contributing to its addictive potential, the speed at which nicotine reaches the brain is known to play the most important role.

5. **The best answer is B.** MDMA's effects on serotonin transmission in the brain are similar to that observed with SSRIs, resulting in transient sexual side effects including erectile dysfunction and anorgasmia. Dopamine, norepinephrine, and oxytocin are all affected by MDMA, though they do not account for this particular side effect.

11 RECREATIONAL DEPRESSANTS

Recreational depressants (also known as "downers") are the yin to the stimulants' yang. Rather than increasing activity and energy, they instead slow down the nervous system and reduce arousal, resulting in feelings of **relaxation** and **sedation**. While most stimulants share a single mechanism (boosting the big three monoamines serotonin, norepinephrine, and dopamine), depressants instead rely upon one of *two* different mechanisms that  lead to similar, albeit distinct, effects: **GABA** and **opioids**. Luckily, we have talked about both of these effects already, so no new knowledge is needed here! As with stimulants, recreational depressants differ from prescription medications less in kind than in degree.

We'll go over three main categories of recreational depressants: alcohol, benzodiazepines, and opioids. The first two act as agonists at **GABA receptors** which you'll remember as the brain's primary inhibitory neurotransmitter, leading to fatigue and sedation (like a gabber who just goes on and on). In contrast, opioids are not depressants in a *scientific* sense, but recreationally they are often lumped together with alcohol and benzodiazepines due to their overall sedating effect.

Some of the other prescription drugs we have talked about so far (including antipsychotics, antihistamines, and anticonvulsants) are notably sedating and could be lumped in as "depressants." (A few, such as quetiapine and gabapentin, even have a street value!) However, there is little to add here that we have not already covered in previous chapters, so for the purposes of simplicity we will limit our discussion to alcohol, benzos, and opioids. As before, keep your focus on recognizing **intoxication** and **withdrawal** states, and be aware of how to treat issues like addiction and overdose related to each drug class!

ALCOHOL

Alcohol is the second most commonly used psychoactive substance in the world, just after caffeine. One-third of the world's population consumes alcohol on a regular basis, whether in the form of beer, wine, mixed drinks, or liquor. The fact that alcohol is legal in many countries does not mean that it is somehow more benign than illicit drugs. In fact, on the scale of all recreational substances, alcohol is among the highest in terms of lethality, addiction, and abuse potential! (This serves as  a reminder that that legality does not equal safety, and vice versa.) While alcohol is not the most harmful drug on a *per capita* basis, given the widespread scale of use it actually ends up causing the most *total* societal damage, surpassing even heroin and methamphetamine!

Alcohol acts primarily by altering the lipid bilayer surrounding the GABA receptor, which changes its conformation and enhances GABA transmission. As you would expect, this has a net **inhibitory** effect on the central nervous system. However, alcohol is a very "dirty" drug that also interacts with serotonin, dopamine, and glutamate receptors in addition to various ion channels. This explains why alcohol is more of a mixed bag than "pure" GABAergic drugs like benzos! While benzos mostly just put people to sleep, alcohol can also be quite stimulating and disinhibiting.

The effects of alcohol will be well-known to most people over the age of 21. Drinkers will initially experience some mild euphoria and relaxation. As intoxication increases, the depressant effect of alcohol becomes clearer, resulting in sedation, slurred speech, delayed reaction times, clumsy movements, and emotional lability. With further intoxication (past a blood alcohol level of 0.10%), drinkers experience increasing confusion, disorientation, and the classic "room spinning" sensation with nausea and vomiting. When the blood alcohol level reaches 0.20% or higher, stupor, unconsciousness, respiratory depression, and even death can occur.

In terms of withdrawal, alcohol follows the First Rule of Neurotransmission: "What goes down must come back up." Rebounding from an *inhibitory* state of alcohol intoxication, people often experience an *excitatory* phase characterized by anxiety, restlessness, and insomnia during withdrawal. While the *psychological* symptoms can be uncomfortable, the *physical* effects of alcohol withdrawal are even more concerning! In severe cases of alcohol withdrawal, overactivation of both the central and autonomic nervous system can lead to **vital sign instability** and even **seizures** which can cause significant morbidity and mortality. In fact, before the time of modern  medicine, patients in severe alcohol withdrawal had a 35% chance of death!

The most feared complication of alcohol withdrawal is **delirium tremens** (also known as DTs). Delirium tremens typically occurs in patients with a long history of alcoholism and, even with medical treatment, is associated with a 5 to 15% risk of dying (often due to prolonged seizures or cardiovascular collapse). Delirium tremens tends to occur about 2 or 3 days after the last drink, although it can occur up to a week later. Diagnosing delirium tremens is based on a characteristic set of signs and symptoms in the context of recent abstinence from alcohol. You can use the mnemonic **DTS are HELL** to remember that this syndrome involves **D**elirium (confusion and altered mental status), **T**remor (uncontrollable shaking and shivering of the body), **S**eizures, **H**allucinations (primarily visual, including the classic "seeing pink elephants" imagery), elevated **E**SR (erythrocyte sedimentation rate, or a marker of inflammation), **L**eukocytosis (high white blood cell count, another marker of inflammation), and abnormal **L**iver function tests (as alcohol is hepatotoxic). Make sure you know how to recognize this clinical picture, as it requires a prompt response including immediate admission to the ICU!

Delirium tremens is a **potentially fatal** outcome of **alcohol withdrawal**.

DTS are HELL:
*D*elirium
*T*remor
*S*eizures
*H*allucinations
*E*SR ↑
*L*eukocytosis ↑
*L*iver function tests ↑

The best treatment for severe alcohol withdrawal (including delirium tremens) is to use **benzodiazepines**. While it may seem counterintuitive to treat GABA withdrawal by giving a drug that activates GABA even more, by dosing GABAergic drugs in a controlled way, you can gradually return the patient to their baseline rather than allow them to be subjected to the erratic swings in vital signs seen in unopposed withdrawal. Benzos with a long half-life (like chlor**diaz**epoxide) are preferred, as they effectively taper themselves. Using a **symptom triggered** approach where benzos are given only when signs of withdrawal emerge (rather than on a pre-scheduled basis) has been shown to decrease the length of hospitalization while using less doses of medication overall.

Delirium tremens must be distinguished from another clinical syndrome known as **alcoholic hallucinosis** that is easily confused for delirium tremens. Both occur during alcohol withdrawal and are characterized by an altered sensorium. However, alcoholic hallucinosis is much more **benign** than delirium tremens and tends to resolve rapidly, with no morbidity or mortality to speak of. Two features will help you distinguish the two! First, alcoholic hallucinosis tends to occur within 24 hours of the last drink, while delirium tremens often occurs 2 or 3 days later. More importantly, alcoholic hallucinosis features **normal vital signs** versus the profound vital sign instability seen in delirium tremens. Knowing whether **vital** signs are affected is **vital** for distinguishing between these two syndromes!

In addition to having immediate effects during intoxication and withdrawal, alcohol can wreak havoc on a long-term basis as well. **Alcohol use disorder** is common, with over 5% of women and 10% of men in the United States showing signs of unhealthy alcohol use in the past year. Excessive alcohol consumption harms not only the drinker's health (with an increased risk of liver disease, cognitive problems, and multiple cancers) but also represents a threat to public health from things like  drunk driving. Given this, clinicians should be mindful to screen for problematic drinking, be aware of the various treatment strategies for alcohol abuse, and be comfortable referring their patients to these services when the need arises.

Treatment for alcohol use disorder consists of an initial **detoxification** followed by **rehabilitation** (or maintenance of sobriety) using various methods, including peer support (the most famous of which is AA or Alcoholics Anonymous), psychosocial therapy (such as cognitive behavioral therapy), and/or medications. The efficacy of these treatments is a matter of ongoing debate, but research seems to indicate that the most successful approach is to match treatments to patient preferences, so it is worth discussing all of the options with each patient to see what they prefer. We'll now talk about a few of the medications that can be used to treat alcohol use disorder.

NALTREXONE
Naltrexone (Revia, Vivitrol) is an **opioid receptor antagonist** that is one of the best medication treatments for alcohol use disorder, as the evidence consistently shows that is able to significantly decrease the amount and frequency of drinking. However, this begs the question... why does blocking the *opioid* receptor have an effect on alcohol which predominantly interacts with *GABA* receptors? In chronic drinkers, most of the pleasure of alcohol comes from the brain producing endogenous opioids in response to drinking (which then cause dopamine to be released, activating the reward pathway). So even though alcohol does not interact with the opioid receptor *directly*, drinking does activate opioid receptors through a downstream effect. By  using naltrexone to block endogenous opioids, the positive feelings associated with drinking are reduced (in essence, **the "carrot" is removed**). Over time, the brain learns to stop associating drinking with pleasure, and the frequency of drinking goes down. Because naltrexone relies on breaking the association between drinking and pleasurable feelings, patients are *not* required to abstain from alcohol before starting (although for some patients this will still be the goal).

There are some caveats to using naltrexone. First, naltrexone has been shown to cause **liver damage** in a dose-dependent fashion, so it is contraindicated in patients with liver disease (get liver function tests before starting!). Further, patients **cannot be taking opioids** when taking naltrexone, as this will precipitate opioid withdrawal. Provided both of these criteria are met, however, naltrexone is one of the best medications we have for treating alcohol use disorder! Finally, it's worth noting naltrexone has a monthly injectable form for patients who cannot or will not take a pill every day. The injection has been shown to work better, so aim for that if possible!

DISULFIRAM

Disulfiram (Antabuse) is a treatment for alcohol use disorder that uses **punishment** to decrease drinking. When someone drinks, most of the ethanol is converted to acetaldehyde. Under normal conditions, this acetaldehyde is then converted to acetate by the enzyme acetaldehyde dehydrogenase. Acetate is easily excreted by the body and does not cause any ill effects. When disulfiram is present, however, the second step  in this process is blocked, which causes ethanol to be converted to acetaldehyde rather than acetate. Acetaldehyde is toxic to the body, causing nausea, vomiting, flushing, tachycardia, shortness of breath, headaches, and a general "sick" feeling.

The hope was that if patients felt sick whenever they drank they would probably give up alcohol pretty quickly. However, the reality is that most patients just end up stopping the *disulfiram* and staying on the alcohol. Because of this, the evidence isn't very strong that disulfiram actually results in reduced rates of drinking over the long-term, which is why it has largely fallen out of favor today. It turns out that removing the carrot (naltrexone) is much more effective than introducing a stick (disulfiram)!

> **Naltrexone** is an **opioid antagonist** that reduces the amount and frequency of drinking in **alcohol use disorder**.
>
> **Removing the carrot** *(naltrexone) is better than* **introducing a stick** *(disulfiram).*

ACAMPROSATE

Chronic alcoholism makes the brain less sensitive to endogenously produced GABA, so many patients with a long history of drinking often live in a state of restlessness and anxiety which makes them crave alcohol even more (they are basically punished for trying to be abstinent!). Acamprosate (Campral) works by binding to GABA receptors and making them *more* sensitive to GABA, allowing those suffering from the effects of chronic alcohol abuse to live more easily without it and reducing rates of relapse. You can remember the function of a-**camp**-rosate by thinking of it as like a **camp**-ing trip: it helps to relax a stressed mind and is far away from the nearest liquor store!

> **Acamprosate** is an **activator of GABA receptors** that helps to **prevent relapse**.
>
> A-***camp***-rosate is like a ***camp***-ing trip: it can ***relax*** a brain in chronic withdrawal!

BENZODIAZEPINES

We covered benzodiazepines in Chapter 6, but it is worth taking another look at them from the perspective of recreational use, as benzos are among the most frequently misused drugs of any kind (prescribed or otherwise). For some patients, the medical nature of benzos can actually make them *more* liable to be abused, as someone who would never dream of "doing drugs" may still use benzos because they are prescribed by a doctor. When talking with patients, it can be helpful to tell them that benzos are basically a **prescription form of alcohol** with a cleaner neurotransmitter profile.

As with any drug that boosts GABA, benzodiazepine intoxication is characterized by both physical and mental relaxation, including sedation, cognitive impairment, poor concentration, and imbalance. Amnesia can occur with some benzos as well.

While benzodiazepines are much safer in overdose than barbiturates, they still pose a risk, especially when combined with other medications that may further depress respiratory drive (particularly opioids). Massive benzodiazepine overdoses can require in-hospital care. Flumazenil (Anexate), a GABA antagonist, was originally developed for use in benzodiazepine overdose; however, there is conflicting evidence on whether it actually improves clinical outcomes, so it is not frequently used. You can remember that flum-**aze**-nil is related to benzodi-**aze**-pines by the **aze** in its name, while the **nil** at the end can remind you flumaze-**nil** turns benzos into **nothing**.

> **Flumazenil** is a **GABA antagonist** that can be used for **benzodiazepine overdose**, although in clinical practice there is little evidence that it improves outcomes.
>
> *Flum-**aze-nil** turns **benzos** into **nothing**.*

Benzodiazepine withdrawal is characterized by increased alertness, anxiety, insomnia, and panic-like symptoms. In severe cases, seizures can occur, requiring ICU care. While not as deadly as alcohol withdrawal, withdrawal from benzodiazepines is still a high-risk time, especially when done abruptly after long-term use. Because of this, a **slow taper** is essential. When deciding on a timeframe for a benzo taper, use the **"break-up rule**!" Just as it takes one month to get over a romantic break-up for every year of the relationship, it generally takes one month to wean for every year that someone has been on benzos!

> **Weaning off** of **benzodiazepines** should be done as a **slow taper**.
>
> Remember **break-up rule**: for **every year** on a benzo, it takes **one month** to quit.

There are **no medication treatments** for benzodiazepine dependence available at this time. Instead, treatment consists of slowly weaning off of the drug then engaging in psychosocial therapies as needed. Because benzodiazepine abuse often occurs in the context of an underlying mental disorder like anxiety or depression, screening for other disorders and then treating them are essential!

OPIOIDS

The last category of "downers" we will cover are opioids. While opioids don't involve GABA in the same way that alcohol and benzodiazepines do, they still cause an overall sedating effect (recall that **D**rowsiness is one of the "**ARMED C**olonialist" symptoms!). For this reason, they are often lumped in together with depressants despite having a completely different mechanism.

Most opioids are more alike than they are different, and both prescription and recreational opioids will produce the characteristic toxidrome as captured in the "**ARMED C**olonialist" mnemonic, with **A**nalgesia, **R**espiratory depression, **M**iosis, **E**uphoria, **D**rowsiness, and **C**onstipation all being seen. In overdose, all of these signs are taken to an extreme, with the slowing of respirations being particularly life-threatening. Consider opioid overdose in any patient presenting with decreased level of consciousness, pinpoint pupils, and respiratory depression! Treatment involves supportive care (including a ventilator, if needed) and administering **naloxone** (Narcan). Nal-**blocks**-one is an **opioid receptor antagonist** that works within minutes to **block** the effects of opioids in the brain. Unlike flumazenil, naloxone *has* been shown to be effective at reducing mortality in opioid overdoses and should be given promptly in *all* cases of suspected opioid overdose.

> **Naloxone** is an **opioid receptor antagonist** that should be given promptly in all cases of **suspected opioid overdose**.
>
> *Nal-**blocks**-one **blocks** the opioid receptor and prevents overdose!*

A quick high-yield tip: **black tar heroin**, a form of cheaply produced heroin, has been known to cause botulism in some cases. Botulism involves widespread inhibition of acetylcholine release at the neuromuscular junction, leading to muscle weakness and paralysis. So when you see all of the "**ARMED C**olonialist" signs and symptoms presenting simultaneously with paralysis, think of **B**lack **T**ar heroin and **B**o**T**ulism!

> **Black tar heroin** is associated with **botulism**. Cases will present with signs of **opioid intoxication** mixed with **paralysis**.
>
> *When you hear **B**lack **T**ar heroin, think of **B**o**T**ulism!*

Opioid withdrawal produces signs and symptoms which are the exact *opposite* of the **ARMED C**olonialist, with nausea, diarrhea, body aches, and elevated vital signs all being common. Treatment of opioid withdrawal involves giving medications to counteract each of the symptoms directly, such as loperamide (Imodium) for diarrhea, acetaminophen or NSAIDs for myalgias, and clonidine (Catapres) for tachycardia and hypertension. Unlike alcohol or benzodiazepines, opioid withdrawal is *not* associated with a high rate of mortality (but it is still highly uncomfortable).

Opioids are some of the most addictive substances known to humankind. They are not only psychologically reinforcing but also are physically addictive. Tolerance develops quickly, requiring higher and higher doses to achieve the same effect. This makes opioid use disorder a particularly **lethal** condition, and deaths due to opioid abuse have risen precipitously over the past couple of decades.

Treatment for opioid use disorder requires both long-term psychosocial therapy as well as medications, with **opioid replacement therapy** using either methadone or buprenorphine being the gold standard of treatment. This involves replacing the abused opioid with a different opioid that is less liable to abuse and more compatible with daily functioning. Opioid replacement can also help to manage drug cravings and alleviate withdrawal symptoms, reducing the risk of relapse.

METHADONE

Methadone is a **high-potency** opioid that is about 5 times stronger than morphine. Despite its potency, methadone's potential for causing euphoria is significantly less than morphine, and today it is more often used to help people detox *off* of opioids than it is as an analgesic (even though it is still effective for that). The secret of methadone's success lies in its **half-life** which, at 24 hours, is longer than most opioids. This means that not only is its onset slower (causing less of a "rush") but its excretion is delayed as well, leading to fewer withdrawal effects. Methadone has been found to be one of the safest and most effective forms of opioid replacement therapy, and many patients can lead functional lives while taking it. You can remember methad-**one**'s long half-life using the same "**one** and done" mnemonic that we used with donepezil!

> **Methadone** is helpful for **opioid use disorder** due to its **long half-life**.
>
> *Methad-"**one** and done" has a long half-life lasting approximately **one** day!*

BUPRENORPHINE

In contrast to methadone's trick of having a long half-life, buprenorphine (Suboxone, Subutex) acts as a **partial agonist**, binding strongly to the opioid receptor but not activating it very much (similar to varenicline's effects on nicotine as discussed in Chapter 10). This leads to milder and less debilitating effects, and patients can lead productive lives even though they are technically "taking drugs" every day. Buprenorphine's strong binding at the opioid receptor also blocks other opioids like morphine from working, which helps to prevent relapse. Buprenorphine is often combined with naloxone to deter people from crushing or injecting the tablets. You can remember the effect of buprenorphine by thinking that "**bup**-renorphine **boops** the morphine."

> **Buprenorphine** is an **opioid partial agonist** used for **opioid use disorder**.
>
> ***Bup**-ren**orphine boops** the **morphine**.*

NALTREXONE

We discussed naltrexone (Revia, Vivitrol) earlier in this chapter when talking about alcohol. Given its mechanism of action as an opioid receptor antagonist, you might expect it to be helpful for treating opioid dependence as well! Paradoxically, however, it is not as helpful for opioid addiction as it is for alcohol, with opioid replacement therapy being preferred in almost all cases. One of the biggest barriers is that patients must be fully abstinent from opioids prior to starting (which can be a tall order!). Even when patients are successfully started on it, the evidence shows it's not as good as opioid replacement therapy, so it is generally not a first-line option for opioid abuse.

Naltrexone and naloxone are both opioid receptor antagonists, so why is naloxone used for opioid *overdose* while naltrexone is for opioid *addiction*? The key lies in the **half-life**. Naloxone has a rapid onset of action, so it is useful in emergency situations requiring immediate reversal of opioid effects. On the other hand, naltrexone has a longer half-life, making it better as a long-term treatment for opioid dependence. To remember the role of nal-**trex**-one in opioid use disorder, think of the patient going on a long **trek** towards sobriety.

Naltrexone is a longer acting opioid antagonist used for opioid dependence.

*Nal-**trex**-one helps with the long **trek** of getting sober.*

PUTTING IT ALL TOGETHER

With recreational stimulants, your role is to be the "guider" rather than the "decider." However, with recreational depressants your role is half "guider" and half "decider." This is because many depressants (including benzos and opioids) are available in prescription form, and medical care can unfortunately be a common place for addictions to start. In addition, alcohol and opioid use disorders both have effective medication-based treatments available, bringing your "decider" role back into play. Keep the following principles in mind when encountering recreational depressants in clinical practice!

1. Depressants are much more deadly than stimulants.
Opioids can be highly lethal in overdose, while alcohol can be deadly in withdrawal. Because of the increased morbidity and mortality associated with these substances, it is crucial to counsel patients on the high potential for harm!

2. Effective medication treatments exist for both alcohol and opioid abuse.
Unlike stimulants, there are effective treatments for both alcohol and opioid abuse. While most treatment for these disorders still takes place in specialized addiction medicine centers, it is important for *all* providers to be comfortable with existing treatments and to utilize them when needed to help our patients get back on track.

REVIEW QUESTIONS

1. A 53 y/o M is admitted to the wards for management of acute pancreatitis. He has been admitted to the hospital on multiple occasions before for previous episodes of pancreatitis. On the second day of hospitalization, he becomes agitated and uncooperative. On exam, diffuse shaking is noted. He appears to be responding to unseen objects around him. Vital signs are HR 118, BP 162/128, RR 22, and T 102°F. What is the most important immediate treatment to start for this patient?
   A. Ethanol
   B. Thiamine
   C. Lorazepam
   D. Disulfiram
   E. Acamprosate
   F. Opioid replacement therapy

2. (Continued from previous question.) The patient is admitted to the ICU. Which of the following lab values is *least* likely to be elevated in this patient?
   A. AST
   B. ALT
   C. ESR
   D. WBC
   E. Vitamin B1

3. A 27 y/o F patient is seen in a methadone clinic for management of opioid use disorder. She has a history of frequent relapses despite methadone treatment. Which of the following options would be most appropriate to switch to?
   A. Naloxone
   B. Naltrexone
   C. Flumazenil
   D. Acamprosate
   E. Bupropion
   F. Buprenorphine

4. A 24 y/o M wakes up on a Monday morning in his bathroom after a weekend spent with friends. He immediately feels a strong urge to defecate and races to the toilet where he experiences severe diarrhea. While sitting, he notices that the skin on his arms is covered in goose bumps as seen below:

He notes also that he feels cold and sweaty. A urine drug screen from this patient is most likely to be positive for what substance?
- A. Alcohol
- B. Cocaine
- C. Amphetamines
- D. Opioids
- E. Benzodiazepines

5. A 46 y/o M with a 25 year history of alcohol abuse is being followed up by his outpatient provider. He has been compliant with his medication regimen and has been attending daily Alcoholics Anonymous meetings. He reports that his last drink was over 1 year ago. When asked about side effects from his medication, he mentions that he had a serious adverse reaction involving headache, nausea, and "violent" vomiting after he "took some Nyquil for a head cold I had." He said that he initially felt "a little drunk" before these symptoms started. Which medication is this patient most likely taking for his alcohol use disorder?
   - A. Naltrexone
   - B. Buprenorphine
   - C. Disulfiram
   - D. Acamprosate
   - E. No medications

1. **The best answer is C.** Given this patient's history of repeated episodes of acute pancreatitis, it is likely that he has a history of alcohol abuse. In this setting, his agitation, altered sensorium, tremor, and vital sign instability is likely to be related to development of delirium tremens. Correct treatment of delirium tremens involves a benzodiazepine taper, with lorazepam (answer C) being a frequently used option. Thiamine (answer B) may be an appropriate treatment for a patient with chronic alcohol dependence, but it is not the most important immediate therapy at this time. None of the other options are indicated for a patient with delirium tremens.

2. **The best answer is E.** Chronic alcoholism is associated with a *decrease* in thiamine (also known as Vitamin B1), not an increase. Delirium tremens is associated with increases in several laboratory values, including liver function tests, ESR, and white blood cell counts (answer A–D). While alcohol use is more associated with increases in AST, ALT (answer B) will still be elevated, albeit to a lesser degree than AST.

3. **The best answer is F.** There are several treatment options besides methadone for patients with chronic heroin dependence. Of these, only naltrexone and buprenorphine are listed. Between these two, buprenorphine has more evidence that it is helpful than naltrexone which is instead more helpful for alcohol use disorders (answer B). Naloxone (answer A) is indicated for acute management for opioid overdose. Flumazenil (answer C) is used rarely for acute management of benzodiazepine overdose as it does not often improve outcomes. Acamprosate (answer D) is indicated for chronic management of alcohol dependence, while bupropion (answer E) is indicated for management of depression and smoking cessation.

4. **The best answer is D.** This clinical vignette closely describes a patient going through opioid withdrawal as evidenced by diarrhea, piloerection, and sweating. Therefore, it is likely that a urine drug screen would be positive for opioids which are detectable in the urine for 2-4 days after last use.

5. **The best answer is C.** This patient's reaction to Nyquil (a common over-the-counter cough suppressant and sleep aid which includes up to 25% alcohol by volume) suggests that he is taking the drug disulfiram. Disulfiram inhibits acetaldehyde dehydrogenase, which prevents the conversion of acetaldehyde into acetate. Acetaldehyde is directly responsible for the unpleasant symptoms he is experiencing. Naltrexone (answer A) would not be expected to cause an adverse reaction to drinking alcohol, as it works by blocking the pleasure of drinking. Acamprosate (answer D) also would not cause this reaction, as it helps to reduce anxiety and distress related to chronic alcohol alcohol use withdrawal. Buprenorphine (answer B) is used to treat opioid use disorder, not alcohol use disorder.

12 HALLUCINOGENS

The next group of recreational drugs that we will cover are the hallucinogens. In contrast to stimulants and depressants, hallucinogens do not split neatly into an "uppers" or "downers" dichotomy, and their effects on the autonomic nervous system are pretty minimal in comparison. Instead, these drugs are notable for their profound impacts on **sensory perception**. More than simply causing hallucinations, these drugs have far-reaching effects on thought, emotions, sense of self, and  consciousness. While the experience of taking hallucinogens differs from person to person, everyone who has taken them will agree that they feel "**altered**" (that is to say, their experience of themselves and the world is different than it is usually) and that their sensory processes (how they see, hear, and feel the world) are drastically different when under their influence. While many people use stimulants and depressants to achieve an immediate effect (either to provide pleasure and/or to relieve distress), people instead use hallucinogens primarily to alter their experience and explore new sensations and thoughts. This makes hallucinogens as a class much less prone to dependence and abuse, as having an altered experience doesn't tend to be as addictive as either pleasure or relief. For this reason, you are less likely to see hallucinogens in clinical settings, although they may come up from time to time!

There are two main classes of hallucinogens: **psychedelic hallucinogens**, which include LSD, magic mushrooms, and peyote, and **dissociative hallucinogens** like ketamine, phencyclidine, and dextromethorphan. While both classes cause altered states and perceptual abnormalities, the neurotransmitters involved (and therefore the clinical effects) differ significantly, so much so that it is just as arbitrary to lump these two classes together as it is to call both benzos and opioids "depressants!" We'll talk about the mechanisms for each, as well as what they mean clinically, more in this chapter.

SEROTONERGIC HALLUCINOGENS

Serotonergic hallucinogens (also known as psychedelic hallucinogens) are famous for their effects on the senses. Use of psychedelics results in **vivid sensory experiences**, with colors becoming more intense and sounds becoming clearer. Distortions such as shape warping, color swirling, and even loss of time perception often occur. Frank hallucinations, such as looking up at the sky and seeing it burst into bright colors or looking at a tree and seeing it grow new leaves, are not uncommon. Many people who  take psychedelics report a feeling that different senses have become connected, with visuals changing in time with music and sound (known as **synesthesia**). Psychedelics are known to increase connectivity in the thalamus (a part of the brain that receives sensory signals) which likely accounts for this effect!

In addition to its sensory effects, many people who take psychedelics report that they feel able to make **new connections** and come to a greater understanding of themselves and of the world (in fact, the word "psychedelic" itself means "revealing the mind or soul"). This ability to come to new realizations has potential therapeutic benefit, with some studies suggesting that psychedelics may help to catalyze improvement in various psychiatric disorders like depression and addiction.

Similarly, psychedelics can provoke **spiritual or philosophical experiences**, with people taking the drug often feeling as though they have had a revelation or are enlightened. For this reason, psychedelic hallucinogens have been used across the world by many different cultures in religious ceremonies (with some calling them "entheogens," meaning "to bring in contact with the divine").

Bright colors, vivid sounds, new connections, spiritual experiences... what does all of this have to do with *serotonin*? After all, "tripping out" is not one of the functions of serotonin we talked about in Chapter 2! Serotonin is believed to play a role in "gating" sensory information by determining what senses come to consciousness and which ones don't. When taking a serotonergic hallucinogen, more sensory information gets to conscious thought which likely explains the vividness of sights and sounds during a trip. This appears to be due to serotonin's actions at $5-HT_{2A}$ receptors (versus the other 5-HT receptors, like $5-HT_{1A}$, that are affected by antidepressants).

In comparison with many other drugs, serotonergic hallucinogens are known to be significantly less harmful. Users can experience nausea and anxiety, and changes in heart rate and blood pressure are common (though rarely dangerous). Even in cases of overdose, little harm tends to befall the user. It is questionable if withdrawal symptoms from serotonergic hallucinogens even exist, and if they do they are highly inconsistent. Because of this, psychedelics are unlikely to come to clinical attention. The one exception to this rule is **hallucinogen persisting perception disorder** (HPPD) which is a side effect which can occur in a small minority of patients who have used these drugs for many years. HPPD is characterized by visual and sensory abnormalities (such as halos surrounding objects, visual "snow," and changes in perceived dimensions) that do not go away even when the drug is stopped, likely resulting from permanent alterations to the serotonin receptors in the brain.

There are many serotonergic hallucinogens, but we will focus on the four that you are most likely to hear about: LSD, psilocybin, mescaline, and DMT!

LYSERGIC ACID DIETHYLAMIDE

The most famous serotonergic hallucinogen is lysergic acid diethylamide (often called LSD, acid, or Lucy). LSD is your prototypical psychedelic, with sensory vividness and distortions coupled with subjective feelings of epiphany and spiritual awakening. LSD is by far the **longest lasting** of the serotonergic hallucinations, with the most intense effects lasting about 12 hours and minor effects lingering even longer than that. Due to its long duration, intoxication with LSD is often called a
trip. Occasionally, users will have a "bad trip" where the perceptual disturbances are frightening or anxiety-producing. Bad trips can be minimized by paying attention to one's mindset and environment (often called "set and setting") before taking the drug.

> **Lysergic acid diethylamide** is the **longest-lasting** serotonergic hallucinogen.
>
> *LSD Lasts a Semi-Day (12 hours).*

PSILOCYBIN

Psilocybin is found in several species of mushrooms and is often called **magic mushrooms** or **shrooms**. It has psychological and perceptual effects similar to LSD, though perhaps a bit milder and with a shorter duration of action (about 4 to 6 hours). Due to its gentler effects, psilocybin is sometimes considered more "social" and less "cerebral" than LSD.

MESCALINE

Mescaline, from the **peyote** plant, is another serotonergic hallucinogen. It has been used by several Native American tribes during religious ceremonies. From a clinical standpoint, mescaline acts similarly to other psychedelics but seems to be associated with stronger "visuals" and more upset stomach.

DIMETHYLTRYPTAMINE

N,N-Dimethyltryptamine (abbreviated DMT) is a serotonergic hallucinogen that is found in the drink **ayahuasca**. In certain parts of South America, plants containing DMT are boiled to make ayahuasca which is then consumed as part of a religious ritual (or for tourists). DMT's effects are similar to other serotonergic hallucinogens, although the experience is said to be more spiritual in nature than other psychedelics. Interestingly, some of the plants in ayahuasca also contain naturally occurring MAO inhibitors which potentiate and prolong DMT's effects. (Recall from Chapter 3 that serotonin and other monoamines are broken down by MAO, so it follows that an MAO inhibitor would help a strongly serotonergic drug to work better!)

DISSOCIATIVE HALLUCINOGENS

Dissociative hallucinogens are similar to serotonergic hallucinogens in that they cause profound sensory distortions, but their subjective effects are experienced quite differently. Dissociatives induce a mental state where the user does not feel like they are connected with their environment. They can also cause **depersonalization** (the sense that one is disconnected from their body or cannot control their own actions) and **derealization** (the feeling that the world is unreal). The experience of taking dissociatives is often described as dream-like and ethereal.

Dissociatives work by **antagonizing NMDA glutamate receptors** (remember **D**issociatives from the NM**D**A mnemonic!). Recall from Chapter 2 that glutamate is an excitatory neurotransmitter in the brain, so blocking glutamate receptors will lead to slowed neural transmission. This may underlie the dissociative effect of NMDA antagonists, as different parts of the brain are prevented from "talking" to each other, leading to a fragmentation of thought. It's important to note that many dissociatives have a very non-specific or "dirty" pharmacologic profile involving multiple other neurotransmitters as well, leading to various effects in the brain (including both stimulatory effects like agitation as well as depressant effects like sedation).

Unlike serotonergics, dissociatives *are* associated with some clinically significant states, and you should be aware of their toxidromes. While there are many drugs that can be classified as dissociatives, we will limit our study to the three that are most likely to be seen clinically: phencyclidine, ketamine, and dextromethorphan.

PHENCYCLIDINE

Phencyclidine (also known as PCP or angel dust) causes pronounced hallucinatory effects. However, it is better known clinically for inducing a state of **excited delirium** characterized by belligerence, impulsivity, agitation, and imperviousness to pain. On tests, you may come across a classic vignette involving a patient who is so agitated and belligerent that it takes 5 people to restrain them. On physical exam, **nystagmus** (or oscillation of lateral eye movements) can be seen. Like meth, phencyclidine has a **long half-life** and duration of action (over a day!). In contrast to other dissociatives, phencyclidine seems to bind strongly to the **D₂ receptor** which may explain its pro-psychotic effects. There were a few high-profile cases of people doing terrible things while on PCP which gave the drug quite a bit of notoriety in the media (most famously in 2002 when music artist Big Lurch murdered his girlfriend and ate parts of her body while under the influence of the drug). Partly due to this reputation, use of PCP has declined, but given its clinical importance you should still be on the lookout on boards and in the emergency room.

> **Phencyclidine** can cause a state of **excited delirium** resulting in agitation, psychosis, and imperviousness to pain. Ocular **nystagmus** can be seen on exam.
>
> *If someone is **being a d*ck** and has **nys**tagmus, they might be on **PCP-nis**.*

KETAMINE

Ketamine (Ketalar) is a dissociative hallucinogen that we have talked about already in the context of depression (as it is increasingly used as a rapid-acting antidepressant, though with transient effects lasting only a few days). However, it also has other clinical and recreational uses, both of which we will discuss here.

Ketamine is used to induce rapid anesthesia in severely injured patients. Within minutes of ketamine administration, patients enter a **trance-like state** in which pain is perceived as being far away or as not happening to one's own body. In comparison with most anesthetics, ketamine does not lower blood pressure and may even help to maintain it, making it  helpful for patients with severe bleeding (for whom other anesthetics might send the patient into circulatory collapse and shock). It also has a bronchodilating effect which can help to preserve the patient's airway. Once the drug's effects wear off, patients will often have little memory of anything that happened during that time, so it is an excellent choice for situations in which **rapid transient analgesia** is needed. For all of these reasons, it is one of the safest anesthetics to use in **children**.

Ketamine is also used recreationally and is known as Special K or just K in this setting. It is generally taken at lower doses than would be used clinically. At these lower doses, depersonalization and derealization occur. At higher doses, users enter what is known as a "**K-hole**" which is characterized by extreme dissociation, euphoria, sensory distortion, and loss of time perception. Ketamine has a relatively **short half-life** compared to other dissociatives, with effects lasting around one or two hours. When used on a short-term basis, there do not appear to be any significant withdrawal effects. Ketamine is not considered to be a highly addictive drug, although some people will have trouble stopping. While ketamine is thought of as a relatively safe drug, bladder and liver toxicity can occur with long-term use.

Overall, you can remember all of the main points about ketamine by thinking of it as **KIDDA**-mine. This will help you to associate it with **K**ids (as it's commonly used as an anesthetic in children), **I**ncreased blood pressure (unlike most anesthetics which tend to lower blood pressure), **D**issociative effects (including both depersonalization and derealization), rapid anti-**D**epressant action, and **A**irway preservation (through its bronchodilating effect).

Ketamine is a **dissociative anesthetic** that can also be used recreationally as a **hallucinogen** or for transient relief of **depression**.

KIDDA-mine:
Kids
Increased blood pressure
Dissociation
Anti-Depressant
Airway preservation

DEXTROMETHORPHAN
Dextromethorphan is found in over-the-counter cough syrups such as Robitussin. It acts on the opioid receptor to suppress the cough reflex, although since it does not have significant activity at the mu opioid receptor it is not an effective analgesic! When taken in doses exceeding the recommended amount, dextromethorphan **antagonizes NMDA receptors**, giving it effects similar to (but often weaker than) ketamine and phencyclidine. Recreational use of dextromethorphan (often called "robotripping" due to its association with the Robitussin brand name) can involve hallucinations, changes in consciousness, euphoria, or even psychosis.

As an over-the-counter medication, dextromethorphan is easily available in the United States, but that does not mean it is safe! Indeed, dextromethorphan misuse can be dangerous, especially considering that it is often sold in combination with acetaminophen which can cause severe liver toxicity in overdose.

PUTTING IT ALL TOGETHER

With the main exception of phencyclidine, you are unlikely to see recreational users of hallucinogens in clinical settings (or, at the very least, it won't be the main problem that they are presenting for). Nevertheless, you should be aware of the common types of hallucinogens and be able to converse knowledgeably with patients who use them. Take note of the following points when discussing hallucinogens with your patients:

1. Serotonergic hallucinogens are generally low-risk from a medical standpoint.
Due to their low potential for personal or societal harm, current medical practice does not involve making a strong recommendation for or against the use of serotonergic hallucinogens. You may still run into mental health practitioners who believe that psychedelics cause problems, but the evidence so far has not supported this notion.

2. Dissociative hallucinogens can be more dangerous.
Compared to serotonergic hallucinogens, dissociative hallucinogens are much more likely to be harmful, and you should have a well-informed discussion on the risks of these drugs with any patients who use them. In addition, you should be able to recognize them in states of intoxication when they come to clinical attention (especially phencyclidine and its association with excited delirium!).

Memorable Psychopharmacology

REVIEW QUESTIONS

1. A 23 y/o F with a history of depression, anxiety, PTSD, and "polysubstance abuse" is seen by a therapist in an addiction medicine clinic for an intake appointment. Her substance history is notable for having used all major classes of recreational substances within the past year. When coming up with a treatment plan, which of the following substances is the *lowest* priority to address?
    A. Alcohol
    B. Cocaine
    C. Amphetamines
    D. Marijuana
    E. Opioids
    F. Benzodiazepines
    G. Serotonergic hallucinogens
    H. Caffeine
    I. Nicotine

2. A 26 y/o M is brought into the ED by police officers responding to a call. According to several 911 calls, the patient was seen wandering through the streets yelling angrily and smashing mailboxes. At present time, he appears calm but disoriented. He does not respond to questions. On exam, oscillations of lateral eye movements are noted. The patient becomes increasingly agitated throughout the exam. He suddenly erupts and begins attacking nearby medical personnel. It takes 6 nurses to finally restrain him. The substance that the patient was most likely taking has what mechanism of action?
    A. GABA agonist
    B. GABA antagonist
    C. Glutamate agonist
    D. Glutamate antagonist
    E. Serotonin agonist
    F. Serotonin antagonist

3. A 46 y/o M has found employment as a truck driver. While on his first drive from California to Florida, he notices that his vision of the west Texas desert is altered. Specifically, the horizon line between the desert ground and the blue sky is not straight but rather appears to be an undulating wave. In addition, he notices several visual halos in the sky. He is concerned by this but decides to keep driving. What substance was most likely to have been used repeatedly earlier in the patient's life?
    A. Marijuana
    B. Mescaline
    C. Methamphetamine
    D. Midazolam
    E. MDMA

1. **The best answer is G.** Multiple studies have demonstrated that the personal and societal harm caused by serotonergic psychedelics can be considered negligible when compared with the other drug classes listed. For this reason, it is generally not a priority for drug treatment.

2. **The best answer is D.** This clinical vignette describes a patient who is intoxicated with phencyclidine as evidenced by his extreme agitation. Phencyclidine is considered to be a potent glutamate antagonist at the NMDA receptor subtype as well as having some effect as a dopamine agonist. None of the other answer choices correctly describes phencyclidine's mechanism of action.

3. **The best answer is B.** This vignette describes a patient who is experiencing hallucinogen persisting perception disorder (HPPD), a syndrome characterized by persistent sensory abnormalities that occur after the patient has stopped taking serotonergic hallucinogens on a long-term basis. Of the answer choices listed, only mescaline is a serotonergic hallucinogen. None of the other drugs listed would be expected to cause HPPD.

13 CANNABIS AND OTHERS

Our final chapter on recreational drugs will cover all the drugs that don't fit neatly into any of the categories we have discussed so far. By far the most common of these are the **cannabinoids** found in marijuana, and this is where we will spend the majority of our time. However, there are some other clinically important substances to be aware of, including **GHB**, **inhalants**, and **anabolic steroids**. While not all of these are taken for an explicitly "psychiatric" reason, they can all have distinct effects on one's mental state so they are worth talking about in any review of psychopharmacology.

You may be hard-pressed to see any unifying themes or concepts in a chapter that is centered around a grab bag of "miscellaneous" substances. Indeed, these drug classes each work by a different mechanism, and some of them don't even involve neurotransmitters! Nevertheless, each of the three core reasons that people use psychoactive substances recreationally that we talked about in Chapter 10 (to feel pleasure, to relief distress, and/or to alter one's mental state) will come into play in various ways with these substances. Cannabis, for example, can help to relieve pain and distract from anxiety, but many people also take it simply for the experience of feeling different than they normally do. As you read through this chapter, pay particularly attention to the reasons why someone might use this substance, as this can help you to make sense of your patient's behaviors as well as provide a window into what is going on in their lives.

In contrast to the chapters on recreational stimulants and depressants, there will be less of a focus on recognition and management of intoxication, withdrawal, and addiction in clinical settings for these substances, as they tend come to clinical attention much less frequently than either stimulants or depressants. However, it is still important that you be able to knowledgeably converse with patients about these!

CANNABINOIDS

Cannabinoids are a class of compounds which bind to **cannabinoid receptors** in the brain. These receptors are normally activated by *endo*genously produced molecules known as endocannabinoids. However, they also bind much more strongly to *exo*genous cannabinoids found in various drugs. (This is roughly analogous to the opioid receptors, which bind weakly to naturally existing endorphins but respond much more strongly to external opioids such as morphine and heroin.) Most cannabinoids  come from the **cannabis** plant, with the drug that is made from the plant being called **marijuana**. However, there are also other forms in which people ingest cannabinoids such as in resins and oils (known as **hash** or **hashish**).

While many cannabinoids exist, the one that is most often associated with the effects of cannabis is **tetrahydrocannabinol** (THC). THC is one of the most widely used psychoactive substances on the planet, with approximately 5% of the world's population having used it at least once in the past year! You can remember the various effects of THC using the mnemonic **HASH PIPER**:

H is for High. Mentally, cannabis causes alterations of consciousness and sensory perception as well as feelings of relaxation and mild euphoria that are collectively referred to as a "high." This is the core alteration in mental state that has made cannabis such a popular drug for millennia!

A is for Anxiety. The effects of cannabis on anxiety are varied. Many people report that cannabis relaxes them, and some will take it as a way of self-medicating an underlying anxiety disorder. However, a significant minority of people who have used cannabis report *increased* feelings of anxiety while under the influence.

S is for Short-term memory loss. Cannabis is associated with immediate effects on short-term memory, with people often having trouble with encoding new information. For someone who is intoxicated with cannabis, even following a single sentence from beginning to end can be a challenge!

H is for Hunger. Increased appetite and food intake (often called "the munchies") is one of the most famous side effects of cannabis. This effect can be helpful clinically, such as using cannabis to stimulate appetite and reduce nausea in patients who have cancer or other diseases that make eating difficult.

P is for Pain relief. Cannabis can be an effective pain reliever for people with chronic pain or spasticity. Given that it is significantly less addictive and harmful than opioids, it can be a reasonable part of a pain management regimen for many patients.

I is for Impairment. Intoxication with cannabis can lead to both cognitive and motor impairment, and people under the influence should be cautioned to avoid driving or otherwise engaging in complex or potentially unsafe activities.

P is for Paranoia. Cannabis can cause a state of paranoia in some people who take it which can even resemble frank psychosis. This effect tends to fade as the drug leaves the body, although for some people (particularly those who take it in large amounts for long periods of time) it can lead to a persistent psychotic disorder.

E is for Energy. Like with anxiety, the effects of cannabis on energy are varied. Some people report increases in energy and sociability, while others say that it knocks them out and will use it as a sleeping aid for this reason. The effect appears to correlate with the particular strain used, with **sativa** strains being more activating and **indica** strains being more sedating. (You can remember this by thinking that s-**active**-a makes you more **active** while **ind**-ica will put you to sleep like reading the **ind**-ex of a book.) Cannabis also tends to lead to decreases in motivation which can present as lethargy and apathy, especially in long-term users.

Sativa and **indica** are two **cannabis strains** that have distinct effects on **energy**.

*S-**active**-a makes you **active** while **ind**-ica is sedating like reading a book **ind**-ex.*

R is for Red eyes. Finally, cannabis can cause conjunctival injection or redness of the eyes which is a tell-tale sign of intoxication. This effect is due to dilation of ocular capillaries and decreased intraocular pressure.

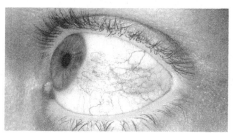

Conjunctival injection related to cannabis use.

Cannabis use results in a wide range of both **physiologic and psychological effects** due to the effect of **THC** on **cannabinoid receptors** throughout the body.

HASH PIPER:
High
Anxiety
Short-term memory loss
Hunger
Pain relief
Impairment
Paranoia
Energy
Red eyes

While THC is the major active cannabinoid in cannabis, there are other compounds in cannabis that exert various effects as well. An important one to know is **cannabidiol** (CBD). In contrast to THC, CBD does not cause any subjective high. Instead, it acts as an *antagonist* at cannabinoid receptors and may actually attenuate some of THC's effects. Because of this, the balance between THC and CBD accounts for the different effects found between particular strains of cannabis, with THC-heavy strains causing more of the "high" while CBD-heavy strains have more analgesic, anti-inflammatory, and anti-anxiety effects. Because it opposes many of the effects that cannabis is known for, you can think of **CBD** as a "**C**annabis **B**ringer **D**owner."

> **Tetrahydrocannabinol** is the active ingredient in **cannabis** while **cannabidiol** acts as a cannabinoid receptor **antagonist**.
>
> *THC is The High Chemical, CBD is the Cannabis Bringer Downer.*

Clinically, knowing about cannabinoids remains important for several reasons. To start with, some cannabinoids have been developed into prescription medications such as dronabinol (Marinol) which are used to reduce nausea and vomiting during chemotherapy, improve appetite in patients  with HIV/AIDS, and treat chronic pain and muscle spasms. While these are the only FDA-approved indications for cannabinoids, some users of cannabis maintain that it is effective for other disorders, including epilepsy, stroke, and a variety of mental illnesses ranging from depression and social phobia to anxiety and PTSD. Unfortunately, there is little high-quality medical research to back these claims up. This does not mean that they are *not* effective; rather, **we simply don't know** whether cannabis works for these purposes. This is because legal regulations have frustrated efforts to perform scientific studies on cannabinoids, so we are left only with anecdotes and other forms of low-quality evidence on which to base our decisions.

Among mental health specialists, there is some concern that cannabis use may induce or exacerbate **psychotic states**, particularly in patients with pre-existing mental disorders or a family history of mental illness. While we don't know if cannabinoids *cause* psychosis per se, there is evidence that it may increase psychotic symptoms in vulnerable individuals. The ratio of THC to CBD plays a large role here, as THC increases psychotic symptoms while CBD actually appears to have an antipsychotic-like effect. In recent years, growers have been selectively breeding marijuana to have higher levels of THC and less CBD, making recent strains more likely to have psychotic effects. A further point of caution is that cannabis use among adolescents is linked to **reductions in IQ**, although the question of correlation versus causation remains unanswered. Nevertheless, these are important points to counsel your patients on!

SYNTHETIC CANNABINOIDS

Synthetic cannabis (sold as Spice, K2, and various other brand names) refers to a variety of cannabinoids that have been designed in a lab to have effects similar to cannabis. Given the immense variety of different compounds that fall under the banner of "synthetic cannabis," it is difficult to make accurate generalizations about them. However, it is safe to say that certain synthetic cannabinoids are much more **potent** than cannabis and have more troubling side effects, including a more clearly defined state of withdrawal and a stronger link to **psychotic** thoughts and behavior (which makes sense, as synthetic cannabinoids generally lack any kind of **C**annabis **B**ringer **D**owner such as CBD). In this way, the relationship of synthetic cannabinoids to cannabis is largely analogous to how synthetic cathinones are often stronger and have more unpredictable effects compared to naturally occurring cathinones like khat (as described in Chapter 10). Also like synthetic cathinones, synthetic cannabinoids are not detectable using urine drug tests, so they should be on your differential for patients presenting with substance-induced psychosis and a **negative drug screen**.

GHB

Gamma-**H**ydroxy**B**utyric acid (better known as **GHB**) is a strange little guy. It acts directly on the GABA receptor, producing mental effects similar to benzodiazepines and for this reason is commonly classified as a depressant. However, users of GHB noted that it was much more *activating* than you would expect from a GABA agonist. This led to the discovery that GHB also binds to its own separate **GHB receptor** which increases downstream levels of glutamate and dopamine, leading to *stimulation* of the central nervous system. In this way, GHB is best thought of as a **combined stimulant and depressant**! It has found a niche in the party scene due to it being not only energy-boosting like stimulants but also sedating and disinhibiting like depressants, with some describing its effects as closest to a combination of alcohol and MDMA.

While people who take it recreationally often liken it to a "best of both worlds" drug, from a clinical perspective GHB can sometimes be more of a "worst of both worlds" situation. In particular, GHB overdose can cause not only inhibitory effects such as respiratory depression but also stimulant-like complications such as seizures. This complicates matters significantly, as the treatment for seizures is to give benzodiazepines, which can further exacerbate both central nervous system and respiratory depression. For these reasons, GHB overdose is considered a medical emergency requiring close monitoring of vitals to prevent further injury or death. Diagnosis is often difficult, as GHB is **undetectable on most urine drug screens**.

GHB is a fast acting drug, with effects lasting a few hours. Withdrawal from GHB resembles benzo withdrawal and appears to involve increased anxiety, insomnia, and restlessness. In extreme cases, in-hospital supportive care may be required.

> **GHB** is a **combined stimulant and depressant** that can be lethal in overdose.
>
> **GHB** = **G**HB **H**as **B**oth *(stimulant and depressant effects).*

INHALANTS

Inhalants as a class can be difficult to define, as there are many different substances and compounds that fall under its banner. However, they generally fall into one of three categories: **solvents**, **anesthetics**, and **nitrites**.

SOLVENTS

Inhaled solvents are found in all sorts of commonly available household items, including glue, nail polish, gasoline, and aerosols. The psychological effects from inhalants vary according to the specific substance, but in general they produce a "**head rush**" where the user feels dizzy and temporarily elated. Perceptual disturbances, such as hallucinations or dissociation, and a loss of motor coordination can occur as well. These effects are very **short-lived** (on the order of seconds to minutes). The specific compounds responsible for these effects differs by the solvent but are generally comprised of hydrocarbons like benzene, toluene, butane, and propane; ketones such as acetone; and chlorofluorocarbons.

While inhalants are commonly available (most can be bought in any grocery store), they are associated with **significant health problems**, both during short and long-term use. The morbidity associated with inhalants vary by the particular substance used but can range from immediate and life-threatening outcomes (such as heart failure, pneumonia, and brain injury) to longer term organ damage (including neuropathy, nephrotoxicity, hepatotoxicity, and carcinogenesis). Depending on the method of inhalation, suffocation can be a significant concern as well.

Sadly, inhalant abuse appears to be particularly prevalent among children without families, the poor, and the institutionalized (for whom as access to other drugs, both recreational and prescription, is quite limited). For this reason, screening for and counseling about inhalant abuse in these populations is essential.

ANESTHETICS

Several gases have historically been used as anesthetics, including nitrous oxide, chloroform, and diethyl ether (or simply "ether"). When inhaled, these gases cause an immediate euphoria (which explains why nitrous oxide is commonly called "laughing gas") as well as disinhibition, memory loss, and decreased consciousness. Compared to solvents, anesthetic gases are not as toxic, though care must be taken to keep ether away from flames as it is highly flammable.

NITRITES

Inhaled nitrites such as amyl nitrite or isobutyl nitrite are commonly called **poppers**. Similarly to other inhalants, they produce an immediate "head rush" lasting several minutes. Poppers, however, are unique in that they are often used for enhancing **sexual experiences**, especially in communities of men who have sex with men. Nitrites work by causing the release of nitric oxide, leading to widespread vasodilation and relaxation of involuntary muscles. The sudden drop in blood pressure that results is accompanied by reflex tachycardia and flushing. These effects are very **transient**, lasting only a minute or two.

While inhalation of nitrites has not been shown to lead to significant long-term health effects, care should be taken to avoid taking nitrites at the same time as phosphodiesterase inhibitors such as sildenafil (Viagra) or tadalafil (Cialis), as the drop in blood pressure from combining poppers with these medications (or any other drugs that rapidly reduce blood pressure) can be life-threatening.

A selection of poppers.

ANABOLIC STEROIDS

Anabolic-androgen steroids (called simply "steroids" by the public) are a bit of an odd duck in the realm of recreational drugs, as people use them less for their effects on the *brain* and more for their effects on the *body*. Steroids increase **muscle mass**, which is useful to gain a competitive edge in sports (although the majority of people who take steroids recreationally do it primarily for aesthetic, rather than athletic, purposes).

Like all steroids (including those used medically), anabolic steroids come with an extensive side effect profile. Mood can become erratic, with increasing swings between depression and mania. Behavior can trend towards impulsivity and aggression (the so-called "roid rage" talked about in the media). Physiologically, long-term steroid use can wreak havoc on multiple organ systems. Steroids cause closure of the epiphyseal growth plates, leading to stunted growth when used in adolescence. Increased acne can offset some of the aesthetic gains. More worryingly, both nephrotoxicity and hepatotoxicity have been reported. Steroids also affect the cardiovascular system, resulting in the "**hyper**" triple threat of cardiac **hyper**trophy, **hyper**tension, and **hyper**lipidemia. Ironically, even when androgenic steroids like

testosterone are used, both virilization and feminization can occur, leading to paradoxical states of increased chest hair growing over newly developed breast buds. Finally, given that the testicles don't have to produce as much endogenous androgens on their own, **testicular atrophy** is seen (which is a high-yield sign on the physical exam if you suspect steroid use). All in all, steroids exact a high price for their promise of larger muscles!

> **Anabolic androgenic steroids** increase **muscle mass** but are associated with multiple **medical** and **psychiatric problems**.
>
> *"I used **steroids** so I could get **a trophy**, but all I got was testicular **atrophy**."*

COMBINING DRUGS

While it is initially helpful to learn about each drug individually, the fact of the matter is that most drug use does not occur in a vacuum. Indeed, **polysubstance use** is the rule rather than the exception, as the majority of people who use drugs recreationally have used more than one (and often in combination with other drugs).

The most frequent pattern of use is to combine two drugs with opposite effects (such as a stimulant and a depressant) to offset the downsides of each. This can range from mixing caffeine with alcohol (as in a Vodka Red Bull) to injecting cocaine and heroin in the same syringe (known as a "speedball" or "powerball"). The resulting effect is characterized by increased energy from the stimulant (without the accompanying anxiety and hyperarousal) as well as the relaxing effect of depressants (without the sedation and drowsiness).

Unfortunately, there is no such thing as a free lunch, and rather than being a happy medium between two extremes, these combinations come with a **higher rate of morbidity and mortality** than either drug alone. This is because the negative effects of each drug (anxiety from stimulants and drowsiness from depressants) all serve as a signal to avoid overuse. When these signals are blocked, users are liable to take in much more of the substance than they had intended, making overdosing much easier. Combining opioids and stimulants has claimed the lives of many, including several high-profile cases such as Chris Farley and Philip Seymour Hoffman. However, even the combination of "weaker" drugs like caffeine and alcohol can be dangerous as well.

PUTTING IT ALL TOGETHER

Now that we have covered the most common recreational drugs, we can review some general principles about them.

1. Be able to recognize both intoxication and withdrawal states for a given drug.
Toxidromes are commonly tested on exams, and for good reason: you can't treat the effects of a substance until you know which substance you are working with. To recognize toxidromes on exams and in real life, remember the phrase, "**It's all in the eyes.**" On questions asking you to recognize different drug states, some information about the eyes will often be given. Dilated pupils suggest stimulant intoxication, while constricted or "pinpoint pupils" point toward opioids. Nystagmus in the context of substance abuse is likely phencyclidine, while conjunctival injection is typically related to cannabis use. Know these well!

Ocular Finding		Related Substance
Dilated pupils	→	Stimulants
Constricted or "pinpoint" pupils	→	Opioids
Nystagmus	→	Phencyclidine (PCP)
Redness of the eyes	→	Cannabis

Examination of the **eyes** helps to recognize both **toxidromes** and **withdrawal** states.

"It's all in the eyes!"

2. Not all recreational drugs are created equal.
There is no shortage of misinformation on recreational drugs. Some people assume that all types of drugs are equally "bad" or that prescription drugs are always safer than recreational substances. Neither is true. Heroin and methamphetamine are clearly associated with more personal and societal harm than hallucinogens, and prescription opioids are a leading cause of death and disability in the United States. Keep this in mind so that you are able to have well-informed conversations with your patients about substance use.

3. Effective treatments for many substance use disorders exist.
If you don't specialize in addiction medicine, it's easy to forget that effective treatments for many substance use disorders *do* exist. In particular, pharmacologic treatments are available to treat cases of **nicotine**, **alcohol**, and **opioid** addiction, and you should not feel shy about prescribing these medications and/or referring to addiction treatment services as necessary.

REVIEW QUESTIONS

1. A 16 y/o M has recently begun smoking marijuana with several of his older friends. Which of the following signs or behaviors is most likely to be observed in this patient while intoxicated?
    A. Decreased eating behavior
    B. Bilateral conjunctival injection
    C. Agitation and belligerence
    D. Reports of depersonalization and derealization
    E. Increase in pain sensation

2. Which of the following effects is *incorrectly* paired with its causative drug?
    A. Mydriasis – Stimulant intoxication
    B. Miosis – Opioid withdrawal
    C. Red eyes – Cannabis intoxication
    D. Nystagmus – Phencyclidine intoxication
    E. Decreased blood pressure – Nitrite intoxication

3. A 22 y/o M is referred to the emergency department after he calls a health hotline to report an erection lasting longer than 4 hours. Detumescence occurs by the time he arrives to the hospital, and no intervention is performed. The patient reports that he has had increasingly longer lasting erections for the past few weeks. Vital signs are within normal limits. General examination reveals male-pattern baldness, as seen below, which he says has only begun in the past several months:

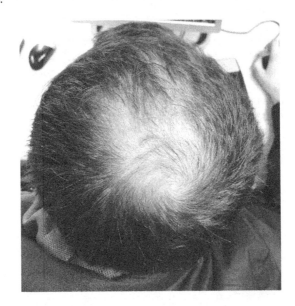

Genitourinary examination reveals a small testicular size of approximately 8 cm^3. His girlfriend confides privately that she has noticed behavior and personality changes in the past 3 months, saying that his mood is "all over the place" and that he easily becomes angry. Urine toxicology is negative. When confronted, the patient admits to drug use. This drug places the patient at increased risk of all of the following outcomes *except*:
    A.   Increased blood pressure
    B.   Skin changes
    C.   Enlargement and thickening of the left ventricle
    D.   Scarring of renal parenchyma
    E.   Elevated blood lipoproteins
    F.   All of the above are known side effects of this drug

4.   A 25 y/o F is brought to the hospital after being found unresponsive on the floor of a dancing club bathroom. Naloxone was administered in the ambulance on the way to the hospital with no effect. In the emergency department, she remains comatose. Initial vital signs are HR 82, BP 134/88, RR 6, and T 96.8°F, though her respirations appear shallow. Several minutes later, she has a generalized tonic-clonic seizure lasting one minute. Intubation is attempted but is unsuccessful due to a strong gag reflex. One hour later, she awakens suddenly and appears to have normal mentation. A urine drug screen is most likely to reveal which of the following substances?
    A.   Cannabis
    B.   *Gamma*-Hydroxybutyric acid
    C.   Chlorofluorocarbons
    D.   Diethyl ether
    E.   Amyl nitrite
    F.   Anabolic steroids
    G.   None of the above

1. **The best answer is B.** Use of cannabis is reliably associated with multiple signs and symptoms. These include reported feelings of euphoria and relaxation, decreased pain sensation (answer E), increased appetite and eating behavior (answer A), feelings of paranoia, and bilateral conjunctival injection. Agitation is seen more with methamphetamines or phencyclidine (answer C), while feelings of depersonalization and derealization occur more often with dissociative hallucinogens (answer D).

2. **The best answer is B.** Opioid intoxication, not withdrawal, is associated with miosis (pupillary constriction). All of the other answer choices are correctly paired with their causative drug.

3. **The best answer is F.** This patient is likely using anabolic steroids as evidenced by mood and behavioral changes, testicular atrophy, and priapism. Anabolic steroids are not routinely detected on urine toxicology tests. Hypertension, acne, cardiac remodeling, renal damage, and hyperlipidemia are all known side effects of anabolic steroid use.

4. **The best answer is G.** This vignette describes a case of GHB overdose. Clues that GHB are involved include the mix of both central nervous system depression (as evidenced by her obtunded mental status) and excitation (as evidenced by her seizure) as well as the rapid emergence from this state within a few hours. However, GHB does not appear on most commonly available urine drug screens (answer B). Inhalants also do not appear on most urine drug screens, but the effects of these drugs tend to wear off in minutes rather than hours (answers C, D, and E). Anabolic steroids would not be expected to cause seizures or coma (answer F). Cannabis is relatively safe in overdose (answer A).

14 DRUG-DRUG INTERACTIONS

And with that, we have officially gone over all the major classes of psychoactive substances! Take a moment to pat yourself on the back. As we approach the end of this book, let's look at all the ways that the drugs we have talked about can interact with each other. At its core, a **drug-drug interaction** is what happens when one drug has an effect on another drug, often in a negative or unintended way. This generally happens by one of two mechanisms: either the two drugs have an effect that is **too strong in combination** or one drug **changes the metabolism** of another drug.

The first type of interaction is seen in something like serotonin syndrome, which occurs when a patient is given two different medications that both increase serotonin. When these two drugs are given together, the body receives too much serotonergic stimulation, and serotonin syndrome can occur (remember Shits and SHIVERS!).

The second type of interaction involves changes in drug metabolism. When a drug enters our bodies, it diffuses through the bloodstream and exerts its intended effects on the target organ (which in the case of psychopharmacology is usually the brain). For example, after someone takes sertraline, it continues to circulate until it is metabolized by the liver, at which point it is rendered inactive and excreted from the body.

However, let's now say that this patient begins also taking a mood stabilizer such as carbamazepine. Carbamazepine is known as an **inducer** because it **speeds up** the metabolism of certain drugs. So for this patient, the metabolism of sertraline will *increase*, leading to an overall net *decrease* in the amount of sertraline in their system.

In contrast, let's say that this same patient instead begins taking a medication for HIV such as ritonavir. In contrast to carbamazepine, ritonavir is **inhibitor** of hepatic enzyme systems and **slows down** the metabolism of certain drugs. So for this patient, the metabolism of sertraline will *decrease*, leading to an overall net *increase* in the amount of sertraline in their system.

An **inducer** will **speed up** metabolism and **decrease drugs levels**, while an **inhibitor** will **slow down** metabolism and **increase drug levels**.

In**D**ucers bring drug levels **D**own, while in**HI**bitors lift drug levels **HI**gh.

While this concept is very simple on the surface, the reality is much more complicated, as there is not just a single system in the liver that is responsible for metabolizing drugs. Instead, there are **multiple enzyme systems** that each go by difficult-to-remember names like 2D6, 3A4, and 1A2. While over 40 different enzyme systems that have been identified, a core group of six have been found to be responsible for the vast majority of all drug metabolism (1A2, 2B6, 2C9, 2C19, 2D6 and 3A4). Most psychotropic drugs are metabolized by each of these systems to varying degrees. For example, sertraline is metabolized by the 3A4 enzyme system, whereas another SSRI like fluoxetine is not. If you gave someone a 3A4 inhibitor, the levels of sertraline in the body would go up, but the levels of fluoxetine would not be affected. In contrast, fluoxetine is metabolized by the 2D6 enzyme system, so if you instead gave someone a 2D6 inhibitor, the levels of fluoxetine in the body *would* go up, while the levels of sertraline would not be affected.

A further complication is the fact that the effect that certain drugs can have on those enzyme systems is not a "yes-or-no," "on-or-off" matter. Rather, there is a **wide range of effects** that a drug can have. For example, among the SSRIs, fluoxetine is a *strong* 2D6 inhibitor, sertraline is a *moderate* 2D6 inhibitor, and citalopram is a *weak* 2D6 inhibitor.

To complicate things even *further*, many enzyme systems in the liver are affected not only by other drugs but by **genetics** as well. For example, the activity of the 2D6 enzyme responsible for metabolizing fluoxetine is determined to a large extent by one's genes. This means that some people are **slow metabolizers** and operate as if they have a built-in 2D6 inhibitor, leading to *higher* levels of medications like fluoxetine even at the same dose as someone else. Other people are inherently **rapid metabolizers**, leading to *lower* levels of fluoxetine at the same dose. (On a clinical level, there are genetic tests available that will tell you a patient's individual metabolic profile. However, this information has not been shown to actually improve clinical outcomes in most cases as you are ultimately titrating to effect rather than a specific dose.)

Finally, to add that last wrinkle of complication, certain drugs (known as **prodrugs**) are actually *activated* by liver metabolism rather than being inactivated. For example, the pain medication codeine is converted into morphine in the liver by the 2D6 system. Codeine itself is not a very powerful analgesic, but morphine *is*. In the presence of a powerful 2D6 inhibitor such as fluoxetine, however, this transformation into morphine is blocked, rendering codeine a rather ineffective analgesic.

Putting this all together, the amount of complexity can become almost overwhelming. The difference between inducers and inhibitors, the multiple enzyme systems, the strength of the interaction, the contribution from genetics, and the distinction between drugs and pro-drugs all combine to make for a seemingly infinite amount of information to know. Because of this complexity, many clinics and hospitals have computerized alert systems that will let you know when you're about to prescribe two drugs that will interact poorly with each other. While helpful in some ways, given the vast number of possible interactions, these systems are prone to "alert fatigue" where clinicians are warned of so many possible interactions that they just start to ignore them all.

When approaching drug-drug interactions, try to use a balanced approach. We can't completely ignore drug-drug interactions because they have the potential to seriously impact patient care. However, trying to memorize every single interaction is also not a realistic goal. Instead, focus your attention squarely on the **most clinically significant interactions**: those where the interaction is *strong*, the outcomes are *bad*, and/or the effect is *not noticeable* until it's too late. We'll go over each of these one by one.

The effect is strong. As mentioned previously, different drugs can have different effects on enzyme systems. For example, a strong inhibitor like fluoxetine can result in drug concentrations that are *five times* higher than normal, while a weaker inhibitor like citalopram will not cause more than a doubling of the concentration.

In psychiatry, there are a few particularly strong inducers you should be aware of. Both carbamazepine (an anticonvulsant mood stabilizer that we covered in Chapter 5) and phenobarbital (a barbiturate that was formerly used to treat anxiety but is rarely used anymore due to its high potential for lethality) are strong inducers of the 3A4 system, and you will see them frequently mentioned in this chapter. You can remember this by thinking of them as your *strong* workout buddies "Carb and Barb."

> **Carbamazpine** and **phenobarbital** are the most commonly encountered **strong inducers** in psychopharmacology.
>
> Remember "**Carb and Barb**," your **strong** workout buddies.

Conversely, there are a few strong inhibitors you should know about. **B**upropion, **F**luoxetine, and **P**aroxetine are each very strong inhibitors of 2D6, which you can remember by thinking that they can cause **B**ig **F**reaking **P**roblems in drug metabolism, as we'll find out soon.

> **Bupropion, fluoxetine,** and **paroxetine** are the most commonly encountered **strong inhibitors** in psychopharmacology.
>
> *Bupropion, Fluoxetine, and Paroxetine can cause Big Freaking Problems.*

The outcomes are bad. Second, we will focus on the interactions where the outcome is particularly tragic. A change in someone's medication for seasonal allergies, for example, can lead to increased sneezing but is unlikely to result in significant harm or death. In contrast, a change in someone's heart failure medications or chemotherapy regimen *can* result in increased chances of a bad outcome or even death.

The effect is not noticeable until it's too late. Finally, we will pay particular attention to those interactions where the effects of our changes are not subjectively noticeable. Changing the metabolism of someone's benzodiazepines, for example, is often noticeable, as the patient will complain of oversedation (with an inhibitor) or of the medication not working (with an inducer). In contrast, changing the metabolism of someone's blood thinning medications is not likely to be noticeable by either the patient or the doctor until things progress to the point where a bad outcome, like a stroke, happens.

To help you remember all of the clinically significant interactions that you will see in the world of psychopharmacology, use the mnemonic "**I Can Have Fun Heartily Out Smarting Warring Drugs.**" On a practical level, you can use this mnemonic as a quick screen when reviewing your patient's problem list and medication regimen. If they have any of these conditions or are taking medications related to them, be extra mindful to look for drug interactions from any medication you start!

I is for Immune. Many antibiotics, such as clarithromycin, are strong inhibitors of certain enzyme systems. In addition, maintaining appropriate levels of immunosuppressants such as tacrolimus or cyclosporine is crucially important for patients with transplanted organs, as too little can cause graft rejection while too much can cause toxicity. Many of these medications are metabolized by 3A4, so carbamazepine and phenobarbital ("Carb and Barb"!) can induce 3A4 and cause drastic reductions in immunosuppressant levels.

Can is for Cancer. The medication tamoxifen (Nolvadex), which is given for certain types of breast cancer, is actually a pro-drug that must be metabolized by the 2D6 system into its pharmacologically active form. If you prescribe your patient a strong 2D6 inhibitor such as **B**upropion, **F**luoxetine, or **P**aroxetine, you can prevent the conversion of tamoxifen into its active form, thereby increasing the risk that your patient will experience a recurrence of cancer. (This is, as the mnemonic will remind you, a **B**ig **F**reaking **P**roblem!) In addition, many other chemotherapy agents, such as irinotecan (Camptosar), interact with the enzyme systems in potentially negative ways, so be extra cautious for any patient being actively treated for cancer.

Have is for HIV. Many of the drugs used to treat HIV can cause clinically significant drug-drug interactions. For example, the protease inhibitors (which includes drugs like atazanavir and ritonovir) are strong 3A4 inhibitors and can interact with a patient's prescribed psychotropics. In particular, benzodiazepines and many antipsychotics will have an increased plasma level in patients taking a protease inhibitor, so you need to be careful to lower their doses to avoid oversedation and extrapyramidal side effects.

Fun is for Fungal medications. Many antifungals agents such as fluconazole, itraconazole, and ketoconazole are strong 3A4 inhibitors and, like the protease inhibitors, can increase the effect of certain benzodiazepines and antipsychotics.

Heartily is for Heart conditions. Several classes of medications that are used to treat heart conditions, including antiarrhythmics like flecainide and lidocaine as well as beta-blockers like carvedilol and metoprolol, are metabolized by the 2D6 system, so their levels can increase drastically in the presence of a strong 2D6 inhibitor such as **B**upropion, **F**luoxetine, or **P**aroxetine. Like with tamoxifen, sudden changes in these medications can lead to arrhythmias, hypotension, and cardiogenic shock, so this can be a **B**ig **F**reaking **P**roblem as well.

Out is for Oral contraceptives. You should be mindful to avoid certain medications for patients taking oral contraceptives to avoid inducing their metabolism and rendering them ineffective. For example, carbamazepine and phenobarbital will inactivate most forms of oral contraceptives, so patients taking these will often need to be given alternative methods of contraception.

Smarting is for Seizures. Many anticonvulsants (including, but not limited to, those used as mood stabilizers as we talked about in Chapter 5) can have significant drug-drug interactions. For patients taking an anticonvulsant, you need to be careful not to give them an inducer which could lower drugs levels and possibly provoke another seizure.

Warring is for Warfarin and other anticoagulants. Warfarin (Coumadin) is a blood thinner that is metabolized by various enzyme systems in the liver. Given the narrow therapeutic window for warfarin, this can result in clinically significant interactions between inducers like Carb and Barb (which can lead to a *sub*therapeutic INR) and inhibitors like valproate and disulfiram (which can cause a *supra*therapeutic INR and lead to pathological bleeding). Warfarin isn't the only anticoagulant that is susceptible to drug-drug interactions, as other drugs such as apixaban (Eliquis) and rivaroxaban (Xarelto) can be affected as well. Finally, there is a theoretical risk that SSRIs and other blockers of serotonin reuptake could interfere with platelet function (remember the **P** in S**P**AROW-tonin!), as platelets cannot synthesize serotonin and instead rely on reuptake to use it for clotting. However, this risk appears to be more theoretical than real, and the evidence that any clinically significant interaction exists is fairly limited.

Drugs is for Diabetes. Finally, several of the medications used for diabetes, and particularly the secretagogues like repaglinide (Prandin) and linagliptin (Tradjenta), are metabolized by the 3A4 system, so our old friends "Carb and Barb" can return to mess things up here as well.

Pay attention to the **most significant interactions** (where the interaction is **strong**, the outcomes are **bad**, and/or the effect is **not noticeable** until it's too late).

I Can Have Fun Heartily Out Smarting Warring Drugs:
Immune
Cancer
HIV
Anti-Fungals
Heart medications
Oral contraceptives
Anti-Seizure drugs
Warfarin and other anticoagulants
Anti-Diabetics

Let's say that you have successfully reviewed your patient's medication regimen and are confident that there won't be any major interactions with the new drug that you are prescribing. However, even after doing this, you may still get the feeling that you're missing something. That's because you might be! Besides the medications we prescribe, there are many other substances that our patients take without our knowledge that can wreak havoc with drug metabolism as well. Pay attention to the "**NAG**ging **WOR**ry" that you've forgotten something despite having checked the medication list and consider counseling your patients on the following substances:

N is for Nicotine. Tobacco use results in induction of the 1A2 system which is responsible for metabolizing many of the drugs we use regularly in psychiatry, including many **antidepressants** and **antipsychotics**. Changes in smoking habits (such as sudden increases or decreases) can cause levels of these medications to  fluctuate wildly. Given that up to 70% of people with schizophrenia in the United States smoke, this is a common occurrence. Interestingly, it is not the nicotine *per se* that induces the enzymes but the aromatic hydrocarbons in tobacco smoke, so a patient switching from cigarettes to nicotine replacement can also experience major shifts in the levels of their psychotropic medications. For this reason, keep smoking in mind for your patients (especially those being prescribed antipsychotics), and make sure to dose appropriately if their smoking status changes!

Smoking induces the metabolism of **antipsychotics** and other psychotropic drugs.

1A2 = 1 thing (smoking) messes up 2 A's (Antipsychotics and Antidepressants).

A is for Alcohol. Acute alcohol use acts as an inhibitor of several enzyme systems in the liver and can increase drug levels. However, *chronic* alcohol causes liver damage which actually acts as an *inducer* of enzyme systems, resulting in the opposite effect.

G is for Grapefruit juice. Grapefruit juice (and juice from similar fruits like pomelo) is a commonly available 3A4 inhibitor. However, just because it can be picked up at any grocery store does not mean that this interaction is any less harmful. Grapefruit juice-related drug interactions include many of the medications that we use in psychiatry, including antidepressants, antipsychotics, benzodiazepines, stimulants, and mood stabilizers.

WOR is for St. John's WORt. St. John's wort is an over-the-counter supplement that is used as an antidepressant, as it appears to increase levels of dopamine, norepinephrine, and serotonin. However, it is also a strong inducer of 3A4 and can interact with many of the conditions mentioned in the "I Can Have Fun Heartily Out Smarting Warring Drugs" mnemonic such as warfarin and birth control. In addition, its serotonergic properties can result in serotonin syndrome when combined with other medications, so make sure to ask about supplements when prescribing any drug that could increase serotonin.

> **Non-prescribed substances** including **recreational drugs** and **supplements** can cause clinically significant interactions as well.
>
> *I've got a **NAG**ging **WOR**ry that I forgot to ask about something:*
> *Nicotine*
> *Alcohol*
> ***G**rapefruit juice*
> *St. John's **WOR**t*

Finally, certain drug-drug interactions have already been covered in more depth in their respective chapters, including serotonin syndrome (Chapter 2), tyramine-induced hypertensive crisis (Chapter 3), QTc prolongation (mostly Chapters 3 and 4), valproate with lamotrigine (Chapter 5), and benzodiazepines that are safer to use in patients with hepatic dysfunction (Chapter 6). Make sure to review these concepts if you're rusty!

PUTTING IT ALL TOGETHER

While we've covered many of the major drug-drug interactions to be aware of, there is simply no way to cover them all while staying concise. However, by keeping a couple of core principles in mind, you can make sure to practice in such a way that meaningful drug-drug interactions are recognized and addressed.

1. Focus on the most clinically important interactions.
While the number of drug-drug interactions is seemingly endless, you can still practice responsibly by taking time to consider the most clinically important interactions for all of your patients. Use the "I Can Have Fun Heartily Out Smarting Warring Drugs" mnemonic to remind yourself of conditions that are particularly high risk for having a significant psychotropic drug-drug interaction.

2. Start low and go slow.
You can avoid a lot of the most significant drug-drug interactions by always keeping your eye on finding the **minimum effective dose**. Because we are titrating to an effect rather than a specific dose in most cases (with lithium and valproate being the most notable exceptions), it's wise to always start at a lower dose range and increase only when it's clear that the current dose is not doing the job. For example, someone prescribed fluoxetine who is also taking a 2D6 inhibitor (or who is a genetically slow metabolizer) may need a much lower dose of fluoxetine than most people (10 or 20 mg instead of 60 or 80). If you aggressively titrate the dose of fluoxetine, however, you would never know that this person could get away with a lot less. By starting low, going slow, and titrating to an effect rather than a specific dose, you can avoid the increase in side effect burden that tends to accompany overmedication.

3. Pay attention to the liver!
As a final high-yield tip, most of the medications used in psychiatry are **hepatically** metabolized. The most notable exceptions to this are **G**abapentin, **A**camprosate, and **L**ithium which are all **renally** metabolized. You can remember this by thinking that the kidneys filter **GAL** drugs just like a **gal**lon of water.

> Most psychiatric medications are **hepatically** metabolized. The biggest exceptions are **gabapentin**, **acamprosate**, and **lithium** which are **renally metabolized**.
>
> The kidneys filter **GAL** drugs (**G**abapentin, **A**camprosate, and **L**ithium) just like they would a **gal**lon of water.

REVIEW QUESTIONS

1. A 25 y/o M with a history of schizophrenia is admitted to the psychiatric hospital with a strict no-smoking policy. He is taking clozapine and was previously residing at a board and care. He has no history of any medical conditions outside of smoking several packs of cigarettes per day. On hospital day 3, the patient has a generalized clonic-tonic seizure and is transferred to the ICU. Labs obtained in the ICU show a plasma clozapine level of 1370 μg/L. Which of the following would have been the most appropriate step to prevent this outcome?
   A. Obtaining a clozapine level upon admission
   B. Prescribing nicotine gum
   C. Prescribing a daily nicotine patch
   D. Lowering the dose of clozapine on admission
   E. Prescribing prophylactic valproate
   F. Nothing could have prevented this outcome

2. A 67 y/o F experiences a recurrence of breast cancer several months after beginning treatment with an antidepressant. She was previously taking only tamoxifen. She sues her psychiatrist for malpractice, saying that he did not warn her that this particular medication could cause a recurrence of her breast cancer. Which of the following medications was most likely prescribed?
   A. Fluvoxamine
   B. Bupropion
   C. Escitalopram
   D. Mirtazapine
   E. This patient has developed a delusional belief and requires counseling

3. A 34 y/o F with a history of depression is frustrated that she cannot get an appointment with a psychiatrist for over 6 weeks. On the advice of a friend, she begins taking over-the-counter St. John's wort supplements. Which of the following medications is *least* likely to interact with St. John's wort?
   A. Oral contraceptives
   B. Warfarin
   C. Meperidine
   D. Cyclosporine
   E. All of these medications are likely to interact with St. John's wort

1. **The best answer is D.** Seizures are a known complication of clozapine toxicity, with case reports showing a substantial risk when plasma levels exceed 1300 µg/L. Clozapine is metabolized by the 1A2 enzyme system which is induced by tobacco smoke. Abrupt smoking cessation can lead to rapid increases in clozapine levels, as occurred in this patient. Therefore, lowering the dose of clozapine on admission could have prevented this outcome. Obtaining a clozapine level on admission (answer A) would not have shown elevated levels, as the patient was still smoking at that time. Prescribing nicotine replacement therapy of any kind (answers B and C) would not have prevented this outcome, as it is the polycyclic aromatic hydrocarbons in tobacco smoke that induce liver enzymes, not the nicotine itself. Adding valproate (answer E) may have prevented this outcome, but adjusting the dose of clozapine is more appropriate than adding an additional medication, especially in a patient with no history of seizures.

2. **The best answer is B.** Of all the listed options, only bupropion is known to be an inhibitor of the 2D6 enzyme system, which is necessary for the conversion of tamoxifen into its active forms. Fluvoxamine, escitalopram, and mirtazapine (answers A, C, and D) are not known inhibitors of the 2D6 enzyme system. This patient is not delusional in her belief, as there is a clear mechanistic link between the newly prescribed antidepressant and the recurrence of her breast cancer (answer E).

3. **The best answer is E.** St. John's wort is an inducer of the 3A4 and 1A2 enzyme systems and has been known to reduce the effectiveness of oral contraceptives, warfarin, and immunosuppressants such as cyclosporine (answers A, B, and D). St. John's wort is also strongly serotonergic and can cause serotonin syndrome when combined with other medications, such as meperidine, that also increase levels of serotonin (answer C). Therefore, combining any of the listed medications with St. John's wort should be done with extreme caution.

15 OTHER MODALITIES

While this is primarily a review of psychopharmacology, it is important to know that there are other treatment modalities available for nearly all psychiatric disorders. These treatments come in a variety of forms, from psychotherapy and support groups to nutrition and exercise. While the efficacy of each treatment varies, many treatments are just as helpful as medications (like various forms of psychotherapy for depression) while others are even *more* effective (such as dialectical behavior therapy for borderline personality disorder). Non-drug modalities also address the many limitations to only using drugs to treat mental disorders including:

Drugs don't change the environment. All mental illnesses have both a biological and environmental component. While drugs can treat the biological side, they cannot change an environment that may be causing or exacerbating a patient's symptoms.

Some drugs are potentially addictive. Opioids, stimulants, and benzodiazepines are all prescription drugs that have significant dependence potential and, in some cases, end up causing more problems than they solve.

Drugs have side effects. All psychiatric medications have adverse effects ranging from relatively minor things like diarrhea all the way to potentially life-threatening complications like agranulocytosis. Even more "benign" side effects can have major implications for your patients' quality of life which should not be ignored.

We often don't know the long-term outcomes. Most studies on psychiatric drugs only assess patients for a few weeks or months. Because of this, questions remains about what effect these drugs have over a ten, twenty, or thirty year span.

For these reasons and others, you should know about non-pharmacologic treatment options for psychiatric illnesses!

PSYCHOTHERAPY

Until the discovery of chlorpromazine and imipramine in the 1950s, psychotherapy was the main intervention that psychiatry could offer. Contrary to popular depictions, psychotherapy does not necessarily involve a Freudian "Tell me about your mother" approach. In fact, there are many types of therapy that are each effective for different disorders in the same way that different drugs work for different conditions. Let's review the major types of psychotherapy as well as what disorders they are used for!

PSYCHOANALYSIS

Psychoanalysis was developed and popularized by Sigmund Freud and was the dominant mode of psychotherapy for much of the 20th century. While its use has decreased since then, you can still find psychiatrists and psychologists who practice it. Research shows that psychoanalysis can be effective for a variety of mental disorders, including mood, anxiety, somatic, and personality disorders. However, these results can also take a long time, with the standard treatment course being several sessions per week over 1 to 2 years.

Because of the cost and the length of treatment required, psychoanalysis is generally **not a first-line therapy** for most patients unless they are independently wealthy.

PSYCHOEDUCATION

Psychoeducation is the process of teaching patients and their families about the given diagnosis, the expected prognosis, and the treatments involved. For example, a patient recovering from their first episode of depression should know that they have a 50% chance of recurrence, while another patient who has had their first manic episode should be educated that they have a 90% chance of having another mood episode in their lifetime! By being informed, the patient is empowered to manage their illness in an appropriate way. Psychoeducation has been shown to reduce rates of **relapse**, **rehospitalization**, and treatment **noncompliance** while improving socio-occupational **functioning**. With few exceptions, psychoeducation should be a key part of *every* interaction with a psychiatrist.

SUPPORTIVE THERAPY

Supportive therapy integrates aspects of many types of psychotherapy, but at its core it relies primarily on building **trust** between the patient and the therapist through **validation** and **encouragement**. Supportive therapy has been shown to be most helpful for **adjustment disorder**. Adjustment disorder is when a patient experiences significant psychological distress related to life events (such as a divorce, job loss, or death of a family member) but does not meet the criteria for major depression. To remember the association between supportive therapy and adjustment disorder, use the rhyming phrase, "For adjustment disorder, add just a supporter."

Supportive therapy is the first-line treatment for **adjustment disorder**.

*For **adjustment disorder**, add just a supporter.*

COGNITIVE BEHAVIORAL THERAPY

Cognitive-behavioral therapy (CBT) is a very high-yield therapy to know, as it has the most evidence behind it of any form of psychotherapy. The list of conditions for which CBT is effective is vast, covering everything from depression and anxiety to PTSD and chronic pain. In contrast to psychoanalysis, it also has an increasing evidence base for its use in schizophrenia as well. It has long been argued that it is impossible to do empirical research on psychotherapy, as there is no way to blind doctors to treatment status or to control for subjective factors like patient-therapist relationship. CBT attempts to overcome this by being a **manualized therapy** where therapists follow a pre-set script to reduce variability between different providers.

The theory behind CBT is that there is a link between one's **thoughts, feelings**, and **behaviors**. In this model, thoughts create feelings, feelings create behavior, and behavior reinforces thoughts as seen in the following diagram:

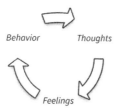

For example, if someone grew up with an abusive parent, they may end up believing that they are worthless and unlovable. These thoughts then begin to repeat in the brain automatically, creating feelings of depression. Feelings influence actions, so someone who believes that they are worthless would end up staying in bed all day, believing that nothing they do is of any value. This behavior of staying in bed all day ensures that they actually *don't* get anything done, further reinforcing the original thoughts of worthlessness that started the cycle.

The goal of CBT is to break this chain by attacking the thoughts and behaviors that began the cycle to begin with. CBT teaches people to identify the automatic negative thoughts that they have, recognize how they are distorted, and replace them with more positive thoughts. Using the example from above, once somebody no longer has automatic thoughts of worthlessness, they may start to feel better, leading to more days spent out of bed doing things of value, which itself may lead to feelings of self-worth.

This is the theory behind CBT, and current evidence seems to suggest that it works! Furthermore, the length of time required for CBT is often much shorter than psychoanalysis, making it cost effective. For this reason, CBT is an excellent **first-line treatment** for **depression** and **anxiety** and can be used effectively in nearly every other mental disorder.

Cognitive behavioral therapy is a **first-line treatment** for **many mental disorders**.

CBT Can't Be Topped (it's a first-line therapy for many conditions!).

EXPOSURE THERAPY

Exposure therapy is a variant of CBT which is used to treat **specific phobias** (such as arachnophobia or fear of spiders). Exposure therapy forces patients to face their fears, but not all at once. Rather, a low-grade stimulus (something related to the specific fear, such as a silly looking spider stuffed animal) is introduced repeatedly. After a while, the fear associated with that stimulus decreases. Once this happens, a new and slightly more frightening stimulus (such as seeing a caged spider from a safe place across the room) is introduced until that fear response is extinguished. This cycle continues until the specific stimulus itself (such as seeing a spider up close) no longer provokes a debilitating fear response.

Exposure therapy for specific phobias is incredibly effective, with high rates of cure even after a single session. Research shows that the effects tend to be long-lasting, with 90% reporting a reduction in fear and 65% saying that it erased their phobia entirely, even years later. Exposure therapy has also proven effective for **PTSD** as well, especially for soldiers with combat-related trauma. One of the primary symptoms of PTSD is avoidance, which prevents patients from forming more positive associations with these memories. By using simulators, exposure therapy can effectively place soldiers back into the situations that triggered their symptoms, which has proven effective at reducing symptoms of PTSD.

DIALECTICAL BEHAVIOR THERAPY

For decades, clinicians were taught that borderline personality disorder was a life-long and unchangeable diagnosis for which no effective treatment existed. However, we now know that this is not the case, as targeted treatments like dialectical behavioral therapy (DBT) can significantly reduce many symptoms of the disorder and results in reduced rates of hospitalizations and suicide attempts.

DBT focuses on teaching a balance between acceptance and change. This balance between opposites is known as a **dialectic**, and it is a core concept of this therapy. People with borderline personality disorder often struggle with self-hatred and lack of identity and can benefit from being encouraged to accept themselves as they are; however, they can also have maladaptive behaviors and personality traits that should be changed. Being able to accept two opposing viewpoints ("I need to accept myself as I am while also needing to change parts of who I am") at the same time is difficult for people with borderline personality disorder, as they tend to see the world in black-and-white terms. Learning how to find the balance between extremes (such as finding the "wise mind" between one's "emotional mind" and "rational mind") is a crucial part of this therapy.

There is much more to DBT than just that (such as learning skills like mindfulness to deal with distress rather than resorting to self-harm), but for your purposes you should remember that **DBT** is "**De-B**orderline **T**herapy."

Dialectical behavior therapy is used to treat **borderline personality disorder**.

DBT = De-Borderline Therapy.

MOTIVATIONAL INTERVIEWING

Motivational interviewing is a set of counseling techniques that clinicians can use to encourage patients to make positive changes. This has made it particularly helpful for treatment of **substance use disorders**, although it can be applied to any scenario  where the patient could benefit from changing their behavior (such as eating less or exercising more). Rather than using guilt or shame to force change, motivational interviewing uses **O**pen-ended questions, **A**ffirmations, **R**eflective listening, and **S**ummarizing (which you can remember using the acronym **OARS**) to build rapport.

Motivational interviewing helps to encourage positive actions in **substance abuse** and other disorders in which behavioral change is needed.

OARS:
***O**pen-ended questions*
***A**ffirmations*
***R**eflective listening*
***S**ummarizing*

Motivational interviewing also relies upon identifying which **stage of change** the patient is in to be able to use the right technique. For example, it doesn't help to tell someone who doesn't think they have a problem with smoking about the risks and benefits of varenicline and bupropion, as they haven't even decided they want to make a change. By matching your approach to the patient's stage of change, however, you can be more effective at helping them to change their behavior.

Stage of Change	Description	Recommended Approach
Precontemplation	No intention to change	Introduce cognitive dissonance
Contemplation	Thinking of change, but hasn't committed	Encourage change
Preparation	Intends to change, but hasn't started	Assist in planning for change, encourage follow-through
Action	Makes the change	Reinforce behavior, offer support and guidance
Maintenance	Continuing with change	Reinforce behavior, prevent relapse

Motivational interviewing is effective, with research showing that it is better at reducing substance use than treatment-as-usual. In addition, it is a relatively short form of treatment, usually requiring only a few 30-minute sessions to be effective.

APPLIED BEHAVIOR ANALYSIS

Applied behavior analysis (ABA) is a type of therapy that uses principles of **operant** and **classical conditioning** to modify maladaptive behaviors. Desired behaviors are reinforced, while undesired behaviors can be replaced by other behaviors. ABA is best known for its use in autism spectrum disorders where it can be used to improve social  functioning (for example, by rewarding children when they engage in appropriate behaviors such as saying hello and goodbye which does not always come naturally to patients with autism). However, it can also be used for any situation where behavior plays a role, whether that is encouraging use of seatbelts or reducing destructive tendencies in a child with oppositional behaviors. The evidence base for this type of therapy is increasing, and you will likely hear more about it in the coming years. For practical purposes, consider **ABA** for **A**utism and other **B**ehavioral **A**nomalies.

> **Applied behavior analysis** uses conditioning to **modify maladaptive behaviors**.
>
> Consider *ABA* for *Autism and other Behavioral Anomalies*.

FAMILY THERAPY

Family therapy is an umbrella term for any type of therapy that seeks to improve the functioning of the family unit, ranging from marital counseling for couples going through a hard time to analyzing family dynamics to identify root causes of a child's behavioral outbursts. Family therapy recognizes the central role that relationships play in one's mental health and attempts to identify maladaptive patterns in these  relationships. Family therapy is generally practiced by marriage and family therapists (MFTs) but can also be practiced by social workers, psychologists, and psychiatrists. Consider family therapy for patients with an unstable or unhealthy home structure or for patients that have illnesses (such as bipolar disorder and schizophrenia) where family support is crucial for recovery.

SUPPORT GROUPS

Finally, support groups for mental health are available for many psychiatric disorders. Involvement in a support group can help to improve outcomes and decrease stigma, although in some cases being around other people struggling with similar problems can lead to back-sliding or relapse. In general, however, support groups can be recommended as a low-risk, potentially high-reward intervention.

PROCEDURES

While psychiatry is not known for being a procedure-heavy field, there are still a few procedures that are effective at treating certain psychiatric conditions.

ELECTRIC BRAIN STIMULATION

Electric brain stimulation is a type of procedure that involves applying electrical currents to the brain. The most famous type of electric brain stimulation is known as **electroconvulsive therapy** (ECT) which involves administering an electric current to the brain in order to induce a seizure. It was first used in 1938 and continued to be used frequently in the mid-20th century before falling out of favor in the 1970s after the release of "One Flew Over the Cuckoo's Nest," a movie which portrayed ECT in a negative light. Since that time, it has made a major comeback, with research showing that ECT is still one of the most effective forms of treatment available for severe depression. Indeed, ECT consistently comes out ahead in head-to-head comparisons with all types of antidepressant medications, making it the **single most effective treatment for depression** that we know of. (ECT is also indicated for schizophrenia, mania, and catatonia, although it is performed more rarely for these purposes.)

Contrary to past depictions, ECT is not a painful procedure and is carried out under general anesthesia. However, there are some important side effects to be aware of, including a risk of **retrograde amnesia** (usually involving loss of memories in the weeks immediately before and during treatment, with important memories from earlier in one's life almost always being preserved). This is a high-yield fact, both for boards and for talking with patients considering ECT! In addition, ECT can be logistically cumbersome for patients, as they need to come to the treatment center 2 to 3 times per week for several months in order to complete a full course of treatment. Further, certain medications that interfere with the seizure threshold (such as benzodiazepines and anticonvulsants) must be discontinued before ECT can start. Finally, as ECT is carried out under general anesthesia, all of the risks associated with that apply here as well. Given all of these factors, ECT is not a first-line option for depression, but for patients who have failed other treatments it can be a lifesaver!

> **Electroconvulsive therapy** is the **most effective** treatment for **severe depression**.
>
> *ECT is shockingly effective.*

While ECT is the most famous form of electric brain stimulation, it is not the only one used in psychiatry. **Transcranial magnetic stimulation** (TMS) uses magnets to generate a current, though in contrast to ECT the goal is not to apply so much current as to induce a seizure but rather to electrically stimulate neurons using lower voltages. This makes TMS safer than ECT, with fewer side effects like amnesia. However, TMS is generally considered to be less effective than ECT (as with less responsibility comes less power!). Nevertheless, TMS can be a good option for patients who have not responded to initial trials of antidepressant medications.

A patient undergoing transcranial magnetic stimulation.

BIOFEEDBACK
Biofeedback is the process of making patients aware of how they are able to **manipulate physiologic functions**, such as heart rate or muscle tone, that are generally considered to be out of voluntary control. It often uses various sensors like electromyographs (EMGs), electroencephalographs (EEGs), and electrocardiograms (EKGs) to show the patient the effect that their mental state has on these processes. Biofeedback has been applied to a multitude of disorders, both medical and psychiatric, with varying degrees of success. The best evidence is for urinary incontinence, ADHD, anxiety, chronic pain, constipation, hypertension, and headache. It's still unclear exactly how biofeedback should fit into a treatment plan, but it can be an option for patients interested in forms of treatment other than (or in addition to) medications and traditional psychotherapy.

PSYCHOSURGERY
Psychosurgery is the application of neurosurgical techniques to treat psychiatric disorders. It generally involves destroying or removing small pieces of the brain with the purpose of reducing psychiatric symptoms such as depression, agitation, or paranoia. The most famous type of psychosurgery, the **lobotomy**, was developed during the 1930s. However, as time went on, it became increasingly clear that these procedures also diminished the patient's personality, individuality, and cognitive abilities, reducing symptoms at the expense of rendering patients essentially lifeless. This realization (combined with rising criticism of the procedure, concerns about consent, and the increasing availability of medications) effectively ended the use of psychosurgery as a method of treatment by the 1970s. While it's easy to condemn the practice of psychosurgery as barbaric and unethical (and it was), it also illustrates the desperation that many doctors felt while trying to treat their patients' psychiatric problems in the pre-medication era. From a clinical standpoint, psychosurgery is almost never used anymore, with the main applications being a cingulotomy for treatment-resistant obsessive-compulsive disorder and implantation of a deep brain stimulator (a device that provides electric brain stimulation) for treatment-resistant depression. Both of these are exceedingly rare, however, with only a few dozen cases being performed each year for psychiatric purposes.

SUPPLEMENTS

Despite the popularity of dietary supplements, the majority have no solid evidence for treating mental illnesses. However, there are four that have been shown to be effective for a variety of these disorders. The first, **St. John's wort**, is helpful for mild depression and even rivals traditional antidepressants in these cases (although antidepressants are superior for moderate to severe cases of depression). Another supplement, known as S-adenosyl methionine or **SAMe**, can be used for the treatment of even severe cases of depression. Next, **omega-3 fatty acids** have gained a modest body of research to support that they may augment traditional antidepressants and mood stabilizers in the treatment of depression and bipolar disorder. Finally, as mentioned in Chapter 6, **melatonin** can be helpful for treating insomnia related to jet lag or shift work disorder.

LIFESTYLE

Finally, there are several lifestyle interventions that have proven effective for treating psychiatric disorders. Nothing here is going to be super high-yield for boards, but from a clinical perspective, it is important to be aware of them, as many of your patients will have questions about them or even be using them already!

NUTRITION

Nutrition plays a role in all aspects of health, and mental health is no exception. In particular, a **Mediterranean diet** (one rich in olive oil, beans, fruits, vegetables, nuts, and fish, along with moderate consumption of dairy,  wine, and meat products) can be effective at preventing depression on a populations level. As with all studies on nutrition, there are some methodological difficulties that prevent these from being the highest quality evidence, but there are enough studies to suggest that there may be a link. In addition, a Mediterranean diet has been shown to reduce the risk of heart disease, stroke, and other major causes of mortality, so there's really no downside to recommending to all of your patients (depressed or not)!

EXERCISE

Exercise is another lifestyle modification that has good evidence showing its efficacy in preventing and treating mental disorders. In addition to better health outcomes overall, people who exercise regularly have improved sleep, increased energy, lower stress, and better mood. Physiologically, exercise increases the amount of circulating **serotonin** and **endorphins**, and this increase continues even several days after  exercise. Of course, for patients with severe depression, just getting out of bed can be a challenge, so this recommendation is not always possible (although even in these cases some form of movement, even if it is just deep breathing, can still be helpful). For mild or moderate cases of depression, however, exercise remains a valuable component of treatment.

YOGA

One form of exercise in particular deserves special mention. Yoga has been shown to be particularly effective at modulating the stress response, which plays a big role in depression, anxiety, borderline personality disorder, and chronic pain conditions such as fibromyalgia. It is thought that, in addition to its role as exercise, yoga also works a form of **mindfulness**, which we talked about before in the context of DBT. This focus on mindfulness has been shown in studies to reduce symptoms of PTSD and depression in up to 70% of patients. For patients who are willing and able to engage, yoga and mindfulness can be excellent adjunctive treatments for psychological stress.

SLEEP

Sleep has a reciprocal relationship with mental health. Not only do many psychiatric disorders worsen sleep, but lack of sleep can trigger both mania and depression. Despite this complexity, the clinical recommendation is simple: **just about everyone should get more sleep**. The pharmacology of insomnia is discussed more in Chapter 6, but several lifestyle and behavioral interventions can improve sleep as well.

Educating patients on sleep hygiene is a good place to start. This includes things like using the bedroom only for sleeping and sex, having a normal bedtime routine (including a consistent sleep time), and avoiding bright lights and screens before bed. Patients should also be aware that the tendency to stay in bed fighting to sleep is

actually bad, as it breaks the association of your bed being a restful place. Rather, it's better to get up and do something restful (like light reading or having a cup of decaffeinated tea) until you feel sleepy. Finally, caffeine or other stimulants should be consumed no later than early afternoon.

For many patients, basic sleep hygiene will lead to significant improvements in both amount and quality of sleep. For those who need additional help, a type of cognitive behavioral therapy has been developed specifically for insomnia, which has proven to be effective and is even available in book form.

EMOTIONAL SUPPORT ANIMALS

Another popular option with patients, emotional support animals are recommended for conditions ranging from PTSD to social phobia. Like service dogs, emotional support animals are protected by law in many states, but unlike service dogs, they are not licensed and do not have to undergo specific training. The evidence thus far is generally in favor of emotional support animals. In any case, for patients who request them, there is generally no harm in permitting emotional support animals.

ACUPUNCTURE

Acupuncture is a popular treatment option, especially for patients seeking more "natural" cures. Acupuncture is thought to work by stimulating the release of endogenous opioids, similar to a runner's high. There is some modest evidence that acupuncture may result in improvement in several **chronic pain** conditions and could potentially help your patients avoid the side effects and risks of dependence associated with opioids. It should be noted, however, that acupuncture has *not* been shown to be effective for any psychiatric condition and shouldn't be recommended for treatment of mental illness.

SOCIAL INTEGRATION
Socializing is a key component (if not *the* key component) of both mental and physical health. Study after study has shown that those who are more socially isolated experience worse health outcomes, are more prone to disease, and recover more slowly from illness. Therefore, encouraging your patients to remain active and social (whether with family and friends or with people from work, school, church, or other places) is **essential** for maintaining health.

PUTTING IT ALL TOGETHER

While this has been a whirlwind tour of various non-medication options to treat mental illness, a few key points should be emphasized.

1. Psychotherapies are not all the same!
There is a tendency to assume that different forms of therapy are essentially equivalent. People will often say something to the effect of, "This patient needs to be in therapy" without specifying what particular type of therapy should be used. However, the evidence shows that different types of therapy are effective in some disorders (such as DBT for borderline personality disorder and supportive therapy for adjustment disorder), so use the knowledge you've accumulated to help your patients find the therapy that will be right for them.

2. Don't discount non-pharmacologic treatments.
This has been stated several times throughout this book, but it bears repeating: therapy and other forms of non-pharmacologic treatments can be just as important as (if not even more important than) medications for many mental disorders. When treating your patients, always consider whether a referral to therapy would be an appropriate part of the treatment plan.

3. ECT is the single most effective option for treatment-resistant depression.
There are few instances in psychiatry where we can say that one treatment clearly works better than another. However, for cases of major depression that have failed multiple treatments, ECT has been shown to work better than any other form of treatment. While the drawbacks cannot be ignored (including logistical difficulties, the possibility of amnesia, and risks of anesthesia), ECT should be considered for nearly all patients with treatment-resistant depression.

REVIEW QUESTIONS

1. A 26 y/o M presents to a primary care clinic saying that he feels "off." He recently moved across the country for work and has not been able to form the same level of social connections that he had before, making him often feel lonely and isolated. He says that he has recently begun having trouble falling asleep. He denies an inability to feel pleasure and does not feel hopeless, saying, "I know things will get better, they just don't feel that great right now." What is the single best treatment recommendation at this time?
    A. No treatment
    B. Citalopram
    C. Trazodone
    D. Supportive therapy
    E. Cognitive behavioral therapy
    F. Psychoanalysis

2. A 67 y/o F is seen in the geriatric psychiatry clinic for long-standing depression. During the interview, she states that she has been depressed "off and on, but mostly on" for the majority of her life beginning in her teenage years. Since the death of a good friend several months ago, she has been increasingly withdrawn. During the interview, she vocalizes a desire to kill herself on multiple occasions. A review of the chart reveals multiple trials of medications and therapy without significant success. Given the patient's history, the decision is made to refer her for ECT. Which of the following is a significant side effect of ECT?
    A. Pain
    B. Muscle cramping
    C. Amnesia
    D. Loss of IQ
    E. Increased risk of myocardial infarction

3. A 22 y/o F is brought to the hospital after she was found unconscious on the floor of her college dormitory with multiple self-inflicted superficial lacerations across both forearms. She receives supportive care for her wounds. She had recently seen a psychiatrist who diagnosed her with major depression and started paroxetine. Her chart indicates that the patient frequently complained of feeling "empty" and had a significant fear of abandonment. She has made suicidal gestures previously on several occasions. Her history is significant for physical and sexual trauma as a child. After stabilizing her acute medical issues, what form of therapy would be most appropriate to recommend?
    A. Dialectical behavior therapy
    B. Cognitive behavioral therapy
    C. Psychoanalysis
    D. Exposure therapy
    E. Supportive therapy

4. A 19 y/o M freshman college student presents to the student health office saying that he feels depressed. He reports difficulty sleeping, decreased appetite, feelings of worthlessness, lack of energy, and trouble concentrating. He denies having a plan for suicide but does state that he wonders "if life is worth it in the end." He denies any history of previous depressive episodes. When asked, he states that he recently failed an entrance examination into the engineering school in which he had hoped to enroll. Which of the following treatments has the best evidence that it will be effective at reducing his symptoms?
    A. Psychoanalysis
    B. Psychoanalysis + citalopram
    C. Cognitive behavioral therapy
    D. Cognitive behavioral therapy + citalopram
    E. Supportive therapy
    F. Supportive therapy + citalopram

5. A 46 y/o F presents to her psychiatric nurse practitioner's office complaining of depressed mood. During the interview, the nurse practitioner confirms that she meets criteria for major depressive disorder, though notably she denies suicidal ideation. When asked about treatment options, she states that she does not want to take any medications and would prefer something more "natural." All of the following non-medical treatment options would likely be effective for depression *except*:
    A. Sleep
    B. Nutrition
    C. Acupuncture
    D. Yoga
    E. Herbal supplements

1. **The best answer is D.** This patient is experiencing adjustment disorder, defined as a negative psychological reaction to adverse life events that does not meet the criteria for a major depressive episode. Patients with adjustment disorder respond well to supportive therapy. No treatment (answer A) is inappropriate, as he is clearly requesting help. Use of antidepressants (answers B and C) would also not be appropriate, as they are not the first-line option for treating adjustment disorder. Cognitive behavioral therapy and psychoanalysis (answers E and F) would not be entirely inappropriate, but they are not as specific to adjustment disorder as supportive therapy.

2. **The best answer is C.** Of all the listed options, only amnesia is recognized as a common clinical side effect of patients undergoing electroconvulsive therapy, with between 20 and 50% of patients reporting that they experienced changes in memory. None of the other answer choices are reliably associated with ECT.

3. **The best answer is A.** This patient likely has borderline personality disorder as evidenced by her recurrent suicidal gestures and self-harm behavior, history of childhood trauma, and self-reported feelings of emptiness and fear of abandonment. For patients with borderline personality disorder, dialectical behavior therapy is the most evidence-based option once all acute medical and psychological issues have been addressed.

4. **The best answer is D.** This patient meets criteria for major depressive disorder. Current research indicates that a patient going through a major depressive episode is most likely to receive the highest benefit from combined use of therapy and medications, with citalopram being an excellent first-line antidepressant. Of the therapy options presented, cognitive behavioral therapy has the most evidence supporting its use in major depressive disorder. Psychoanalytic therapy (answers A and B) tends to take longer, is harder to find, and is often more expensive, so it is generally not a first-line option. Supportive therapy (answers E and F) may be helpful to a limited extent, but for someone with a diagnosis of depression rather than adjustment disorder it is likely to be insufficient to treat his disorder.

5. **The best answer is C.** Many non-medical treatments for depression have found support through research, including sleep, nutrition, exercise, yoga, and herbal supplements such as St. John's wort. While acupuncture has some evidence suggesting that it may be helpful for chronic pain, there is insufficient evidence that it improves outcomes in depression or any other mental disorder.

16 FINAL REVIEW

Use of psychoactive substances (either for medical or recreational purposes) is widespread, as over 90% of your patients will have used at least one in the past month. In addition, these drugs can have powerful effects on both mental and physical health. Because of this, every healthcare provider should be familiar with the most common drugs and should be able to **knowledgeably converse** with your patients about them, whether that is in the role of a "decider" (for prescription medications) or as a "guider" (for recreational drugs). This review has hopefully helped you to reach that level, regardless of your intended field of practice.

For those who are not going into psychiatry as a profession, a distinction should be made between situations that can reasonably be handled by a general practitioner and those that will require a higher level of care. For example, a healthy young adult presenting with depressive symptoms and no suicidality can generally be prescribed an antidepressant and/or referred to psychotherapy without needing to involve a psychiatrist. However, other clinical situations will need someone specialized in the treatment of mental illness to provide appropriate care. Use the mnemonic **ABC PSYCH** to remember those situations that require a referral to a higher level of care:

A is for Addiction. Comorbid recreational drug abuse complicates treatment of nearly every psychiatric illness, so a referral to a higher level of care (such as a dual diagnosis program) should be considered.

B is for Bipolar disorder. Bipolar disorder, especially type 1, should be treated by a specialist in the majority of cases. This is especially important for drugs requiring close monitoring like lithium or valproate.

C is for Complexity. While some cases are fairly straightforward to diagnose, others can be complicated or unclear. When diagnostic clarity is needed, consider a referral to a specialist.

P is for Psychosis. Psychotic disorders such as schizophrenia will likely require a specialist for long-term management and monitoring, especially if more intensive drugs like clozapine are being prescribed.

S is for Suicidality. Patients who are having thoughts of suicide or have attempted suicide in the past should almost always be referred to a higher level of care.

Y is for "whY isn't this working?" Perhaps you've tried prescribing an antidepressant or two, but the patient does not seem to be getting any better. In situations where the standard of care doesn't seem to be making much of a difference, a referral to a specialist is probably in order.

C is for Comorbidity. Patients with more than one psychiatric disorder should generally receive a specialized level of care, both to assure diagnostic accuracy and to ensure that the treatments used for one disorder are not interfering with the other.

H is for Homicidality. Patients who have a history of agitation or violence as a result of a mental disorder will likely need a higher intensity of treatment.

> While some **psychiatric disorders** can be treated in **general medical settings**, certain conditions will require a referral to a **specialist in mental health**.
>
> Remember the **ABC PSYCH** criteria for referral to a mental health specialist:
> **A**ddiction
> **B**ipolar disorder
> **C**omplexity
> **P**sychosis
> **S**uicidality
> "Wh**Y** isn't this working?"
> **C**omorbidity
> **H**omicidality

And that's it! Take some time to review the key points from every chapter, then proceed to the final set of review questions to comprehensively test your knowledge. These final review questions are designed to be **challenging** and will often require you to have knowledge about diagnosing and treating illnesses (both medical and psychiatric) that have not been explicitly covered in this book. It is not so important to be getting all the answers correct; rather, try to think critically about each question and use them to learn about your strengths and weaknesses. Good luck!

FINAL REVIEW QUESTIONS

1. A 47 y/o overweight F presents to her primary care provider with a chief complaint of intense right cheek pain when brushing her teeth. The pain "feels electrical" and happens several times per day. It has increased to the point where she is afraid of eating or brushing her teeth for fear of triggering the pain. What is the best treatment option?
   A. Ibuprofen
   B. Percocet
   C. Carbamazepine
   D. Gabapentin
   E. Topiramate
   F. Cognitive behavioral therapy

2. A 72 y/o F with a history of breast cancer s/p bilateral mastectomy is discovered to have a recurrence in her lungs. She is undergoing chemotherapy which has resulted in a 20-lb weight loss secondary to severe nausea and lack of appetite. During a visit with her oncologist, she endorses having difficulty "dealing with" this diagnosis and often cannot fall asleep at night due to persisting thoughts about what she "did to deserve this." She has stopped enjoying activities that previously brought her pleasure and has become more isolated from her friends and family. While she denies thoughts of suicide, she often thinks that it might be better if she stopped treatment "so I won't be such a drain on everyone." Which of the following options would be *most* appropriate to prescribe for this patient?
   A. Bupropion
   B. Mirtazapine
   C. Duloxetine
   D. Fluoxetine
   E. ECT
   F. None of the above

3. A 21 y/o F college student with no past medical history comes into the emergency room complaining of chest pain and shortness of breath. She was studying for her finals when she began sweating profusely and became diffusely tremulous. Her chest pain is precordial, "stabbing," and unrelated to exertion. Vital signs are within normal limits except for HR 104 and RR 18. EKG shows no abnormalities. Initial troponins are negative. Which of the following is the best initial treatment?
   A. Inhaled nitrites
   B. Propranolol
   C. Buspirone
   D. Lorazepam
   E. Sertraline
   F. None of the above

4. (Continued from previous question.) The patient is discharged with a 14-day supply of medication and a referral to an outpatient psychiatrist. She presents to her appointment 10 days later saying that she has run out of her medication because she is "having panic attacks all the time." Which type of treatment has the best efficacy for long-term treatment of panic disorder?
   A. SSRIs
   B. Benzodiazepines
   C. Buspirone
   D. Beta-blockers
   E. Caffeine
   F. Psychotherapy

5. A 28 y/o F presents to a dentist's office for the first time in several years. She worked as a club promoter for the past 6 years and only recently acquired dental insurance upon finding a new job. Upon examination, the dentist notices significant attrition of the teeth, as shown below:

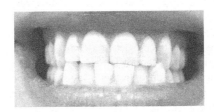

The patient denies any knowledge of frequently grinding her teeth. She reports engaging in adequate dental hygiene, including brushing and flossing. Which of the following substances would best account for these dental findings?
   A. Caffeine
   B. Alcohol
   C. Nicotine
   D. MDMA
   E. Methamphetamines
   F. None of the above

6. A 12 y/o F is brought to the hospital by ambulance after her foster mother returns from work to find her unresponsive in her room. CPR is started on the way to the hospital. In the emergency department, she is evaluated by two physicians and determined to be brain dead. An autopsy is performed which reveals multiple chemical burns in the nasal and oral passages as well as a plastic bag trapped in her airway. Analysis of the residue on the inside of the plastic big is *least* likely to reveal which of the following chemicals?
   A. Acetone
   B. Toluene
   C. Diethyl ether
   D. Chlorofluorocarbons
   E. Butane
   F. All of the above substances are equally likely to be found

7. A 21 y/o F college student comes to a psychiatrist to establish care. She states that she has been diagnosed with bipolar disorder and has "daily" manic episodes lasting several minutes or hours. During these episodes, she becomes very mad at her boyfriend and throws items around the house. She is not on any medications other than lorazepam 1 mg which she takes 1-2 times per day as needed for "panic attacks." Further interview reveals several hospitalizations as a teenager for cutting. She states she is "always suicidal," especially when her boyfriend threatens to break up with her, but flatly states that she's "no more a danger to myself now than any other time." She is on birth control and has no intention of becoming pregnant at this time. Which of the following medications would help most to change the trajectory of this patient's illness?
    A. Fluoxetine
    B. Lithium
    C. Valproate
    D. Risperidone
    E. None of the above

8. A 28 y/o F is admitted to the inpatient psychiatric unit after she is found by police. She has been missing for two weeks during which time she had been sleeping on a park bench two cities away. Prior to her disappearance, she had begun gluing newspapers to the windows of her house and yelling at her family members when they tried to remove them, saying, "Don't you get it? *They* are coming!" One month before this, she quit her job at a coffee shop, stopped bathing, and cut off contact with everyone outside of her family. Urine toxicology is negative. Risperidone is started. On day 5 of treatment, the patient is observed pacing up and down the hallways. When asked to sit down, the psychiatrist notices that she is unable to do so, as she continues to move her legs back and forth constantly. Her family is concerned about this new behavior and asks for an explanation. Which of the following statements would be appropriate to make?
    A. "We are not sure what is causing this behavior."
    B. "This is likely a manifestation of her psychotic thought process."
    C. "This side effect is usually not permanent."
    D. "There are no effective treatments for this condition."
    E. "All medications in this class have an equal chance of causing this."
    F. None of the above

9. (Continued from previous question.) The patient is switched to quetiapine. After two weeks of treatment at therapeutic doses, the pacing and restlessness have resolved. However, no significant change in psychotic symptoms is observed. What is the most reasonable next step?
    A. Olanzapine
    B. Clozapine
    C. ECT
    D. Desipramine
    E. Lithium
    F. None of the above

10. A 23 y/o F graduate student in violin performance is anxious about her upcoming recital and requests a medication from her doctor to help "calm my nerves." She takes this medication prior to her performance and finds that it is helpful for her. While walking home in the cold air, she becomes short of breath and begins wheezing. The medication's effects on which of the following receptors is the cause of her dyspnea?
    A. α-1
    B. α-2
    C. β-1
    D. β-2
    E. β-3
    F. None of the above

11. A 44 y/o F with a history of bipolar disorder, hyperlipidemia, obesity, osteoarthritis, and allergic rhinitis presents to the emergency department after she vomited bright red blood. She reports that over the past few months she has had "gnawing" pain in her upper abdomen after eating. Over-the-counter antacids have not alleviated the pain. Thirty minutes ago, she felt "suddenly very ill" and ran to the bathroom where she vomited blood. She currently has 10/10 constant epigastric pain and reports feeling lightheaded. Vital signs are HR 122, BP 78/40, RR 18, and T 99.9°F. Labs are pending. CXR is shown below:

    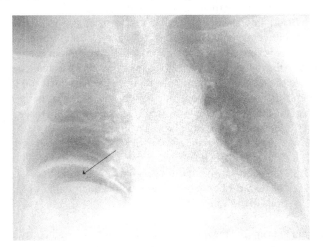

    With further history taking and lab analysis, it is discovered that her current presentation is related to treatment for one of her existing medical conditions. Treatment for which of the following conditions is most likely implicated?
    A. Bipolar disorder
    B. Hyperlipidemia
    C. Obesity
    D. Osteoarthritis
    E. Allergic rhinitis
    F. None of the above

12. (Continued from previous question.) Which of the following could have prevented this outcome?
    A. Using acetaminophen
    B. Using celecoxib
    C. Altering diet
    D. Antibiotic therapy
    E. None of the above

13. A 35 y/o M filmmaker comes for his first appointment at his new psychiatrist's office. He previously saw another psychiatrist who managed him on lithium for bipolar disorder. However, this medication was discontinued when he developed stage 3 chronic kidney disease several years ago. He has been untreated for bipolar disorder since that time. Which of the following medications would *not* require modified dosing for this patient?
    A. Acamprosate
    B. Lithium
    C. Gabapentin
    D. Lorazepam
    E. None of the above

14. (Continued from previous question.) The patient denies having had a manic episode in the past several years. His current complaint is that he feels "terribly depressed" and has not had the energy or the motivation to complete his work. Which of the following would *not* be considered an acceptable monotherapy for the patient at this time?
    A. Lurasidone
    B. Carbamazepine
    C. Quetiapine
    D. Lamotrigine
    E. Olanzapine
    F. None of the above

15. (Continued from previous question.) After discussing the various options available to him, the patient looks displeased. "One of my best friends took sertraline for his depression and said it worked wonders for him. Can I go on that instead? I don't know what any of these other drugs are." What is the most appropriate response?
    A. "The best medication is the one the patient believes in. Let's start sertraline."
    B. "Sertraline is an effective antidepressant for many people, but in your case it is unlikely to work."
    C. "I would be concerned about sertraline flipping you into a manic episode."
    D. "Sertraline is unlikely to work, but another antidepressant may."
    E. "Sertraline would not be a good choice for you given your kidney problems."
    F. None of the above

16. A 25 y/o M with no significant medical history presents to his primary care doctor for an annual physical. Labs are reviewed and are generally within normal limits. A flu vaccine is administered. The physician reviews a depression screen that was given to the patient in the waiting room and sees that the patient indicated that he has been feeling depressed. When asked about it, the patient is initially reluctant to discuss the matter. The physician asks whether the patient has had changes in sleep, appetite, energy, or concentration, and the patient denies all of these symptoms. The patient also denies having thoughts of guilt, hopelessness, or suicide. The patient then says, "Well, if you have to know... I just got a girlfriend after years of being alone, and it's been wonderful! We really love each other. But I've realized that I just don't... last that long, you know... in bed?" The physician reviews the treatment options, and the patient says he is open to trying medications. Which of the following medications would be appropriate in this case?
    A. Triazolam
    B. Gabapentin
    C. Paroxetine
    D. Propranolol
    E. Hydroxyzine
    F. None of the above

17. A 25 y/o F with a history of depression and anxiety watches a documentary on the medical industry and decides to stop taking all of her medications. Two days later, she feels increasingly anxious, restless, and is unable to fall asleep until 4 o'clock in the morning. The next day at work, she has a "panic attack" but is unable to identify a particular stressor. That evening while making dinner at home, she becomes diaphoretic and experiences sudden chest pain. She calls 911 and is taken to the hospital. On her way to the hospital, she has a generalized-tonic clonic seizure lasting 5 minutes. Withdrawal from which of the following medications is most likely to account for her symptoms?
    A. Fluoxetine
    B. Paroxetine
    C. Venlafaxine
    D. Quetiapine
    E. Risperidone
    F. Diazepam
    G. Oxazepam
    H. Buspirone
    I. Lithium
    J. None of the above

18. (Continued from previous question.) The patient is admitted to the hospital. Which of the following is the best treatment for her condition?
    A. Oxazepam
    B. Alprazolam
    C. Chlordiazepoxide
    D. Phenobarbital

E. Ketamine
F. Flumazenil
G. None of the above

19. A 36 y/o F comes into the primary care clinic for a routine visit. During the interview it is discovered that she has a 20 pack-year smoking history. However, she is unwilling to quit because she is worried she will "look like an elephant." Further history taking reveals that she suffers from recurrent depression and was admitted to an inpatient psychiatric unit as a 26-year-old due to a suicide attempt via overdose. She is not currently on any medications except for a skin cream for acne. What treatment strategy would be most appropriate here?
    A. Nicotine replacement therapy
    B. Varenicline
    C. Bupropion
    D. Motivational interviewing
    E. Group support

20. A 27 y/o F is brought to the ED by a friend at 3:00 on a Sunday morning complaining of profuse diarrhea and headache over the past few hours. She has never had these symptoms before. During the interview, she is noted to become confused, often stopping the doctor and saying, "Wait, what?" Even when the question is repeated, she still is unable to answer. She is oriented to person and place only. Physical exam reveals damp skin diffusely over her body. Vital signs are HR 122, RR 20, BP 146/82, and T 100.9°F. The patient's friend admits that they were "out partying" when they noticed that the patient was becoming more confused. Chart review reveals that she has been prescribed fluoxetine for depression and had been prescribed tramadol after a recent dental procedure. What additional physical exam findings would be expected?
    A. Pupillary size <2 mm
    B. Sudden jerks and twitching of the body
    C. Increased intraocular pressure
    D. Right-sided paresis
    E. Involuntary movements of the mouth
    F. None of the above

21. A 67 y/o M with a history of hypertension, hyperlipidemia, and chronic low back pain presents to a primary care office to establish care. When asked about recreational substance use, he admits to using poppers to "enhance my sexual experience." What is the most appropriate response from the physician?
    A. "Inhalants like those are very dangerous. You should stop right away."
    B. "Thanks for telling me. Poppers are generally safe and shouldn't cause you any problems."
    C. "Tell me more about the other medications you are taking."
    D. "Are you sure that's the real reason you're using them?"
    E. "Have you experienced any chest pain recently?"
    F. None of the above

22. A 49 y/o M sees his psychiatrist for help with depressed mood. He reports that he has felt depressed since his wife filed for divorce two years ago. He admits that his excessive drinking played a large role in the divorce, and despite the losses he has suffered he continues to imbibe 3 or more alcoholic drinks per night. He says, "Once I take a single drink I start to feel good, and before I know it I've downed the whole bottle." He was started on duloxetine for depression but notes that it hasn't made much difference. His psychiatrist explains that his depression is unlikely to improve while he continues to abuse alcohol. The patient expresses a desire for help to cut down on drinking, noting that he has not been able to do it through willpower or Alcoholics Anonymous groups. He is interested in medication. Which of the following options would be most appropriate to recommend?
    A. Naloxone
    B. Naltrexone
    C. Disulfiram
    D. Acamprosate
    E. Gabapentin
    F. None of the above

23. (Continued from previous question.) All of the following statements would be appropriate for the psychiatrist to say *except*:
    A. "You cannot drink at all while taking this medication."
    B. "We may need to draw some labs before starting."
    C. "It's important to know what other medications you are taking."
    D. "If you find it difficult to take a pill, there are other options available."
    E. "This medication does best when it is paired with other forms of support."
    F. All of the above would be appropriate

24. A 70 y/o M is brought to his geriatrician after his wife becomes concerned that he is "getting dementia." She notes that he has become increasingly sluggish, has lost interest in activities, and often seems to "zone out" while she is trying to talk with him. Recent labs are generally within normal limits with the exception of elevated LDL. The geriatrician performs a MoCA on which he scores a 16/30 (although he gives up halfway through after becoming visibly frustrated and says, "Ugh, I can't do this, what's the point?"). His activities of daily living appear to be intact, although his wife says that he won't eat unless prompted and will often get up early in the morning and "just walk around the house." The wife does not remember other times when he has had symptoms similar to this but also notes that they have been married only 6 years. Which of the following appears to be the most appropriate treatment at this time?
    A. Memantine
    B. Donepezil
    C. Rivastigmine
    D. Galantamine
    E. Risperidone
    F. None of the above

25. A 42 y/o M with a history of schizophrenia managed on olanzapine since his early twenties presents to his psychiatrist's office for follow-up. He has a history of hospitalizations in the past when he has run out of medications. He reports that he recently found a new case worker who has set him up with a job through a local agency that seeks to find employment for the mentally ill. He takes olanzapine at night and would normally sleep until around noon. This was not a problem while he was unemployed, but since starting work it has been difficult for him to be awake enough to do his job. He requests a change to a different medication that "won't make me feel so tired at work." Which of the following options would be best for this patient?
    A. Discontinue olanzapine
    B. Discontinue olanzapine and start haloperidol
    C. Discontinue olanzapine and start clozapine
    D. Continue olanzapine and add modafinil
    E. Continue olanzapine and add methylphenidate
    F. None of the above

26. (Continued from previous question.) The patient's case worker phones the psychiatrist several weeks later to say that it would be preferable if the patient were on a long-acting injectable form of medication, as the patient finds it very difficult to remember to take medications since starting work. The patient is also on the phone and says he is amenable to this change. What is the best response?
    A. "A long-acting injectable antipsychotic would be contraindicated for this patient."
    B. "We can do that, but we would need to switch back to olanzapine."
    C. "We can do that, but we would need to switch to a new antipsychotic."
    D. "We can do that provided he is tolerating the oral medication well."
    E. "We can do that, but I think it would be better if he could just remember on his own."
    F. None of the above

27. (Continued from previous question.) The patient is switched to monthly injections. The psychiatrist follows this patient longitudinally over the next decade. At a routine follow-up visit, the psychiatrist notices that the patient appears to be grimacing constantly throughout the interview. When he asks the patient about it, the patient states that he is not bothered by it. Which of the following would most likely have prevented this outcome?
    A. Conducting regular in-office assessments of involuntary movements
    B. Having a neurologist as part of the care team
    C. Choosing a different antipsychotic
    D. Adding clozapine
    E. Adding propranolol
    F. None of the above

28. A 57 y/o M with a history of bipolar disorder presents to his primary care doctor complaining of increased urination. He says that he has been peeing "like a race horse" and drinking lots of water. His doctor asks him how often he has been

awakening at night to urinate, and he responds, "At least two or three times." Vital signs are HR 112, BP 94/50, RR 12, and T 98.3°F. Digital rectal examination reveals a markedly enlarged prostate with prominence in the middle lobe. The physician prescribes tamsulosin and orders a CBC, BMP, A1c, and PSA; he then says that he will contact the patient if a prostate biopsy needs to be done. Later that evening, the same patient is brought to the emergency department after he was found to be unable to walk. He is severely confused and has urinated on himself. Fingerstick glucose is 120. Lab studies from earlier in the day are reviewed. An abnormality in which of the following labs is most likely to account for his symptoms?
- A. Electrolytes
- B. Hemoglobin A1c
- C. White blood cell count
- D. Platelets
- E. Prostate specific antigen
- F. None of the above

29. A 30 y/o F living in New Mexico stumbles into the emergency department saying that she is seeing double. Her speech is noticeably slurred, and soon she is unable to give responses to any questions asked. Vital signs are within normal limits except for RR 4. Physical exam reveals bilateral drooping of the eyelids and facial muscles, pupils that are 2 mm bilaterally and non-responsive to light, and dry oral mucosa. Needle marks are seen on the skin over her right antecubital fossa. A neurologic examination is performed and reveals diffuse bilateral weakness of skeletal muscles in both the upper and lower extremities. During the exam, her breathing stops, and a code blue is called. She is admitted to the ICU on a ventilator. CT scan of the head shows no ischemic injury or hemorrhage. Which of the following drug classes is most likely to be positive on a urine drug screen?
- A. Organophosphates
- B. Anticholinergics
- C. Cocaine
- D. Methamphetamines
- E. Opioids
- F. None of the above

30. A 26 y/o M is brought to the hospital by his roommate after he was found at home in his underwear crawling around on the floor. He screamed when his roommate entered, then said that he was being "slowly eaten by rats" and "burned by embers." In the hospital, he is severely confused and oriented to name only. Vital signs are HR 102, BP 144/86, RR 18, and T 99.5°F. Physical examination is unremarkable, with pupils 5 mm bilaterally and reactive to light. CBC, BMP, and urine toxicology are negative. His roommate says that the patient has no known psychiatric history. The patient is admitted to the hospital for monitoring. His mental status returns to baseline within 24 hours. He admits to being at a party in the hours before his roommate returned. He is unsure what he consumed, saying only that he "took what they offered me." Which substance is most likely involved?

A. Cocaine
B. Heroin
C. Cannabis
D. Synthetic cannabis
E. Synthetic cathinones

31. A 44 y/o M presents to his psychiatrist's office for follow-up. His BMI is 31.3 kg/m², increased from 27.2 kg/m² prior to starting a medication six months ago. Hemoglobin A1c from one week ago is 6.4%. He desires a switch to a medication which will not cause him to gain as much weight. Which of these medications is *least* likely to be weight gaining?
    A. Mirtazapine
    B. Olanzapine
    C. Aripiprazole
    D. Quetiapine
    E. Valproate

32. A 45 y/o M is started on a new antidepressant for treatment of major depression after having failed several trials of SSRIs and SNRIs. As the dose is titrated, he begins experiencing multiple side effects, including dry mouth and dizziness when standing quickly. At a visit with his urologist, he is noted to have a distended bladder. A catheter is placed and drains 600 mL of urine. Laboratory analysis reveals a creatinine of 2.2. Which of the following effects of this antidepressant likely accounts for his urinary retention?
    A. Serotonergic effects
    B. Noradrenergic effects
    C. Dopaminergic effects
    D. Anticholinergic effects
    E. Antihistaminergic effects
    F. None of the above

33. A 62 y/o M presents to the ED with intermittent chest pain for the past several days. The pain is precordial, lasts 10-15 minutes, and is not associated with activity. She has had similar symptoms before. On chart review, a previous coronary angiogram performed one month ago shows normal vasculature. She refuses to provide a urine sample. Vital signs reveal tachycardia and tachypnea but normal temperature. Ocular examination is shown below:

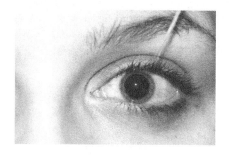

Initial troponins are positive. EKG reveals ST elevation. CXR is normal. An echocardiogram is performed and shows normal EF and absence of fluid in the pericardial cavity. What is the most likely etiology of this patient's chest pain?
   A. Accumulation of foam cells on coronary vessels
   B. Inflammation of the myocardium
   C. Spasm of the coronary arteries
   D. Infiltration of blood into the tunica media of the aorta
   E. Psychosomatic manifestation of anxiety
   F. None of the above

34. A 60 y/o M presents to his primary care doctor complaining of increasing tremor in his right hand at rest. The tremor improves with activity. His wife notes that his writing has become smaller and more difficult to read. He is otherwise healthy. Examination reveals decreased emotiveness of the face, cogwheel rigidity bilaterally, and bradykinesia. The primary care doctors make a referral to a neurologist for further evaluation. Decreased output in which of the following areas of the brain would most likely be found on histologic examination?
   A. Ventral tegmental area
   B. Tuberoinfundibular pathway
   C. Nigrostriatal pathway
   D. Raphe nuclei
   E. Locus ceruleus
   F. None of the above

35. (Continued from previous question.) Similar neurologic findings can be induced in an otherwise healthy subject by giving which of the following medications?
   A. Fluoxetine
   B. Fluphenazine
   C. Flumazenil
   D. Fluvoxamine
   E. Flunitrazepam
   F. None of the above

36. A 7 y/o M is referred to a child psychiatrist after a screening test for ADHD at school is positive. In taking the history from the patient's mother, she endorses easy distractibility, high levels of activity, and impulsive behavior in the home as well. Neuropsychological testing shows mild to moderate inattentiveness and hyperactivity. When discussing treatment options, the patient's mother is concerned about the idea of putting her child on stimulants. The decision is made to start guanfacine along with behavioral therapy. What side effect should the psychiatrist warn the mother about?
   A. Hypertension
   B. Sedation
   C. Growth restriction
   D. Increased risk of cardiac events
   E. Potential for abuse
   F. None of the above

37. A 29 y/o M army veteran presents to a post-deployment clinic for a second appointment after returning from a tour of duty. While overseas, he experienced combat directly and was involved in an explosion that resulted in the loss of two of his friends. Since returning, he has been plagued by nightmares nearly every night involving the incident. He feels like he cannot relax and says that he no longer knows what to talk about with his old friends who have never "tasted combat." He was prescribed prazosin which has had some effect on his nightmares. He admits to smoking marijuana daily, saying that it helps him to "finally be able to chill out for once." He then says, "You're gonna tell me to stop, aren't you doc?" What is the most appropriate response?
    A. "Yes, smoking marijuana is harmful, and you should stop immediately."
    B. "I would recommend stopping because marijuana isn't helpful for PTSD, but I understand if you need it for now."
    C. "Marijuana may or may not be helpful for PTSD. The fact is we really don't know enough to say definitively."
    D. "Actually, marijuana can be helpful for PTSD as long as you are aware of the risks."
    E. "No. As a matter of fact, I would encourage you to continue using marijuana as it's been shown to help with some PTSD symptoms."
    F. None of the above

38. A 47 y/o F requests an urgent OB/GYN appointment for severe vaginal pain over the past two days. She denies dysuria or cloudy urine. Pelvic examination reveals significant tenderness at the superior aspect of the vulva, with prominent engorgement of the clitoris. She was recently prescribed a sleeping pill by her primary care doctor but cannot remember the name. Which medication was most likely prescribed?
    A. Zolpidem
    B. Hydroxyzine
    C. Temazepam
    D. Trazodone
    E. Mirtazapine
    F. None of the above

39. A 13 y/o F with a history of depression and self-harm is brought to the hospital after she told her mother that she overdosed on a bottle of pills the previous evening. She reports that she ingested "a whole bottle of pills from my mom's medicine cabinet" and then went to sleep expecting not to wake up again. She awoke in the morning and did not notice any effects from her overdose and decided not to tell anyone about it. Later that evening, she began to feel ill, with right upper quadrant abdominal pain and nausea. She vomited several times before asking her mother to take her to the hospital. Vital signs are HR 118, BP 88/48, RR 14, and T 99.0°F. Pupils are 5 mm bilaterally and reactive. Abdominal examination reveals exquisite tenderness in the RUQ. CMP, CBC, and coags are ordered and reveal elevations in bicarbonate, AST, ALT, bilirubin, and INR. Which of the following medications was most likely ingested?

A. Ibuprofen
B. Acetaminophen
C. Oxycodone
D. Lithium
E. Amitriptyline
F. None of the above

40. (Continued from previous question.) What is the best initial treatment?
    A. N-acetylcysteine
    B. Organ transplantation
    C. Hemodialysis
    D. Intubation
    E. Surgical intervention
    F. None of the above

41. A 68 y/o retired M with a history of hypertension, hyperlipidemia, and two strokes is brought to see his geriatrician. His wife is concerned by increasing memory difficulties which she believes coincided with his strokes. His first stroke occurred 2 years ago after which he had problems remembering the topic of conversation. His second stroke occurred 3 months ago, and since then he has needed more assistance with managing finances and housework. A MoCA performed in the office is 19/30. Which medication would have the best chance of preventing further decline in his cognitive abilities?
    A. Memantine
    B. Donepezil
    C. Galantamine
    D. Rivastigmine
    E. Some medications can prevent further decline in his cognitive abilities, but they are not listed above
    F. No medications can prevent further decline in his cognitive abilities

42. A 30 y/o F with a history of bipolar disorder presents to her psychiatrist's office for follow-up. She states that she recently has become more depressed and wishes to start treatment for this. When asked about symptoms, she complains of persistent fatigue, depressed mood, and difficulty concentrating. She notes that her appetite has decreased, yet she still has gained 25 pounds over the past year. "Maybe it's because I'm all stuffed up," she jokes. "I poop maybe once or twice a week." The psychiatrist notices that the patient's voice is deeper than he remembers. Vital signs are within normal limits except for a heart rate of 54. The patient is not currently pregnant and is on birth control. She has no other medical problems. What is the most appropriate treatment?
    A. Mirtazapine
    B. Sertraline
    C. Phenelzine
    D. Imipramine
    E. Bupropion
    F. None of the above

43. (Continued from previous question.) The diagnosis is explained to the patient. She asks, "Does this mean I have to stop taking my current medication?" What is the best response?
    A. "Yes, we must stop it immediately."
    B. "Yes, we must stop it immediately and replace it with another medication."
    C. "No, we can continue the medication as is."
    D. "No, we can continue the medication as is but we have to add another medication."
    E. "We don't know for sure until we do some imaging studies."
    F. None of the above

44. A 31 y/o M with a history of alcohol use disorder presents for an annual physical. When the physician asks about his current level of alcohol intake, the patient becomes very defensive and says, "What business of that is yours? It's no one's problem but my own!" The physician responds by saying, "It's clear to me that this is a big problem for you. Let's set a quit date." The patient becomes enraged and leaves the office. This visit may have gone better if the physician had used techniques from which of the following forms of therapy?
    A. Cognitive behavioral therapy
    B. Dialectical behavior therapy
    C. Exposure therapy
    D. Supportive therapy
    E. Motivational interviewing
    F. None of the above

45. A 30 y/o F with a history of bipolar disorder is started on a mood stabilizer. She presents to a follow-up appointment four months later with a different psychiatrist as her previous prescriber is on leave. She admits to having missed two previously scheduled appointments. When asked how the medication is going, she admits that she stopped taking "that poisonous drug" after she gained 15 pounds and started pulling out large patches of hair while showering. She also complains of mild RUQ abdominal pain. She is open to trying another medication "as long as it's not that one again." When reviewing her chart, the psychiatrist notes that no labs were obtained before starting this medication. All of the following labs should have been ordered *except*:
    A. BMP
    B. CBC
    C. LFTs
    D. Urine pregnancy
    E. No labs are required for this medication

46. (Continued from previous question.) The psychiatrist discusses various treatment options with the patient. At this time, she reports feeling depressed and lacking in energy. She finds it difficult to concentrate at work, has not been eating as much, and has poor sleep. The patient and her psychiatrist agree on starting a different anticonvulsant mood stabilizer. When discussing this medication with her, the

psychiatrist notes, "This medication can help with your depression, but it's not likely to do anything to prevent a manic episode." Which of the following labs should be ordered specifically for this medication?
   A. BMP
   B. CBC
   C. LFTs
   D. Urine pregnancy
   E. No labs are required for this medication

47. (Continued from previous question.) The patient is started on the new mood stabilizer. Labs are ordered to assess for side effects from her previous medication. Her LFTs are within normal limits. However, a urine pregnancy test is positive. Ultrasonography reveals a 14-week intrauterine pregnancy. A maternal serum alpha-fetoprotein test is positive. Repeat ultrasonography performed several weeks later is shown below:

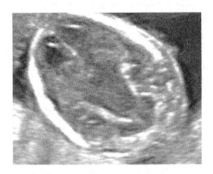

What fetal malformation is most likely to be present?
   A. Transposition of the pulmonary artery and aorta
   B. Displaced tricuspid valve leaflets
   C. Lumbar myelomeningocele
   D. Protrusion of abdominal contents through the anterior abdominal wall
   E. Fewer than five fingers on the hands
   F. Bilateral renal agenesis

48. A 34 y/o F living in rural China is brought to the hospital after she was found by her husband with shortness of breath, abdominal cramping, and diarrhea. On interview, she refuses to answer questions. Her husband reports that they recently had a fight. Vital signs are HR 48, BP 92/50, RR 22, T 99.8°F. Physical exam reveals pupillary size of 2 mm bilaterally, saliva oozing from her mouth, bilateral wheezing, diffuse clammy skin, and urine staining her pants. Which of the following treatments should be administered promptly?
   A. Sodium bicarbonate
   B. Naltrexone
   C. Naloxone
   D. Flumazenil
   E. None of the above

49. A 50 y/o M is admitted to the hospital for severe depression after his wife discovered that he had purchased a gun with the intention of shooting himself later that week. During the initial interview with the psychiatrist, the patient says, "It doesn't matter if you hospitalize me. My beard is going to grow into my mouth and suffocate me tonight anyway." He references this idea several times throughout the interview. When asked how he knows this, he says that he saw it on a television show and "knew that angels had put that message on the TV at exactly that moment for me to see it." He is not currently taking any medications and has no significant medical history outside of obesity and chronic low back pain. Which of the following is the single best treatment for this patient?
    A. Escitalopram
    B. Desipramine
    C. Phenelzine
    D. Risperidone
    E. Clozapine
    F. More than one of the above

50. A 19 y/o M is brought to the emergency department by his college roommates after he begins "acting strangely" for the past three hours. He is observed to be staring at the wall and says he is "watching it move." On interview, he is fully oriented but does suddenly yell, "Oh!" and look off in another direction when being asked about the date. When asked about what he is seeing, he says, "I'm talking to a tree. The tree is telling me that we are all here, we all have roots in the same soil, inspiring and expiring the same atmosphere, and with the same sun shining on us." Physical examination is unremarkable. Vital signs are HR 78, BP 118/74, RR 12, and T 97.9°F. Urine toxicology is negative. Which of the following substances is most likely to have been used?
    A. Methamphetamines
    B. Hydromorphone
    C. Lysergic acid diethylamide
    D. Phencyclidine
    E. Tetrahydrocannabinol
    F. Methylenedioxymethamphetamine
    G. None of the above

51. A 33 y/o F from Vietnam with a history of bipolar disorder is started on a new medication by her psychiatrist to treat mania. Two weeks after starting, she starts to feel ill and develops a sore throat, diffuse pain in her joints, and chills. She presents to her local urgent care hoping to get antibiotics. Physical examination reveals the following lesions on her tongue:

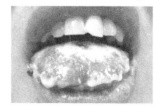

Which of the following is the most important for the doctor to do at this time?
- A. Discontinue the new medication
- B. Provide an antibiotic
- C. Start intravenous fluids
- D. Take a social and family history
- E. Transport the patient immediately to the emergency department
- F. No action is required

52. A 44 y/o M comes to the ED complaining of worsening blurry vision for the past two days. On review of systems, he also reports frequent nocturia with "frothy" urine which began at the same time as his blurry vision. BP is 212/124. Serum creatinine is 5.2. Intravenous labetalol is started. On further questioning, he denies a history of hypertension. His only medications are atorvastatin and phenelzine for depression. He notes that his outpatient psychiatrist recently switched him from fluoxetine to phenelzine. Which of the following interventions would have prevented this outcome?
    - A. Educating on lifestyle changes
    - B. Recommending smoking cessation
    - C. Adding an antihypertensive medication
    - D. Waiting 5 weeks after discontinuing fluoxetine to start phenelzine
    - E. Nothing could have prevented this outcome

53. A 25 y/o M with a history of schizophrenia and Crohn's disease is admitted to the psychiatric hospital. He is extremely paranoid and refuses to eat, drink, or take any medications, including steroids for his inflammatory bowel disease. It is now hospital day 5, and the patient has developed severe abdominal pain and loose bloody stools that are consistent with previous exacerbations of his inflammatory bowel disease. He still refuses to eat or drink. His family is concerned and says that, when he is on his medications, he becomes less paranoid and will take medications. Given the concern for his medical stability, a court order is granted permitting involuntary psychiatric treatment of this patient. Even when told about the court order, however, he still refuses to take any pills. Which of the following options would be most appropriate in this situation?
    - A. Olanzapine
    - B. Risperidone
    - C. Lurasidone
    - D. Clozapine
    - E. Quetiapine

54. A 16 y/o F is brought to the ED reporting significant anxiety and difficulty breathing. She reports that she first became short of breath while playing sports in her school gym, which had recently opened after some remodeling. Vital signs are HR 102, BP 114/78, RR 26, pulse ox 84%, T 99.2°F. She repeatedly says, "Help me, help me, it feels like I'm dying," and appears very distressed. The resident prescribes a medication that results in rapid resolution of her symptoms. After treatment, vital signs are HR 96, BP 116/80, RR 14, pulse ox 98%, T 99.3°F. Which of the following treatments was most likely administered?

A. Propranolol
B. Prazosin
C. Mirtazapine
D. Gabapentin
E. Lorazepam
F. None of the above

55. A 46 y/o F living in San Francisco begins going to therapy. During her twice weekly sessions, she faces away from the therapist while lying on a couch. Specific topics explored are her relationship with her mother and father, her use of rationalization and sublimation to deal with stress, and her dreams. What type of therapy is the patient engaging in?
    A. Psychoanalysis
    B. Cognitive behavioral therapy
    C. Dialectical behavior therapy
    D. Exposure therapy
    E. Supportive therapy
    F. None of the above

56. A 72 y/o M with a long history of depression presents to a tertiary care center for a second opinion. He has become increasingly depressed since the death of his wife several years ago, saying that he does not enjoy doing anything and typically isolates himself without seeing anyone for weeks at a time. He has difficulty both falling and remaining asleep, with significant fatigue during the day. He remains independent with his daily activities. His psychiatrist has prescribed paroxetine 40 mg daily, mirtazapine 15 mg qhs, and bupropion 300 mg daily. He has been prescribed fluoxetine, sertraline, nortriptyline, quetiapine, and aripiprazole in the past but does not feel that any of them have worked for him. He denies plans to commit suicide but says repeatedly that he longs to be with his wife. Which of the following interventions would have the best chance of improving his depression?
    A. Adding venlafaxine
    B. Increasing bupropion to 450 mg daily
    C. Discontinuing paroxetine
    D. Adding olanzapine
    E. Recommending ECT

57. A 38 y/o M is brought to the emergency department by police after he was found banging on car windshields at a busy intersection. A new intern is assigned to see him. He is highly confused on exam and talks about "the lab in Arizona" incessantly. He ignores questions when asked. Physical exam reveals a pupil size of 8 mm bilaterally and tachycardia. The patient then becomes agitated and screams, terminating the exam. He continues to scream obscenities constantly whenever someone tries to approach him. It is not possible to obtain a urine sample at this time. Due to ongoing agitation, the patient is placed in 4-point restraints. Despite this, he continues to scream and spit at others around him. He is seen straining against his restraints. Which of the following is the most appropriate treatment?

A. Haloperidol
B. Risperidone
C. Aripiprazole
D. Lurasidone
E. Quetiapine
F. None of the above

58. (Continued from previous question.) The intern orders this medication which noticeably calms the patient in several minutes. Thirty minutes later, the patient begins moaning loudly. He is no longer pulling at his restraints but is seen twisting his neck into a bent position as pictured below:

The nurse runs to find the intern. What is the best next step?
A. Administer lorazepam
B. Administer diphenhydramine
C. Administer another dose of the original medication
D. Administer another dose of the original medication along with lorazepam
E. Administer another dose of the original medication along with diphenhydramine
F. None of the above

59. A 48 y/o M is meeting with his psychiatrist to discuss starting a medication. While reviewing his chart, the psychiatrist notices that a recent EKG showed an elevated QTc of 500 ms. Which of the following medications would be most reasonable to prescribe for this patient?
A. Ziprasidone
B. Citalopram
C. Olanzapine
D. Haloperidol
E. None of the above

60. A 66 y/o M is brought to the hospital after his wife becomes concerned that he "looks drunk." When asked to elaborate, his wife reports that his gait has become more unsteady and his speech progressively slurred over the past two weeks. The patient denies alcohol ingestion over this period. His past medical history is significant for bipolar disorder, hypertension, and osteoarthritis. When asked about any recent changes, his wife says, "We went to his primary care doc a few weeks ago who changed his blood pressure meds and switched him from Tylenol to Aleve because his joints were really hurting him. Would Aleve cause this?"

Physical exam reveals drowsiness, ataxia, slurred speech, and bilateral upper extremity tremor. Vital signs are within normal limits. Which component of his history is most likely to reveal the cause of his current symptoms?
A. Medication history
B. Allergies
C. Social history
D. Family history
E. Review of systems
F. None of the above

61. (Continued from previous question.) Mood stabilizer levels are obtained and are elevated to 5 times the therapeutic level. What is the best immediate treatment?
A. Activated charcoal
B. Organ transplantation
C. Hemodialysis
D. Intubation
E. Surgical intervention
F. None of the above

62. A 66 y/o M presents to the emergency department with chest pain. While awaiting evaluation, he has a syncopal episode and is found to be in cardiac arrest. He is rapidly intubated and admitted to the ICU. To induce sedation, the anesthesiologist would like a benzodiazepine whose effects can be rapidly reversed when the medication is stopped. Which of the following options would be best suited for this purpose?
A. Lorazepam
B. Diazepam
C. Midazolam
D. Chlordiazepoxide
E. Alprazolam
F. None of the above

63. A 49 y/o M with a history of hypertension, hyperlipidemia, coronary artery disease, obesity, and gout presents to his primary care office. He complains of low back pain and knee pain, both of which have been persistent and unchanged for the past 10 years. His substance use consists of alcohol (1 or 2 drinks per night most nights of the week), tobacco (smoking 2 packs per day with a 50 pack-year history), and occasional marijuana use (3 or 4 times per month). He has access to a firearm. He endorses fatigue and depressed mood but no hopelessness or suicidal ideation. He has no history of manic episodes. Which of the following interventions would be most likely to result in the greatest increase in years of life?
A. Starting an antidepressant
B. Treating his substance use disorder
C. Management of coronary artery disease
D. Weight loss through diet and lifestyle modification
E. Removing his firearm

64. A 33 y/o F with a history of daily alcohol use for the past 8 years is admitted to the hospital after a car crash. Twenty hours into her admission, she asks her nurse, "Did you see that? That was the largest lion I've ever seen." She denies being fearful or anxious. The resident on-call is paged for evaluation. Vital signs are HR 92, BP 122/76, RR 14, and T 98.8°F. Which of the following is the most appropriate immediate treatment?
    A. Ethanol
    B. Triazolam
    C. Lorazepam
    D. Alprazolam
    E. Chlordiazepoxide
    F. None of the above

65. Which of the following second generation antipsychotics has the greatest antagonist effect on dopamine receptors in the tuberoinfundibular pathway?
    A. Olanzapine
    B. Risperidone
    C. Quetiapine
    D. Aripiprazole
    E. Clozapine

66. A 22 y/o F working at a coffee shop presents to her psychiatrist's office reporting that she has "gotten the wind knocked out" of her. She reports that for the past three weeks she has had to call in sick to work several times due to oversleeping her alarm. She reports fatigue throughout the day despite sleeping over 10 hours per night and says that waking up in the morning is "so much work, like my arms are made of bricks." She also reports weight gain of 10 lbs secondary to eating "like a pig." She denies purging, restricting, or a history of eating disorders. She says that she feels worthless, saying, "I can't do anything right, like, how hard is serving coffee?" When asked about recent stressors, she reports that she has been interested in a co-worker and asked him out several days ago; however, he has not returned her interest. When asked if her mood fluctuates, she says that on her birthday one week ago she felt "like the cloud had lifted, I was with all my family and friends, it was a great day." Since then, however, her poor mood has returned. Which of the following treatments is most likely to be effective?
    A. Sertraline
    B. Venlafaxine and aripiprazole combination
    C. Mirtazapine
    D. Bupropion
    E. Selegiline
    F. None of the above

67. A 78 y/o F with a history of Alzheimer's dementia is brought into the hospital for agitation. UA is positive for both leukocyte esterase and nitrite. Urine culture is pending. She is admitted to the medicine service. Overnight, she is awake and screams constantly. The RN staff pages the overnight intern who consults his guidebook and gives a verbal order for intravenous medication. This occurs

several times over the course of the night. Around 4:00am, the RN pages again saying that the patient is screaming more and has become tachycardic, hypotensive, and diaphoretic. The intern orders an EKG and comes to the bedside. Upon arriving, he finds the patient unconscious and immediately calls a code blue. If an EKG had been done prior to the patient becoming tachycardic, which part of the reading would most likely be abnormal?

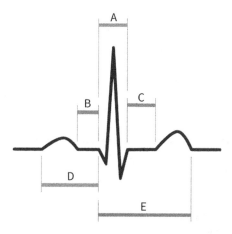

68. A 23 y/o M presents to his primary care doctor's office reporting that he feels anxious about "everything." He graduated from college with a degree in business one year ago but is currently unemployed after he was let go from a recent internship. When asked about this, the patient says, "I couldn't get anything done. My boss would give a project, but I'd keep worrying that it would never be good enough, so I'd spend all my time thinking about how bad it would be and not actually get anything done." He recognizes that this is maladaptive. When asked about whether his anxiety affects other domains in his life, he reports that he worries constantly about his mother's health, saying, "My dad died a few years ago, I couldn't stand to lose mom too." He also worries about his finances despite his mother's assurances that he will be taken care of financially. The doctor says, "I'm going to give you a medication to help with anxiety. It has one of the longest half-lives of any drug of its type, so it should reduce your anxiety throughout the day." Which of the following medications was most likely recommended?
    A. Clonazepam
    B. Diazepam
    C. Lorazepam
    D. Triazolam
    E. Alprazolam
    F. None of the above

69. (Continued from previous question.) When discussing the risks and benefits of treatment, the patient becomes alarmed, saying, "I don't want anything that could be addictive!" Despite attempts to reassure the patient, he is adamant that he does not want this medication. The doctor then provides him with a referral to a psychiatrist to discuss it further. All of the following alternative options would have been appropriate to discuss with this patient *except* for:
    A. Buspirone
    B. Prazosin
    C. Fluoxetine
    D. Cognitive behavioral therapy
    E. Venlafaxine
    F. All of the above are acceptable treatments for this condition

70. A 66 y/o M is brought to the hospital after a friend noticed that the right side of his face was drooping. Blood pressure is 188/92. Non-contrast CT of the head reveals a stroke in the left hemisphere. The patient had told the friend earlier over coffee that he had recently switched to a new antidepressant. Which of the following medications was most likely started?
    A. Sertraline
    B. Venlafaxine
    C. Mirtazapine
    D. Trazodone
    E. Aripiprazole

71. A 27 y/o F with a history of major depression as a teenager experiences her second major depressive episode. In discussing the various treatment options, the patient and her doctor decide on an SSRI. The patient is worried because she took paroxetine as a teenager and experienced severe anxiety, insomnia, headaches, and "brain zaps" when it was abruptly discontinued. She wishes to avoid a similar outcome this time and requests a medication that could potentially be discontinued without significant withdrawal symptoms. Which of the following medications should the doctor prescribe?
    A. Fluoxetine
    B. Paroxetine
    C. Escitalopram
    D. Venlafaxine
    E. Chlordiazepoxide
    F. None of the above

72. A 26 y/o F is brought into the ED after having been found by her ex-husband asleep next to a bottle of pills. She is obtunded and is unable to answer any questions. Vital signs are HR 78, BP 118/72, RR 6, O2 sat 80%, and T 98.9°F. Her ex-husband reveals that her medical history is positive for depression and fibromyalgia. She had recently undergone a dental procedure. Physical examination reveals absent pupillary reflexes to bright light bilaterally. EKG is shown below:

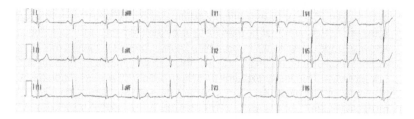

What is the most likely medication involved?
- A. Phenelzine
- B. Amitriptyline
- C. Duloxetine
- D. Ibuprofen
- E. Hydrocodone

73. (Continued from previous question.) What is the most appropriate treatment at this time?
    - A. Flumazenil
    - B. Sodium bicarbonate
    - C. Naltrexone
    - D. Intravenous fluids
    - E. Diltiazem
    - F. None of the above

74. A 15 y/o M with a history of ADHD is reported to his school principal after he is caught attempting to sell his prescribed Adderall to a classmate. His mother brings him in for an appointment with his psychiatrist. She is distraught by this news and wants to know what will happen next. This patient has been under this psychiatrist's care for several years during which time his dose has escalated steadily over time. In addition, the last two prescription refills have been issued early as the patient reports that he "lost the bottle." Neuropsychological testing was performed several years ago which strongly suggested both inattentiveness and hyperactivity. At previous visits, both the patient and his mother have reported that this medication was effective for him. What would be a reasonable response to his mother?
    - A. "We will need to stop treating your son for ADHD because of this."
    - B. "It would be best to continue this medication because it has worked for him in the past."
    - C. "We should switch to a different medication called methylphenidate."
    - D. "We should switch to a different medication known as atomoxetine."
    - E. "We need to stop the medication and have your son do behavioral therapy only."
    - F. None of the above

75. A 40 y/o M presents to an addiction clinic requesting assistance with quitting substances. He states that he uses his drug of choice to feel "more alert and alive" and also appreciates that this drug helps him to "keep the weight off." However, he feels it is harming his health. He has not been able to quit on his own despite a few attempts. The doctor explains that there are effective medication treatments available for this particular drug. Which of the following drugs does the patient most likely take?
    A. Nicotine
    B. Methamphetamines
    C. Alcohol
    D. Heroin
    E. Psilocybin
    F. None of the above

76. A 36 y/o F presents to her primary care doctor for routine follow-up. She has a history of uterine fibroids and moderate depression but has declined to seek treatment for either. She says that she is trying to manage both of these conditions by altering her eating patterns and is currently eating only pre-packaged nutritional supplements. Which of the following is the most appropriate response?
    A. "Keep doing what you're doing."
    B. "The best thing for depression is to eat only raw fruits and vegetables."
    C. "I would recommend a diet with lots of olive oil, legumes, unrefined cereals, fruits, and vegetables."
    D. "Avoiding gluten is a good way of reducing depression and anxiety."
    E. "No specific diet has been shown to help with depression in any way."
    F. None of the above

77. A 44 y/o M with a long-standing history of depression presents to his psychiatrist appearing frustrated. Despite treatment, his PHQ-9 score indicates severe depression and is unchanged from two months ago. He appears exasperated, saying, "Nothing has worked!" Review of his chart shows a history of multiple medication trials, including fluoxetine, citalopram, sertraline, bupropion, venlafaxine, aripiprazole, and desipramine. He is referred for ECT. Which of the following medications can be continued during ECT?
    A. Carbamazepine
    B. Diazepam
    C. Olanzapine
    D. Gabapentin
    E. Lorazepam
    F. Valproate
    G. Oxazepam
    H. None of the above

78. A 24 y/o F arrives late for an intake appointment with her new psychiatrist. Due to time constraints, the psychiatrist is unable to take a complete psychiatric history. Her primary complaint is ongoing depression, and after further interview she is diagnosed with major depressive disorder. Bupropion is prescribed and titrated to 300 mg/day. Two weeks later, the psychiatrist is alerted that the patient is in the hospital after suffering a seizure. Which aspect of the patient's history is most likely to reveal the cause of her seizure?
    A. Prior medication trials
    B. Allergic or adverse reactions to medications
    C. History of suicide attempts
    D. Anxiety symptoms
    E. Psychotic symptoms
    F. History of trauma
    G. Diet and nutritional intake
    H. Social and occupational status
    I. Family history of psychiatric illness

79. A 25 y/o F presents to her psychiatrist's office. She reports having been diagnosed with bipolar disorder at age 18 and has been hospitalized for manic episodes three times, including twice within the past year. During this time, she has not had a consistent psychiatrist managing her medications. Her current regimen consists of lithium, quetiapine, lamotrigine, topiramate, and sertraline. She reports feeling depressed, saying, "I can't concentrate on anything, I feel really stupid all the time." She sleeps around 7-8 hours per night. Mental status exam reveals a dysthymic affect, linear thought process, normal speech patterns, and absence of suicidal ideation. She desires to simplify her medication regimen. Which of her medications would be most appropriate to discontinue at this time?
    A. Lithium
    B. Quetiapine
    C. Lamotrigine
    D. Topiramate
    E. Sertraline
    F. None of her medications should be discontinued

80. A 22 y/o M is brought to the hospital for agitation and bizarre behavior. The clinical picture is consistent with a diagnosis of substance-induced psychosis given reports from his friends that his change in mental status coincided with use of substances several hours ago. However, his urine drug screen is negative. Which of the following substances is most likely to be involved?
    A. Crack (freebase cocaine)
    B. Adderall (prescription amphetamines)
    C. Bath salts (synthetic cathinones)
    D. Special K (Ketamine)
    E. None of the above

1. **The best answer is C.** This is a classic case of trigeminal neuralgia. In addition to its use in epilepsy and bipolar disorder, carbamazepine is helpful in treating trigeminal neuralgia. The other options are not as specific for treatment of trigeminal neuralgia. *(Chapter 5—Anticonvulsant Mood Stabilizers)*

2. **The best answer is B.** This patient is clearly suffering from a major depressive episode and should be offered treatment with an antidepressant. Mirtazapine is an excellent choice for a patient with poor appetite, weight loss, and difficulty sleeping. The other antidepressants (answers A, C, and D) could be reasonable options, although the presence of these other side effects makes mirtazapine a better choice. ECT (answer E) would not be a first-line treatment for this patient and would likely be difficult considering her medical comorbidities. *(Chapter 3—"Atypical" Antidepressants)*

3. **The best answer is D.** Benzodiazepines like lorazepam are highly effective in treating acute episodes of panic disorder, which this patient is likely experiencing given the lack of objective findings on exam and laboratory analysis. Inhaled nitrites (answer A) are used for angina pectoris but would not be appropriate for a patient in the absence of a cardiac etiology. Propranolol (answer B) has some anxiolytic effects but is more specific for performance anxiety. Both buspirone and sertraline (answers C and E) can be used for long-term treatment of several anxiety disorders but do not work rapidly enough for acute treatment. *(Chapter 6—Benzodiazepines)*

4. **The best answer is F.** Cognitive behavioral therapy has the strongest and most consistent evidence for a complete and long-lasting effect on treating panic disorder, with nearly 90% of patients experiencing a complete recovery. SSRIs (answer A) are helpful but are considered a second-line treatment after cognitive behavioral therapy. Benzodiazepines (answer B) are helpful for short-term treatment but often make panic disorder worse in the long-term. Buspirone, beta-blockers, and alpha-blockers (answers C, D, and E) are not first-line options for treating panic disorder. *(Chapter 6—How to Use Anxiolytics and Hypnotics)*

5. **The best answer is D.** Withdrawal from MDMA is associated with bruxism. With repeated use over a long period of time, this can result in dental attrition as pictured. None of the other substances cause significant dental attrition (although caffeine and nicotine can both cause staining). *(Chapter 10—MDMA)*

6. **The best answer is C.** This case describes a tragic outcome of inhalant abuse. Inhalants take a variety of forms but can be roughly categorized into three general categories: solvents and gases, anesthetics, and nitrites. Of these, solvents are far and away the most common, as they can be produced legally and cheaply from items in nearly any grocery store. Acetone is found in nail polish remover, toluene in glue, chlorofluorocarbons in hair spray, and butane in lighters (answers A, B, D, and E). In contrast, anesthetics like diethyl ether and chloroform tend to be more highly regulated, making them much less likely to be accessible by children and adolescents. *(Chapter 13—Inhalants)*

7. **The best answer is E.** This patient likely has borderline personality disorder which has been misdiagnosed as bipolar disorder. As such, the primary treatment that will alter the trajectory of her illness is dialectical behavior therapy. Medications can help symptomatically but will not improve the underlying features of her disorder. *(Chapter 15—Psychotherapy)*

8. **The best answer is C.** Unlike tardive dyskinesia, akathisia is typically not permanent (although in rare cases it can be). Treatment consists of propranolol, a benzodiazepine, or an anticholinergic drug (answer D). The relationship between akathisia and antipsychotics like risperidone is well established (answers A and B). Certain antipsychotics such as haloperidol and risperidone have a higher chance of causing akathisia than others like olanzapine or quetiapine (answer E). *(Chapter 4—Antipsychotic Effects)*

9. **The best answer is A.** Current guidelines suggest switching to clozapine after two failed trials of antipsychotics. While both risperidone and quetiapine have been used to treat this patient, risperidone cannot be considered an adequate trial as it was discontinued early due to a side effect (rather than lack of efficacy). Because of this, at least one more antipsychotic should be trialed prior to clozapine. ECT could be considered as it is effective in treating schizophrenia, but due to logistical issues and problems with consent, it should probably be reserved until more options have been tried. Neither desipramine (answer D) nor lithium (answer E) are indicated for schizophrenia. *(Chapter 4—Second Generation Antipsychotics: The "-Apines")*

10. **The best answer is D.** This patient most likely was prescribed propranolol, a non-selective β-blocker. By preventing the sympathetic nervous system's dilatory effects on the bronchioles (mediated by β-2 receptors), propranolol can exacerbate asthma for certain patients. None of the other receptors are implicated in the pathogenesis of asthma. *(Chapter 2—Norepinephrine)*

11. **The best answer is D.** This patient's history is consistent with a perforated gastric ulcer, with the chest x-ray showing free air under the diaphragm. This is a life-threatening complication of chronic NSAID use. None of the commonly used treatments for any other disorder listed has gastrointestinal perforation as a known side effect. *(Chapter 8—Non-Opioid Analgesics)*

12. **The best answer is A.** Acetaminophen is not associated with peptic ulcers and is preferred over an NSAID for patients at high-risk for this complication. Use of a histamine blocker (such as ranitidine) or a proton-pump inhibitor can also be used to prevent this complication. Celecoxib (answer B) does have a lower rate of peptic ulcers than other NSAIDs but is still associated with a risk of ulcers compared to no treatment. Diet (answer C) was long thought to be associated with ulcers, but this is no longer believed to be the case. Antibiotic therapy (answer D) is helpful for patients with gastric ulcers secondary to H. pylori but does not help in NSAID-induced ulceration. *(Chapter 8—Non-Opioid Analgesics)*

13. **The best answer is D.** Acamprosate, lithium, and gabapentin (answers A, B, and C) are all metabolized renally. While lorazepam is safe to give in cases of liver dysfunction, it is not renally metabolized and would not require modified dosing for this patient. *(Chapter 14—Putting It All Together)*

14. **The best answer is B.** All of the options listed have some evidence for efficacy in bipolar depression except carbamazepine which instead is used to treat bipolar mania. *(Chapter 5—Anticonvulsant Mood Stabilizers)*

15. **The best answer is B.** While there is some degree of controversy on this, the most consistent evidence regarding the use of antidepressants in bipolar disorder is not that they cause a switch into mania (answer C) but that they simply are not effective as monotherapy for bipolar depression. Prescribing a medication that the patient believes in can help to improve the chance of that treatment working but should not be the only reason to prescribe (answer A). Sertraline is no more or less effective than other antidepressants (answer D) and would not be contraindicated in a patient with chronic kidney disease given that it is hepatically metabolized (answer E). *(Chapter 5—Antidepressants)*

16. **The best answer is C.** While delayed ejaculation is considered to be an adverse effect of SSRIs, in certain cases it can actually be a desired effect, and SSRIs like paroxetine are indicated as one of the primary medical treatments for premature ejaculation. While this patient likely has distress over his situation, use of an antianxiety medication would not be indicated (answers A, B, D, and E). *(Chapter 2—Serotonin)*

17. **The best answer is G.** This describes a case of benzodiazepine withdrawal as evidenced by rebound insomnia, increased anxiety, panic symptoms, and seizures. Of the two benzodiazepines listed, only oxazepam would be expected to produce symptoms within two days given its short half-life. Diazepam (answer F) has a long half-life and would not produce symptoms of withdrawal in such a short period of time. Withdrawal from SSRIs and SNRIs (answers A, B, and C) can also result in insomnia and anxiety but would not be expected to produce seizures; in addition, fluoxetine's long half-life makes it very unlikely to precipitate withdrawal symptoms. Withdrawal from antipsychotics (answers D and E) or mood stabilizers (answer I) is not associated with significant anxiety or seizures but may precipitate increased psychotic and/or manic symptoms. Withdrawal from buspirone (answer H) is generally benign and is not associated with seizures. *(Chapter 6—Anxiolytic Effects)*

18. **The best answer is C.** Treatment of benzodiazepine withdrawal involves giving benzodiazepines, often one with a long half-life such as chlordiazepoxide to allow for a slower and more controlled taper. It is not necessary to use the same benzodiazepine that is being withdrawn (answer A). Alprazolam is an intermediate-acting benzodiazepine and would not be as helpful as a long-acting one. Flumazenil is used rarely in cases of benzodiazepine overdose, not withdrawal (answer F). Phenobarbital would help to reverse some of the signs

and symptoms of benzodiazepine withdrawal but is significantly more dangerous than benzodiazepines and would not be a first-line treatment. Ketamine (answer E) has no place in the treatment of benzodiazepine withdrawal. *(Chapter 11—Benzodiazepines)*

19. **The best answer is D.** While smoking cessation would likely be beneficial for this patient, she has not yet voiced readiness to make this change. For this reason, offering interventions at this time is premature. Motivational interviewing is indicated to help the patient move to the preparation stage of change. Once she is ready to make this change, any of the options listed are likely to be helpful. Varenicline (answer B) is the most effective medication for helping her quit smoking, though bupropion (answer C) could offer additional support as an antidepressant. *(Chapter 10—Nicotine and Chapter 15—Psychotherapy)*

20. **The best answer is B.** The patient appears to be in serotonin syndrome, likely precipitated by MDMA use in combination with her existing fluoxetine and tramadol use. Serotonin syndrome is characterized by diffuse hyperreflexia and myoclonus. Recent use of MDMA would be associated with pupillary dilation rather than constriction (answer A). Increased intraocular pressure is not found with either serotonin syndrome or MDMA intoxication (answer C). Right-sided paresis would not be expected unless if the patient was having a stroke (answer D). Tardive dyskinesia is an effect of chronic antipsychotic use and would not be expected to present as acutely (answer E). *(Chapter 2—Serotonin)*

21. **The best answer is C.** Alkyl nitrites, otherwise known as poppers, are generally not considered harmful (answer A) when used recreationally. The exception is when they are combined with phosphodiesterase inhibitors such as sildenafil (Viagra), as the combination can drop blood pressure to dangerously low levels. Because of this, finding out about concurrent medication use (especially in an older male patient) is essential before declaring it to be safe (answer B). The patient is accurately describing the most common reasons that nitrites are used recreationally (answer D). Nitrite use does not predispose one to chest pain or heart disease, and in fact nitrites are used to treat angina pectoris (answer E). *(Chapter 13—Inhalants)*

22. **The best answer is B.** Out of the existing pharmacologic treatments for alcohol use disorder, naltrexone is recommended as a first-line option given it is more effective and generally well tolerated. Disulfiram, acamprosate, and gabapentin (answer C, D, and E) have all been used for this purpose but are not considered to be as effective as naltrexone. Naloxone (answer A) is used for emergency treatment of opioid overdose, not for alcohol use disorder. *(Chapter 11—Alcohol)*

23. **The best answer is A.** Unlike disulfiram, it is not required that patients taking naltrexone abstain from alcohol, and indeed, some have argued that it is actually helpful to drink alcohol while taking naltrexone in order to uncouple alcohol use from its positive reinforcement effects. Naltrexone cannot be used in patients with severe liver damage (answer B) or in patients taking opioids (answer C). It is

available as a pill or an intramuscular depot (answer D). Finally, research shows that medication treatment combined with psychosocial therapies results in the best outcomes (answer E). *(Chapter 11—Alcohol Abuse)*

24. **The best answer is F.** This patient has many symptoms consistent with a diagnosis of major depression, including changes in appetite, early morning awakening, anhedonia, and depressed mood. While his MoCA score is in the range to suggest cognitive impairment, this appears to be secondary to poor effort. Clinicians have used the term "pseudodementia" to describe cases like this. Treatment with an antidepressant and/or psychotherapy should be initiated. No antidementia agents (answers A, B, C, and D) would be appropriate here, and risperidone (answer E) would not be expected to improve outcomes in depression. *(Chapter 9—Other Drugs Used in Dementia)*

25. **The best answer is B.** While olanzapine is a highly sedating medication, discontinuing an antipsychotic is not recommended for a patient who has been stabilized on it (answer A) without replacing it with something else, especially in a patient with a clear history of hospitalizations secondary to medication discontinuation. The patient has not failed olanzapine, so clozapine would not be indicated and is itself quite sedating (answer C). Haloperidol is less sedating than olanzapine and represents a reasonable switch. Continuing olanzapine and adding either modafinil (answer D) or a stimulant (answer E) could be considered if the patient does not tolerate a switch to another antipsychotic, but probably should not be attempted first to avoid polypharmacy and adding additional side effects. *(Chapter 4—Antipsychotic Effects)*

26. **The best answer is D.** Haloperidol is available in a long-acting injectable form so there is no need to switch back to olanzapine (answer B) or another antipsychotic (answer C). In addition, there are no specific contraindications to long-acting forms of antipsychotics provided that the patient has demonstrated tolerance to the oral form of the medication (answer A). Finally, it would be inappropriate to push back against a plan that the patient has formulated alongside his case worker in the absence of any legitimate contraindications (answer E). *(Chapter 4—Putting It All Together)*

27. **The best answer is C.** As a strong dopamine blocker, haloperidol has a high risk of causing tardive dyskinesia. Choosing a different antipsychotic would confer a lower risk of causing tardive dyskinesia. While conducting in-office assessments of involuntary movements such as the Abnormal Involuntary Movement Scale (AIMS) is recommended to facilitate detection, it would not have prevented this outcome (answer A). Similarly, having a neurologist as part of the care team may have facilitated detection but also would not have prevented it from occurring (answer B). While switching patients with tardive dyskinesia to clozapine is a good next step, adding clozapine does not necessary prevent tardive dyskinesia (answer D). Propranolol is indicated as treatment for akathisia, not as prevention against tardive dyskinesia (answer E). *(Chapter 4—Antipsychotic Effects)*

28. **The best answer is A.** A patient with a history of bipolar disorder presenting with polyuria and polydipsia should raise your suspicion for lithium-induced nephrogenic diabetes insipidus. He is now presenting with altered mental status secondary to hypernatremia, which would be evident in his electrolytes. His markedly enlarged prostate on exam could very well be a sign of benign prostatic hyperplasia, but this diagnosis alone would be insufficient to account for his polydipsia and vital sign abnormalities. While diabetes mellitus can cause polyuria and polydipsia, a relatively normal fingerstick glucose would argue against this being the cause of his altered mental status (answer B). His WBC may be transiently elevated due to a stress response, but this is not as likely to be abnormal as his sodium level (answer C). Platelets are unlikely to be changed (answer D). His prostate specific antigen level may be elevated secondary to benign prostatic hyperplasia but would not account for his altered mental status (answer E). *(Chapter 5—Lithium)*

29. **The best answer is E.** This vignette describes a case of botulism as evidenced by paralysis combined with signs of opioid intoxication such as respiratory depression. The needle marks on her forearm suggest intravenous drug use. Botulism is associated with black tar heroin, an impure form of heroin. Organophosphates would result in increased salivation and muscle activity, not decreased (answer A). The effect of anticholinergic drugs overlap with botulism to some degree but would not cause paralysis to the same degree; in addition, anticholinergic toxicity would be expected to cause more vital sign instability (such as tachycardia and hypertension) as well as dilated pupils. Neither cocaine nor methamphetamines (answers C and D) would produce the muscle paralysis seen here. *(Chapter 11—Opioids)*

30. **The best answer is D.** This vignette describes a case of substance-induced psychosis as evidenced by the lack of psychiatric history and rapid resolution of symptoms. Tellingly, the urine toxicology is negative which argues against cocaine, heroin, and cannabis (answers A, B, and C). Synthetic cannabis can result in substance-induced psychosis with a negative urine toxicology screen. Other designer drugs like synthetic cathinones (answer E) can also result in substance-induced psychosis with a negative urine toxicology screen, though as stimulants they would be expected to result in more signs and symptoms suggestive of sympathetic nervous system activation such as tachycardia, hypertension, and mydriasis. *(Chapter 13—Cannabinoids)*

31. **The best answer is C.** Aripiprazole is generally weight neutral. All of the other options are associated with weight gain. *(Chapters 3, 4, and 5)*

32. **The best answer is D.** The patient was likely started on a tricyclic antidepressant such as amitriptyline. Tricyclics are serotonergic, noradrenergic, anticholinergic, and antihistaminergic. However, it is the anticholinergic effect that causes urinary retention by opposing the effects of the parasympathetic nervous system, which enables urination. None of the other effects could account for urinary retention in this case. *(Chapter 3—Tricyclic Antidepressants)*

33. **The best answer is C.** The patient in this case likely used cocaine recently, which is associated with coronary vasospasm. In this case, the vasospasm has resulted in a STEMI. Coronary artery disease is incorrect, as atherosclerosis would likely be noted on her recent angiogram (answer A). Myocarditis would likely be associated with fever and pericardial effusion (answer B). Aortic dissection would likely reveal widening of the mediastinum on CXR (answer D). A panic attack is unlikely to cause the physical exam findings and imaging results seen here (answer E). *(Chapter 10—Cocaine)*

34. **The best answer is C.** The patient's history of resting tremor and micrographia are suggestive of Parkinson's disease, and the physical exam findings only further support this diagnosis. Parkinson's disease is associated with damage to dopaminergic neurons in the substantia nigra which communicates with the striatum via the nigrostriatal pathway. Both the ventral tegmental area and the tuberoinfundibular pathway (answers A and B) are associated with dopaminergic neurons but are not directly involved in the pathophysiology of Parkinson's disease. The raphe nuclei (answer D) are the location of serotonin production, while the locus ceruleus (answer E) is the site of norepinephrine production. *(Chapter 2—Dopamine)*

35. **The best answer is B.** Fluphenazine is a first generation antipsychotic and, like other antipsychotics, can produce parkinsonism as a side effect by blocking dopamine. None of the other medications listed have parkinsonism as a side effect. *(Chapter 4—Antipsychotic Effects)*

36. **The best answer is B.** Guanfacine is a non-stimulant that can be used to treat ADHD. Potential side effects include sedation and hypotension rather than hypertension (answer A). To avoid sedation during the day, it is usually dosed at night. Growth restriction and potential for abuse (answers C and E) are both seen with stimulants but not non-stimulants. There is no clear risk of cardiac events from either stimulants or non-stimulants (answer D). *(Chapter 7—Non-Stimulants)*

37. **The best answer is C.** With the exception of reducing nausea and vomiting during chemotherapy, improving appetite in patients with HIV/AIDS, and treating chronic pain and muscle spasms in certain conditions, there is a significant lack of high-quality evidence for or against using cannabis to treat medical illnesses. Patients should be made aware of this. Saying that cannabis definitely does (answer E) or does not (answer A) help is a hardline approach that doesn't accurately reflect the current state of knowledge. More moderate responses are not completely wrong but are not as accurate as admitting that there is a lack of high-quality medical evidence (answer B and D). *(Chapter 13—Cannabinoids)*

38. **The best answer is D.** Trazodone is associated with priapism, or sustained erections lasting longer than 4 hours. This can occur in both males and females. None of the other options are associated with priapism. *(Chapter 3—"Atypical" Antidepressants)*

39. **The best answer is B.** The patient's abdominal tenderness and liver function abnormalities strongly suggest hepatic damage which would be expected in cases of acetaminophen toxicity. Her elevated bicarbonate suggests metabolic acidosis which can develop in cases of severe poisoning. Ibuprofen and lithium (answers A and D) would both be expected to cause renal damage rather than hepatotoxicity. Oxycodone (answer C) would result in sedation, slowing of respirations, and miosis, none of which are observed here. Amitriptyline (answer E) is unlikely to present with hepatic toxicity. *(Chapter 8—Non-Opioid Analgesics)*

40. **The best answer is A.** The indicated treatment for acetaminophen toxicity is N-acetylcysteine. While N-acetylcysteine is most effective if given within 8 hours after ingestion, it can still be helpful up to 24 hours post-ingestion. Hemodialysis would not be expected to be helpful in a patient with normal creatinine (answer C). Intubation, transplantation, and surgical intervention are all not indicated at this time (answers B, D, and E). *(Chapter 8—Non-Opioid Analgesics)*

41. **The best answer is E.** This patient has vascular dementia as evidenced by the step-wise decline in his cognitive abilities coinciding with the timing of his cerebrovascular accidents. While memantine (answer A) and the acetylcholinesterase inhibitors (answers B, C, and D) can help symptomatically, they are not disease-modifying and cannot prevent a further decline in his cognitive abilities. Rather, only medications that prevent future strokes such as statins or antihypertensives would be expected to prevent further decline in his cognitive abilities, although they would not be expected to reverse current deficits. *(Chapter 9—Other Drugs Used in Dementia)*

42. **The best answer is F.** This patient's clinical history, including depressed mood, weight gain, constipation, deepening of the voice, and bradycardia, strongly suggests hypothyroidism. This is likely secondary to lithium, as nearly 10% of patients taking lithium experience low thyroid function. Given this, treatment with an antidepressant would not be appropriate (answers A through E). *(Chapter 5—Lithium)*

43. **The best answer is D.** Treatment for hypothyroidism (regardless of its etiology) involves thyroid hormone replacement. This does not require that lithium be discontinued (answers A and B). It would be inappropriate to continue lithium and leave the hypothyroidism untreated (answer C). Finally, imaging studies are not required to diagnose or treat hypothyroidism. *(Chapter 5—Lithium)*

44. **The best answer is E.** While this patient is in the pre-contemplation stage of change, the physician attempted to use a strategy more in line with the preparation stage, leading to a poor outcome. Had the physician been more familiar with the principles of motivational interviewing, they may have been able to respond with a technique that worked better for the pre-contemplation stage of change. *(Chapter 15—Psychotherapy)*

45. **The best answer is A.** This patient was likely started on valproate as evidenced by her weight gain, hair loss, and abdominal pain suggestive of hepatic damage. Suggested labs before starting valproate are CBC, LFTs, and urine pregnancy (answers B, C, and D). BMP is not required, although it is not necessarily wrong to order it to be thorough. *(Chapter 5—Anticonvulsant Mood Stabilizers)*

46. **The best answer is E.** The patient was likely prescribed lamotrigine, as it is the only mood stabilizer that is helpful for bipolar depression but does not treat or prevent manic episodes. Lamotrigine is generally well tolerated and does not require any particular labs before starting. The patient should be counseled on the risk of rash and Stevens-Johnson syndrome. *(Chapter 5—Anticonvulsant Mood Stabilizers)*

47. **The best answer is C.** A positive maternal serum alpha-fetoprotein in the context of valproate use during the first trimester of pregnancy is highly suggestive of a neural tube defect such as a myelomeningocele. Displaced tricuspid valve leaflets, known as Ebstein's anomaly, are seen with intrauterine lithium exposure (answer B). Transposition of the great arteries (answer A), gastroschisis (answer D), oligodactyly (answer E), and renal agenesis (answer F) are not known complications of in utero valproate exposure. *(Chapter 5—Anticonvulsant Mood Stabilizers)*

48. **The best answer is E.** This patient is showing signs of parasympathetic nervous system overactivation, likely due to a suicide attempt using organophosphates given her history. The correct treatment is with an anticholinergic such as atropine. Sodium bicarbonate is used to treat tricyclic antidepressant overdose; however, tricyclics are anticholinergic which would produce the opposite findings as seen here (answer A). Naltrexone and naloxone are opioid receptor antagonists; however, opioid overdose would produce respiratory depression rather than hyperventilation as seen here (answers B and C). Benzodiazepines overdose is unlikely to produce the autonomic signs and symptoms observed here (answer D). *(Chapter 2—Acetylcholine)*

49. **The best answer is F.** This patient is suffering from major depression with psychotic features as evidenced by his mood-congruent delusions, including ideas of reference. The standard of care for treatment of depression with psychotic features is to use both an antidepressant and an antipsychotic, meaning that there is no single best treatment (answers A through E). *(Chapter 3—Additional Options)*

50. **The best answer is C.** The patient is likely under the influence of a serotonergic hallucinogen given the acute onset of perceptual disturbances along with normal vital signs and an unremarkable physical exam. Of these options, only lysergic acid diethylamide (LSD) falls into this category. Stimulants like methamphetamine or MDMA (answers A and F) can also produce perceptual disturbances but would likely be associated with vital sign abnormalities, mydriasis, and greater impairment in orientation and cognition. Opioids (answer

B) would not be expected to result in the same degree of perceptual disturbances or hallucinations. Phencyclidine would likely produce nystagmus on exam and is typically associated with a higher degree of agitation or even aggression. Cannabis (answer E) does not regularly cause hallucinations. *(Chapter 12—Serotonergic Hallucinogens)*

51. **The best answer is E.** This patient was likely started on carbamazepine and has developed Stevens-Johnson syndrome which is characterized by separation of the epidermis from the dermis. While a rash is the classic presentation of this illness, mucosal involvement is frequently seen and should raise suspicion for this disease in patients recently started on certain medications such as carbamazepine. Stevens-Johnson syndrome is considered a life-threatening emergency and requires prompt admission to the hospital. While discontinuing the new medication is important, getting the patient to the emergency department takes precedence. None of the other options are necessary at this time (answer B, C, and D), and taking no action is absolutely not the best next step (answer F). *(Chapter 5—Anticonvulsant Mood Stabilizers)*

52. **The best answer is A.** This patient is experiencing a hypertensive crisis, most likely as a result of ingesting an aged food or drink (such as cheese or wine) while taking an MAOI (phenelzine in this case). Education on lifestyle changes such as avoiding aged foods and drinks containing tyramine could have prevented this outcome. Smoking cessation would not have any impact on hypertensive crisis as nicotine is not involved (answer B). While antihypertensive medications could lower blood pressure, they would likely only lower it by 10-20 mm Hg which is not enough to make it a safe blood pressure (answer C). While waiting 5 weeks to switch from fluoxetine to phenelzine should absolutely have been done, this patient is not currently suffering from serotonin syndrome which would instead present with diarrhea, shivering, and hyperreflexia, among other signs (answer D). *(Chapter 3—Monoamine Oxidase Inhibitors)*

53. **The best answer is A.** Olanzapine is the only medication listed that has a short-acting injectable form which may be required in this situation given the patient's refusal to take medications by mouth. While risperidone (answer B) has a long-acting injectable form, that would not result in the immediate stabilization required in this case. Lurasidone, clozapine, and quetiapine do not have either short- or long-acting injectable formulations. *(Chapter 4—Putting It All Together)*

54. **The best answer is F.** The resident most likely administered a β-2 agonist such as albuterol to relieve this patient's asthma attack. A non-specific β-blocker like propranolol (answer A) would be contraindicated for a patient with an asthma attack and would result in greater changes in vital signs. Lorazepam (answer E) might be given in the case of a panic attack, but the patient's vital signs (such as her low oxygen saturation) suggest that something more is going on. Prazosin, mirtazapine, and gabapentin (answers B, C, and D) are not indicated for emergency treatment of asthma or anxiety. *(Chapter 2—Norepinephrine)*

55. **The best answer is A.** This vignette describes a stereotypical style of psychoanalysis as evidenced by its focus on relationships, defense mechanisms, and the unconscious. *(Chapter 15—Psychotherapy)*

56. **The best answer is E.** ECT is the single most effective treatment for major depressive disorder that has not responded to multiple trials of medications. Making changes to his existing medication regimen may have an effect, but it is not likely to be as effective as ECT. *(Chapter 15—Procedures)*

57. **The best answer is A.** This patient is likely suffering from methamphetamine-induced psychosis, and his level of agitation should be considered a behavioral emergency. He is unlikely to take medications by mouth, so a short-acting intramuscular formulation is recommended. Of the options available, only haloperidol is available in this form. *(Chapter 4—Putting It All Together)*

58. **The best answer is B.** This patient is likely experiencing an acute dystonic reaction in response to use of haloperidol. The standard treatment for acute dystonia is to use a highly anticholinergic medication such as diphenhydramine or benztropine. Lorazepam would likely sedate the patient but not reverse the dystonic reaction (answer A). Administering another dose of haloperidol in a patient experiencing a dystonic reaction would only exacerbate the dystonia (answers C, D, and E). In many cases, haloperidol is administered alongside diphenhydramine from the beginning to prevent dystonic reactions, although this might have been forgotten by an intern early in their training. *(Chapter 4—Antipsychotic Effects)*

59. **The best answer is C.** Out of the options listed, only olanzapine has not been shown to prolong the QTc in a clinically significant way. The other options should be avoided in this patient with pre-existing prolongation of the QTc. *(Chapters 3 and 4)*

60. **The best answer is A.** This patient is likely in lithium toxicity which can be precipitated by use of NSAIDs such as naproxen when combined with various blood pressure medications. In this patient, it is likely that a change in blood pressure medication along with a concurrent switch to naproxen resulted in reduced renal clearance of lithium. None of the other components of his history would clarify the diagnosis more than knowing his current medication regimen. *(Chapter 5—Lithium)*

61. **The best answer is C.** Emergent hemodialysis is indicated for cases of severe lithium toxicity to facilitate clearance of the medication from the system. Activated charcoal is used for toxicity from certain substances but would not be the best option in this case (answer A). Renal transplantation may be necessary in the future depending on whether the damage to his kidneys is permanent but would not be the most important immediate step (answer B). Intubation and surgical intervention do not have a place in the treatment of lithium toxicity (answers D and E). *(Chapter 5—Lithium)*

62. **The best answer is C.** Of the options listed, only midazolam is considered a short-acting benzodiazepine, with an elimination half-life of less than two hours. This makes it a good choice for producing a state of sedation that can be rapidly reversed when the medication is stopped. Lorazepam and alprazolam (answers A and E) are both considered to be intermediate-acting benzodiazepines, while diazepam and chlordiazepoxide (answers B and D) are both long-acting benzodiazepines. *(Chapter 6—Benzodiazepines)*

63. **The best answer is B.** Tobacco use is the single greatest cause of preventable death worldwide. With few exceptions, treatment of tobacco use is the most effective intervention for increasing the patient's years of life by reducing the risk of cancer, lung disease, heart disease, stroke, and infectious illnesses. Obesity secondary to poor diet and physical inactivity (answer D) is the second leading cause of preventable death. Management of his coronary artery disease may result in a greater quality of life but would not have the same effect on all-cause mortality as smoking cessation. Antidepressants have not been shown to reduce the risk of mortality (answer A). Removing the firearm from a patient without thoughts of suicide may result in a decreased chance of harm but would not necessarily be appropriate or legal (answer E) and would not reduce his risk of death as much as smoking cessation. *(Chapter 10—Nicotine)*

64. **The best answer is F.** This patient is experiencing alcohol hallucinosis which often occurs within 24 hours of the last drink, involves visual hallucinations, and often spontaneously resolves within 48 hours. Tellingly, her vital signs are within normal limits. Alcoholic hallucinosis in and of itself does not require prompt treatment, although it does suggest that she needs to be monitored closely for developing other signs suggestive of delirium tremens or vital sign instability. *(Chapter 11—Alcohol)*

65. **The best answer is B.** Out of the options presented, risperidone is most associated with hyperprolactinemia, which is caused by antagonism of dopamine receptors in the tuberoinfundibular pathway. This can manifest as gynecomastia and lactation in both males and females. Olanzapine, quetiapine, aripiprazole, and clozapine do not have the same effect on prolactin (and in fact, aripiprazole can be used clinically to reduce prolactin levels in patients with risperidone-induced hyperprolactinemia). *(Chapter 2—Dopamine and Chapter 4—Second Generation Antipsychotics: The "-Idones")*

66. **The best answer is E.** This vignette describes a stereotypical case of atypical depression as evidenced by the patient's mood reactivity, leaden paralysis, hypersomnia, and hyperphagia. MAOIs such as selegiline or phenelzine have some evidence that they are more effective than other antidepressant classes when used for atypical depression. While any of the other antidepressants could potentially work, only selegiline is an MAOI. *(Chapter 3—Monoamine Oxidase Inhibitors)*

67. **The best answer is E.** This patient developed torsades des pointes, a potentially life-threatening complication of QTc prolongation. In this case, the most likely culprit is intravenous haloperidol which is associated with both QTc prolongation and torsades des points. None of the other points labeled correlate with the QT interval. *(Chapter 4—First Generation Antipsychotics)*

68. **The best answer is B.** Out of all the options listed, only diazepam is considered to be a long-acting benzodiazepine. Triazolam (answer D) is a short-acting benzodiazepine, while clonazepam, lorazepam, and alprazolam (answers A, C, and E) are all intermediate-acting benzodiazepines. Keep in mind that, despite this doctor's recommendation, benzodiazepines are not the first-line treatment for generalized anxiety disorder. *(Chapter 6—Benzodiazepines)*

69. **The best answer is B.** SSRIs (answer C), SNRIs (answer E), and buspirone (answer A) have all been shown to be effective at treating generalized anxiety disorder. Out of all the options, cognitive behavioral therapy (answer D) should be the first-line treatment (either alone or in combination with medications), as it is the most likely to produce sustained improvement and has no side effects. Only prazosin does not have evidence for its use in generalized anxiety disorder and is instead used to reduce nightmares in post-traumatic stress disorder. *(Chapter 6—Other Anxiolytics and Hypnotics)*

70. **The best answer is B.** Venlafaxine is associated with increases in blood pressure in a dose-dependent fashion, especially towards the beginning of therapy. This is due to the involvement of norepinephrine. While not normally a cause for concern, in a patient with pre-existing hypertension, blood pressure can raise to alarming levels. None of the other medications listed have any effect on blood pressure. *(Chapter 3—Serotonin-Norepinephrine Reuptake Inhibitors)*

71. **The best answer is A.** Out of the SSRIs listed, fluoxetine has the longest half-life. Because of this, it is associated with a much less severe discontinuation syndrome compared to medications with a shorter half-life such as paroxetine or venlafaxine (answers B and D). Escitalopram (answer C) has a medium half-life and could be a reasonable choice but is not as helpful for this indication as fluoxetine. Chlordiazepoxide (answer E) is a benzodiazepine and should not be used as monotherapy for treatment of depression. *(Chapter 3—Serotonin-Specific Reuptake Inhibitors)*

72. **The best answer is E.** This patient likely overdosed on hydrocodone as evidenced by her low respiratory rate and absent pupillary reflex (as would be expected if the pupils were already maximally constricted). She likely obtained hydrocodone from her dentist following her recent procedure. The EKG shown is normal. Had the EKG shown widening of the QRS, a tricyclic might be involved (answer B). Duloxetine would possibly be used to treat comorbid depression and fibromyalgia but would not produce these signs or symptoms in overdose (answer C). Phenelzine or ibuprofen would not produce the combination of signs and symptoms seen here (answers A and D). *(Chapter 2—Opioids)*

73. **The best answer is F.** In a case of opioid overdose, the most important initial treatment is administering naloxone and supporting respirations if necessary. Naltrexone (answer C) is an opioid receptor antagonist but has too long of a half-life to be useful in emergency situations. Flumazenil can be used in select cases of benzodiazepine overdose (answer A), while sodium bicarbonate would be used for tricyclic antidepressant overdose (answer B). Neither intravenous fluids (answer D) nor diltiazem (answer E) play a role in management of opioid overdose. *(Chapter 11—Opioids)*

74. **The best answer is D.** In a patient who is diverting and possibly abusing a prescription stimulant, switching to a non-stimulant with less abuse potential is recommended. Stopping treatment for ADHD would not be appropriate (answer A). Adding behavioral therapy in addition to medications is also recommended but given the patient's previous good response to medications it should be done in addition to, rather than in place of, making medication changes (answer E). While methylphenidate (answer C) does have slightly less abuse potential than amphetamines, the risk is still higher than with a non-stimulant like atomoxetine. Continuing the medication in light of the discovery of diversion and possible abuse would not be advisable (answer B). *(Chapter 7—Non-Stimulants)*

75. **The best answer is A.** This case describes a stimulant, as these increase levels of alertness and decrease appetite. Of the stimulants listed (answers A and B), only nicotine has evidence-based treatments. Alcohol and heroin (answers C and D) both have evidence-based treatments but would not be expected to make someone feel more alert or decrease appetite. Psilocybin (answer E) and other hallucinogens would not result in the symptoms described, nor do they have effective treatments. *(Chapter 10—Nicotine)*

76. **The best answer is C.** This describes a Mediterranean diet which has been shown in population-based studies to lower the risk of depression. While the evidence is limited by methodological difficulties, a Mediterranean diet is associated with many other cardiovascular benefits, making a recommendation of this diet very low-risk. No other diets have been empirically shown to improve outcomes in depression. *(Chapter 15—Lifestyle)*

77. **The best answer is C.** With the exception of olanzapine, all of the medications listed are used to treat or prevent seizures and would therefore be inappropriate to continue for a patient who is scheduled to undergo electroconvulsive therapy. Olanzapine and other atypical antipsychotics have not been shown to impact the seizure threshold. *(Chapter 5—Anticonvulsant Mood Stabilizers and Chapter 6—Benzodiazepines)*

78. **The best answer is G.** This patient's seizure was most likely caused by giving bupropion to a patient with active bulimia nervosa. Assessment of the patient's diet for evidence of disordered eating patterns should be done for all patients being started on bupropion. None of the other aspects of the history would be as likely to reveal a cause for her seizures. *(Chapter 3—"Atypical" Antidepressants)*

79. **The best answer is D.** For a patient with bipolar disorder, polypharmacy is the rule rather than the exception. However, this patient's case likely represents overmedication. Out of the drugs she is prescribed, lithium, quetiapine, and lamotrigine (answers A, B, and C) all have evidence for their use in bipolar disorder. Topiramate and sertraline do not. Between these two options, discontinuing topiramate will likely alleviate the patient's cognitive dulling and should be attempted first. *(Chapter 5—The "Not Mood Stabilizers")*

80. **The best answer is C.** Synthetic cathinones and synthetic cannabinoids can cause psychotic states but are not detected on most urine drug screens. Cocaine and amphetamines would be picked up on most urine drug screens (answers A and B). Ketamine is not often picked up on urine drug screens, but given that the patient's substance use began several hours ago, it is unlikely that he would still be under the influence of ketamine as its mental effects only lasts 1 or 2 hours (answer D). *(Chapter 10—Cathinones and Chapter 12—Dissociative Hallucinogens)*

ALPHABETICAL INDEX OF DRUG NAMES

Abilify. *See* aripiprazole
acamprosate, 157
acetaminophen, 120, 123, 159
acetylsalicylic acid, 119
acid. *See* LSD
Adderall. *See* amphetamine
Advil. *See* ibuprofen
alcohol, 154, 180, 190
Aleve. *See* naproxen
alprazolam, 95
Ambien. *See* zolpidem
amitriptyline, 40
amphetamine, 44, 105, 108, 144
Anafranil. *See* clomipramine
Anexate. *See* flumazenil
Antabuse. *See* disulfiram
Aricept. *See* donepezil
aripiprazole, 44, 64, 67
armodafinil, 110
asenapine, 61
aspirin, 122
Aspirin. *See* acetylsalicylic acid
Atarax. *See* hydroxyzine
Ativan. *See* lorazepam
atomoxetine, 109, 113
Austedo. *See* deutetrabenazine
ayahuasca. *See* DMT

bath salts. *See* cathinone
Belsomra. *See* suvorexant
Benadryl. *See* diphenhydramine
benztropine, 53
blow. *See* cocaine
brexipiprazole, 64
bromocriptine, 56

buprenorphine, 160
bupropion, 34, 110, 143, 187
Buspar. *See* buspirone
buspirone, 37, 96

caffeine, 141, 180
Campral. *See* acamprosate
cannabidiol, 176
cannabis, 119, 124, 174, 177, 180
carbamazepine, 78, 87, 187
cariprazine, 65, 83
Catapres. *See* clonidine
cathinone, 147
CBD. *See* cannabidiol
Celebrex. *See* celecoxib
celecoxib, 122
Chantix. *See* varenicline
chlordiazepoxide, 94, 155
chloroform, 178
chlorpromazine, 59, 67
citalopram, 133
clomipramine, 40
clonazepam, 95
clonidine, 110, 113, 159
clozapine, 61, 210
Clozaril. *See* clozapine
cocaine, 145, 180
codeine, 120, 186
Cogentin. *See* benztropine
Concerta. *See* methylphenidate
crack. *See* cocaine
crystal meth. *See* methamphetamine
Cymbalta. *See* duloxetine
Cytomel. *See* liothyronine

Dantrium. *See* dantrolene
dantrolene, 56
Daytrana. *See* methylphenidate
Demerol. *See* meperidine
Depakene. *See* valproate
Depakote. *See* valproate
Desyrel. *See* trazodone
deutetrabenazine, 55
Dexedrine. *See* dextroamphetamine
dexmethylphenidate, 108
dextroamphetamine, 109
dextromethorphan, 170
diamorphine, 180
diazepam, 94
Dilaudid. *See* hydromorphone
diphenhydramine, 53, 58, 97
disulfiram, 157
divalproex. *See* valproate
DMT, 167
donepezil, 131
doxepin, 40
doxylamine, 97
dronabinol, 176
duloxetine, 33, 124
Duragesic. *See* fentanyl

ecstasy. *See* MDMA
Effexor. *See* venlafaxine
Elavil. *See* amitriptyline
Emsam. *See* selegiline
escitalopram, 31
Eskalith. *See* lithium, *See* lithium
eszopiclone, 100
ethanol. *See* alcohol
ether, 178

Exelon. *See* rivastigmine

Fanapt. *See* iloperidone
fentanyl, 121
Fetzima. *See* levomilnacipran
flumazenil, 158
fluoxetine, 30, 42, 187
fluphenazine, 67
fluvoxamine, 31
Focalin. *See* dexmethylphenidate

gabapentin, 82, 98, 124
galantamine, 132
Geodon. *See* ziprasidone
GHB, 177
guanfacine, 110, 113

Halcyon. *See* triazolam
Haldol. *See* haloperidol
haloperidol, 58, 67
hash. *See* cannabis
hashish. *See* cannabis
heroin, 159
Hetlioz. *See* tasimelteon
hydrocodone, 120
hydromorphone, 121
hydroxyzine, 97

ibuprofen, 119
iloperidone, 63
imipramine, 39
Inderal. *See* propranolol
indica (cannabis strain), 175
Ingrezza. *See* valbenazine
inhalants, 178
Intuniv. *See* guanfacine
Invega. *See* paliperidone

isocarboxazid, 41

K2. *See* cannabis
Kapvay. *See* clonidine
Ketalar. *See* ketamine
ketamine, 43, 169
khat. *See* cathinone
Klonopin. *See* clonazepam

Lamictal. *See* lamotrigine
lamotrigine, 80, 87
Latuda. *See* lurasidone
levomilnacipran, 33, 124
Lexapro. *See* escitalopram
Librium. *See* chlordiazepoxide
liothyronine, 44
lisdexamfetamine, 109
lithium, 44, 73, 87, 123, 210
Lithobid. *See* lithium
lorazepam, 58, 95
LSD, 167
Lunesta. *See* eszopiclone
lurasidone, 63, 83
Luvox. *See* fluvoxamine
Lyrica. *See* pregabalin

marijuana. *See* cannabis
Marinol. *See* dronabinol
Marplan. *See* isocarboxazid
MDMA, 144
melatonin, 101, 203
memantine, 132
meperidine, 120
mescaline, 167
methadone, 160
methamphetamine, 146
methylphenidate, 44, 105, 108, 144

midazolam, 94
milnacipran, 33
Minipress. *See* prazosin
mirtazapine, 35
modafinil, 110
molly. *See* MDMA
morphine, 120
Motrin. *See* ibuprofen
MS Contin. *See* morphine
mushrooms. *See* psilocybin

N-acetylcysteine, 124
naloxone, 159, 161
naltrexone, 156, 161
Namenda. *See* memantine
Naprosyn. *See* naproxen
naproxen, 119
Narcan. *See* naloxone
Nardil. *See* phenelzine
nefazodone, 36
Neurontin. *See* gabapentin
nicotine, 142, 190
nicotine replacement, 143
nitrites, 178
nitrous oxide, 178
Norco. *See* hydrocodone
nortriptyline, 40
Nuvigil. *See* armodafinil

olanzapine, 60, 67, 83
olanzapine/fluoxetine, 84
oxazepam, 94
oxcarbazepine, 82
oxycodone, 120
OxyContin. *See* oxycodone

paliperidone, 62, 67
Pamelor. *See* nortriptyline
paracetamol. *See* acetaminophen
Parlodel. *See* bromocriptine
Parnate. *See* tranylcypromine
paroxetine, 30, 187
Paxil. *See* paroxetine
PCP. *See* phencyclidine
Percocet. *See* oxycodone
pethidine. *See* meperidine
peyote. *See* mescaline
phencyclidine, 168, 180
phenelzine, 41
phenobarbital, 187
poppers. *See* nitrites
prazosin, 99
pregabalin, 98, 124
propranolol, 54, 99
Provigil. *See* modafinil
Prozac. *See* fluoxetine
psilocybin, 167

quetiapine, 44, 60, 83

ramelteon, 101
Razadyne. *See* galantamine
Remeron. *See* mirtazapine
Restoril. *See* temazepam
Revia. *See* naltrexone
Rexulti. *See* brexpiprazole
Risperdal. *See* risperidone
risperidone, 62, 67
Ritalin. *See* methylphenidate
rivastigmine, 131
Rozerem. *See* ramelteon

SAMe, 203
Saphris. *See* asenapine
sativa (cannabis strain), 175
Savella. *See* milnacipran
selegiline, 41
Serax. *See* oxazepam
Seroquel. *See* quetiapine
sertraline, 31, 133
Serzone. *See* nefazodone
shrooms. *See* psilocybin
Sinequan. *See* doxepin
solvents, 178
Sonata. *See* zaleplon
speed. *See* methamphetamine
Spice. *See* cannabis
St. John's wort, 191, 203
steroids, 179
Strattera. *See* atomoxetine
Sublimaze. *See* fentanyl
Suboxone. *See* buprenorphine
Subutex. *See* buprenorphine
suvorexant, 100
Symbyax. *See* olanzapine/fluoxetine

tasimelteon, 101
Tegretol. *See* carbamazepine
temazepam, 95
Tenex. *See* guanfacine
THC. *See* cannabis
Thorazine. *See* chlorpromazine
tobacco. *See* nicotine
Tofranil. *See* imipramine
Topamax. *See* topiramate
topiramate, 82
tramadol, 120

tranylcypromine, 41
trazodone, 36
triazolam, 94
Trileptal. *See* oxcarbazepine
Trintellix. *See* vortioxetine
Tylenol. *See* acetaminophen

Ultram. *See* tramadol
Unisom. *See* doxylamine

valbenazine, 55
Valium. *See* diazepam
valproate, 76, 81, 87, 133
valproic acid. *See* valproate
varenicline, 143
venlafaxine, 32, 124
Versed. *See* midazolam
Vicodin. *See* hydrocodone
Viibryd. *See* vilazodone

vilazodone, 37
Vistaril. *See* hydroxyzine
Vivitrol. *See* naltrexone
vortioxetine, 37
Vraylar. *See* cariprazine
Vyvanse. *See* lisdexamfetamine

Wellbutrin. *See* bupropion

Xanax. *See* alprazolam

zaleplon, 100
ziprasidone, 44, 63, 67
Zoloft. *See* sertraline
zolpidem, 100
zopiclone. *See* eszopiclone
Zyban. *See* bupropion
Zyprexa. *See* olanzapine

ATTRIBUTIONS

The fonts **Oswald** and Source Sans Pro were used for the cover and inside text, respectively. They were accessed from Google Fonts under an open-source license.

All images displayed in this book are under the public domain, with the following exceptions. Use of this content does not suggest that the content's original creator(s) endorse this book or its author in any way.

COVER AND BACK
- Cover and back design by Stephen Sauer (SingleFinDesign.com).
- Images and icons designed by Iconfinder.

CHAPTER 2 | NEUROTRANSMITTERS
- "Male with very severe gynecomastia." Credit: No author information (Creative Commons Attribution-Share Alike 3.0 Unported license).

CHAPTER 3 | ANTIDEPRESSANTS
- "Tricycle." Credit: Stephanie Heendrickxen, CA (Creative Commons Attribution 3.0 license).
- "Washing hands." Credit: Medvedka (Shutterstock.com).

CHAPTER 4 | ANTIPSYCHOTICS
- "Fortune teller with ears on her hands." Credit: Ekaterina Tutynina (© 123RF.com).
- "Medication forms." Credit: LHF Graphics (Shutterstock.com).
- "Prolactinoma on MRI." Credit: S Bhimji MD (Creative Commons Attribution 4.0 International license).

CHAPTER 5 | MOOD STABILIZERS
- "Ebstein's anomaly." Credit: Luis Muñoz-Castellanos et al. (Creative Commons Attribution 2.0 Generic license).
- "Stevens-Johnson Syndrome." Credit: Dr. Thomas Habif (Creative Commons Attribution-Share Alike 3.0 Unported license).
- "Cyanotic neonate." Credit: Jules Atkins, Supplied by: Brandi Catt.

CHAPTER 10 | RECREATIONAL STIMULANTS
- "Insufflating cocaine." Artist: KUCO (Shutterstock.com).
- "Lines of cocaine." Artist: LHF Graphics (Shutterstock.com).
- "Injecting drugs." Artist: KUCO (Shutterstock.com).
- "Khat leaves." Credit: ©2010CIAT/NeilPalmer (Creative Commons Attribution-ShareAlike 2.0 Generic license).
- "Bath salts." Credit: National Institute on Drug Abuse; National Institutes of Health; U.S. Department of Health and Human Services.
- "Photograph of an areca nut vendor on the island of Hainan, China." Credit: Rolfmueller (Creative Commons Attribution-Share Alike 3.0 Unported license).

CHAPTER 11 | RECREATIONAL DEPRESSANTS
- "Motivational carrot." Artist: LHF Graphics (Shutterstock.com).
- "Heroin and spoon." Artist: KUCO (Shutterstock.com).

CHAPTER 12 | HALLUCINOGENS
- "LSD on the tongue." Artist: KUCO (Shutterstock.com).

CHAPTER 13 | CANNABIS AND OTHERS
- "Cannabis leaf." Artist: LHF Graphics (Shutterstock.com).
- "Hyperemia of the superficial blood vessels of the conjunctiva." Credit: Thepawn1 (Creative Commons Attribution-Share Alike 3.0 Unported license).
- "Smoking cannabis." Artist: KUCO (Shutterstock.com).
- "Needle in hand." Artist: KUCO (Shutterstock.com).

CHAPTER 15 | OTHER MODALITIES
- "Sigmund Freud, 1856-1939." Credit: David Webb (Creative Commons Attribution 2.0 Generic license).
- "Mediterranean diet foods." Credit: G.steph.rocket (Creative Commons Attribution-Share Alike 4.0 International license).

CHAPTER 16 | FINAL REVIEW
- "QRS widening." Credit: James Heilman, MD (Creative Commons Attribution-Share Alike 3.0 Unported license).
- "Dilated pupils." Credit: Sophie Riches (Creative Commons Attribution-Share Alike 3.0 Unported license).
- "Free air under the diaphragm." Credit: James Heilman, MD (Creative Commons Attribution-Share Alike 3.0 Unported license).
- "Banana sign at 16 weeks." Credit: Dr. Wolfgang Moroder (Creative Commons Attribution-Share Alike 3.0 Unported license).
- "A person with medication induced dystonia." Credit: James Heilman, MD (Creative Commons Attribution-Share Alike 3.0 Unported license).

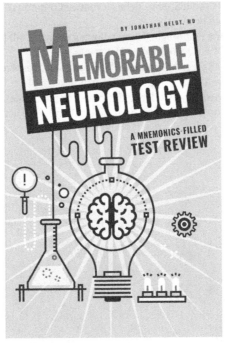

INTERESTED IN LEARNING MORE?

Get *Memorable Psychiatry* and *Memorable Neurology*, both available now from the same author!

Memorable Psychiatry

The best and most effective way to learn about psychiatry! **Memorable Psychiatry** breaks down the complex but fascinating world of mental health using simple explanations, frequent mnemonics, visual aids, and a focus on mechanisms over memorization to catch you up to speed and put you ahead of the curve on the art and science of psychiatric diagnosis.

Memorable Neurology

The nervous system can be a scary place to explore without a guide! **Memorable Neurology** gives you the tools you need to understand the structure, function, and potential dysfunction of the most complex organ system in the body. **Memorable Neurology** combines a solid foundation in neuroanatomy with a focus on clinical diseases to give you a leg up in the field of neurology. A generous helping of mnemonics, visuals, and practice questions makes learning the material simple, straightforward, and enjoyable.

BOTH AVAILABLE NOW ON AMAZON.COM!

ABOUT THE AUTHOR

Jonathan Heldt is currently on faculty at the UCLA Semel Institute for Neuroscience & Human Behavior. He completed his Bachelor's degree in Biochemistry at Pacific Union College, his medical degree at the Loma Linda University School of Medicine, and his residency at the UCLA Psychiatry Residency Training Program. He is interested in both mental health and medical education and hopes that this book will inspire these interests in others. He has no conflicts of interest to disclose.

For questions, comments, and updates, please visit **memorablepsych.com**
or email **memorablepsych@gmail.com**.

Memorable Psychopharmacology by Jonathan Heldt

Neurotransmitters

Serotonin	Dopamine	Norepinephrine
"Broad-spectrum antineurotics" **S**PAROW-tonin **S**leep and energy **P**latelet dysfunction **A**bdominal upset **R**eproductive effects **O**verdose (serotonin syndrome) **W**eight gain **Ray**-phe nuclei bringing **rays** of light	**DOPAMINE** **D**rug addiction **O**utcomes **P**sychosis **A**ttention **M**ovement **I**nhibition of prolactin **N**ausea **E**nergy **Dopaminergic Pathways** +Sx: Meso**limb**ic (**limbs** for thumbs-up), −Sx: Mesocortical Tubero**I**nfundibular Pathway = **T**his **I**nhibits **P**rolactin **V**entral **T**egmental **A**rea = **V**ery **T**iring **A**ddiction **N**igro**S**triatal **P**ath = i**N**voluntary, **S**tuttering, **P**arkinsonism	"Oh FFFFFF!" **F**ear **F**ocus **F**ired up **F**asting **F**eedback pain inhibition **F**ull body response Locus **cer**uleus (being **cer**-rounded) **Noradrenergic Receptors** α-1 receptors found **α-11** over the place α-2 takes SNS from **A–Z** (ends its effects) You **beta** have **1 heart** and **2 lungs** It's β-2 (better to) **relax**

Acetylcholine	Histamine	Other Neurotransmitters
Muscarinic: SLUDG-E BM **S**alivation **L**acrimation **U**rination **D**iaphoresis **G**astrointestinal activation **E**mesis **B**radycardia **M**iosis **Anticholinergic** **Blind** as a bat, **dry** as a bone **Hot** as a hare, **stuck** on the throne **Red** as a beet, **heart** in the zone **Mad** as a hatter when ACh goes **Nicotinic:** Nic's muscle memory	**H₁S+A-mine** H₁ receptor involved in **S**leep **+** **A**llergies **Opioids** **ARMED** Colonialist **A**nalgesia **R**espiratory depression **M**iosis **E**uphoria **D**rowsiness **C**onstipation Mu for **m**orphine!	**GABA** Inhibitory (a **gabber** puts everyone to sleep) **Glutamate** Excitatory (gluta**mate**-ing is exciting!) **Oxytocin** **BLOC**-ytoxin: **B**irth **L**actation **O**rgasm **C**onnection **Orexin** **Go-rex**-in = on-the-**go** (awake) and hungry like a T. **rex!**

Antidepressants

Discontinuation Syndrome	SSRIs	SNRIs
FINISH **F**lu-like symptoms **I**nsomnia **N**ausea **I**mbalance **S**ensory disturbances ("brain zaps") **H**yperarousal	**Flu**oxetine (lasts 1-2 weeks, like the **flu**) **Par**oxetine (fast like a **pair** of **ox**en) **Squirt**-raline (diarrhea, breastfeeding) **Seat**-alopram (car seat = electro-**car**-diogram for QTc prolongation) Fluvoxamine (messy interactions)	Ve**N**lafaxine (**N**orepinephrine, hyper**teN**sion, fast like a **fax** but takes a while to go away) **Dual/Dull**-oxetine (dual mechanism, ↓ pain) Milnacipran/Levomilnacipran (strongest NE)

Atypical Antidepressants	TCAs (Trans, Chans, and Ans)	MAOIs
Bupropion (**bu-DA-NE** = ↓ sex sfx, ↓ smoking, cx in **bul**imia) **Meal**-tazzzapine (↑ appetite, sedating) **Trazzo-bone** (sedation, priapism) **Nefa**-zodone (**nefa**-rious liver toxicity) **Villain**-zodone (partial agonist) **Vortex**-etine ("swirl" of different effects)	I'm-**peeing**-ramine (bedwetting) **Clom**-ipramine (best for obsessive-**clom**-pulsive disorder) Amitriptyline (depression, pain) **No-trip**-tyline (↓ sedation, orthostatics) Doxepin (↑ sedation)	**Inhibits MAO-A and B = ↑ SE, NE, DA** Phenelzine (Nardil) Tranylcypromine (Parnate) Isocarboxazid (Marplan) **Inhibits MAO-B only = ↑ DA only** **Sele**-giline (**sele**-ctive)

Antipsychotics

FGAs	"-Apines" (↑ Sedation, ↑ Wt Gain)	"-Idones" (↑EPS, ↓Wt Gain)
Haloperidol (twisting IV = torsades) **Snore**-promazine (highly sedating) **Flu**-phenazine (knocks you out, lasts a few weeks)	**Olanz**apine (**O**besity) **Queti**-apine (sedating for "**quiet** time") **Cloz**-apine (watch agranulocytosis **cloz**-ely) **S-N**-apine (↑ **S**erotonin + ↑ **N**orepinephrine)	**Rise-pair**-idone (↓ sedation, gynecomastia) **Zip**-rasidone (**zip**py car for electro-**car**-diogram) **Low**-rasidone (bipolar depression) **High-low**-peridone (orthostatic hypoTN)

"IPRs" (Partial Agonists)	Short-Acting IMs	Long-Acting IMs
Light & airy-piprazole (30% blockade, wt neutral, ↓ depression) **Bricks**-piprazole (heavier 50% blockade) Cariprazine (bipolar depression)	"Into the **CHAOZ flew** an IM!" **C**hlorpromazine **H**aloperidol **A**ripiprazole **O**lanzapine **Z**iprasidone **Flu**phenazine	"**OPRAH flew** through a long acting career" **O**lanzapine **P**aliperidone **R**isperidone **A**ripiprazole **H**aloperidol **Flu**phenazine

Memorable Psychopharmacology by Jonathan Heldt

Mood Stabilizers

Lithium	Valproate	Carbamazepine
LITHIUM SFX **L**ow therapeutic index **I**ntestinal upset **T**eratogenicity **H**ypothyroidism **I**nteractions **U**rination **M**uscle weakness **S**kin **F**atigue **X**tra pounds (weight gain)	**VALPROIC SFX** **V**omiting **A**lopecia **L**iver damage **P**ancreatitis **R**ebound seizures **O**varian cysts **I**nteractions **C**BC abnormalities **S**pina bifida **F**atigue **X**tra pounds (weight gain) Target dose = 20 mg/kg/day (wt in lbs × 10)	**CBZ** **C**ranial nerve pain (trigeminal neuralgia) **B**ipolar disorder sei**Z**ures **CARB SFX** **C**BC abnormalities **A**djustments **R**ash **B**aby (neural tube defects) **S**odium abnormalities **F**atigue **X**tra pounds (weight gain)
Target level = ~1	Target level = ~100	Target level = ~10

Lamotrigine	"Not Mood Stabilizers"	Antipsychotics in Bipolar Disorder
Treats **bipolar depression** (less like a lion and more like a **lamb**) Lamotr-**itch**-gine → itchy rashes (10%), SJS (1%) **Val**-**hal**-**la** (if using **val**-proate, **hal**-f dose of **la**-motrigine)	**Dope**-iramate (wt loss, cognitive dulling) Gabapentin (↓ anxiety) Oxcarbazepine ("maybe" mood stabilizer) **Antidepressants in Bipolar Disorder** Not effective! Risk of mania highest from ↑NE	**Antimanic** = All of them **Antidepressive** = Carries quiet, low, and old **Cari**-prazine **Quiet**-apine **Low**-rasidone **Old**-lanzapine

Anxiolytics/Hypnotics

Short-Acting Benzodiazepines	Intermediate-Acting Benzodiazepines	Long-Acting Benzodiazepines
TOM **T**riazolam **O**xazepam* **M**idazolam	**Lure a CAT** **L**or-azepam* **C**lonazepam **A**lprazolam **T**emazepam*	Works for días ("days" in Spanish) Chlor-**diaz**-epoxide **Diaz**-epam *OK w/ liver dysfx (**O**utside **T**he **L**iver)

Other Anxiolytics	Antihistamines	Hypnotics
SRIs (broad-spectrum antineurotics) **Bus**-pirone (GAD, "missing the bus") **Gaba-PEN**-tin (**P**ain, **E**pilepsy, **N**ervous) Pregaba-**lean** (faster lean-er gabapentin) Pro-**ban**-it-**all** (perform anx, **bans all** β) Pr-**a**-zos-**in** (α-1 **in**-hibitor, ↓ nightmares)	Diphen-**H₁**-dramine (+++ anticholinergic) H₁-**drowsy**-zine (+ anticholinergic) Doxylamine (++ anticholinergic)	**Z**-drug half-life is alphabetical: **Z**aleplon (4 hours) **Z**olpidem (6 hours) **Z**opiclone (8 hours) **Soothe**-orexant (orexin antagonist) Mela-**turn-in** (turn in for the night)

Stimulants

Stimulant Side Effects	Stimulant Classes	Non-Stimulants
RACING **R**estlessness **A**ppetite suppression **C**ardiovascular effects **I**nsomnia **N**arcotic potential **G**rowth restriction	Methylphe-**N**-i-**DA**-te (NE+DA reuptake inhib) "Weaker" **Amp**-phetamines (NE+DA releasing agent) "Stronger"	**Atom**-oxetine (NRI, smaller effects) Cl-**awn**-idine and gu-**awn**-facine (make you yawn and put weight on) Modafinil (**mo'** time for **da final**)

Analgesics/Antidementia

Opioids	Non-Opioid Analgesics	Antidementia
Low-Potency **Low**-deine Tramadol (tram it all in = multiple NTs) Me-**pair**-idine (**pairs** with other NTs) **Medium-Potency** Morphine Hydrocodone Oxycodone **High-Potency** Hydro**morphone** ("Mighty Morphone Power Rangers") **Vent**-anyl (you'll need a **vent**-ilator)	**NSAIDs** ↓ COX-1 (stomach) and COX-2 (pain) **N**ephrons/**S**tomach **A**re **I**ncidentally **D**amaged **Select**-coxib (select-ive for COX-2) **Ass**-**pair**-en (an **ass** to a **pair** of en-zymes) **Acet**-aminophen ("Have acet!" to eat liver) Tx overdose = N-**acet**ylcysteine **Antidepressants** **Dul**l-oxetine, other NRIs **Anticonvulsants** **Gaba-PEN**-tine (**P**ain), pregabalin **Cannabinoids**	**ACEIs** **Done**-pezil (one and done-pezil = once daily) **River**-stigmine (fast like a river) Galantamine (medium half-life) **NMDA Antagonist** **Mem**-antine (hold onto **mem**-ories)

Memorable Psychopharmacology by Jonathan Heldt

Major Side Effects and Toxic States

Serotonin Syndrome	Neuroleptic Malignant Syndrome	Delirium Tremens (Alcohol Withdrawal)
Shits & SHIVERS **Shits** (diarrhea) **Shi**vering **H**yperreflexia **I**ncreased temperature **V**ital sign instability **E**ncephalopathy **R**estlessness **S**weating	**FEVER** **F**ever **E**ncephalopathy **V**ital sign instability **E**levated WBC and CPK **R**igidity Tx: **Dan**(trolene) or **Bro**(mocriptine) Dan the Bro with dance FEVER	**DTS** are **HELL** **D**elirium **T**remor **S**eizures **H**allucinations **E**SR ↑ **L**eukocytosis **L**iver function tests ↑
Extrapyramidal Side Effects	**TCA Overdose**	**Hypertensive Crisis**
AD-A-P-T **A**cute **D**ystonia (hours) **A**kathisia (days) **P**arkinsonism (weeks) **T**ardive Dyskinesia (years)	Overdose = Wide QRS (2/2 ion channels) Antidote = Sodium bicarbonate (**bi-car** runs over **tricycle**)	Proposing to **Tyra Mine** on **Maui** over **wines** and **cheeses** = high **blood pressure**!

Recreational Substances

Stimulants	Depressants	Hallucinogens
Caffeine (brings you out of a-den-osine) **Smoking Cessation** Very-**nic**-clean (clean from **nic**-otine) Nico-**team** replacement (2+ forms!) Bupropion (remember budane lighter) **MDMA/Ecstasy** **XTC** = o**X**ytocin, Bru**X**ism **Cocaine** "Stronger Ritalin" **Co**caine **co**nstricts **co**ronaries **Methamphetamine** "Stronger Adderall" **Cathinones** (khat, Africa & Middle East) **Arecoline** (betel nut, SE Asia & Pacific)	**Tx Alcohol Use Disorder** Naltrexone ("removes the carrot" = best!) Disulfiram ("introduces a stick" = not as good) A-**camp**-rosate (relaxing like **camp**ing) **Tx Benzo Use Disorder** Break-up rule: 1 mo to quit / 1 yr on a benzo **Tx Opioid Use Disorder** Nal-**blocks**-one (OD rescue med) Methad-"**one and done**" (half-life of 1 day) **Bup**-renorphine (**boops** the morphine, partial agonist) Nal-**trex**-one (long **trek** of getting sober)	**Serotonergic** LSD (Lasts a Semi-Day=long half-life) Psilocybin (mushrooms, shorter, gentler) Mescaline (peyote, stronger visuals, ↑ upset stomach) DMT (ayahuasca, more spiritual effects) **Dissociative** Phencyclidine (PCP-nis = excited delirium, nystagmus) **KIDDA**-mine (**K**ids, **I**ncrease BP, **D**issociation, anti-**D**epressant, **A**irway preservation) Dextromethorphan ("robotripping")

Cannabis and Others

Cannabis	Other Substances	Drug-Drug Interactions
HASH PIPER **H**igh **A**nxiety **S**hort-term memory loss **H**unger **P**ain relief **I**mpairment **P**aranoia **E**nergy **R**edness of the eyes **T**HC = **T**he **H**igh **C**hemical **C**BD = **C**annabis **B**ringer **D**owner S-**active**-a (**activ**ating) **Ind**ica (sedating like book **ind**ex)	**GHB** (GHB **H**as **B**oth stim + depress effects) **Inhalants** Solvents (short "head rush," dangerous) Anesthetics (euphoria, flammable) Nitrites (used during sex, ↓ BP) **Steroids** ↑ muscle mass but many med/psych issues, testicular atrophy **"It's All in the Eyes"** Dilated pupils = Stimulants "Pinpoint" pupils = Opioids Nystagmus = Phencyclidine (PCP) Red eyes = Cannabis	In**D**ucers bring **D**own, in**HI**bitors raise **HI**gh Inducers = **Car**bamazepine, Phenobar**b**ital ("**Carb and Barb**") Inhibitors = **B**upropion, **F**luoxetine, **P**aroxetine (**B**ig **F**reaking **P**roblems) Smoking induces 1A2 (**A**ntipsychotics and **A**ntidepressants) Major interxn ("I **C**an **H**ave **F**un **H**eartily **O**ut **S**marting **W**arring **D**rugs") OTC interxn (**NAG**ging **WOR**ry = **N**icotine, **A**lcohol, **G**rapefruit juice, St. John's **WOR**t) Renally metabolized psych drugs (**GAL** = **G**abapentin, **A**camprosate, **L**ithium)

Other Modalities

Types of Psychotherapy	Procedures	Supplements
Psychoanalysis (long and expensive) Psychoeducation (every patient!) Supportive therapy (adjustment d/o) **CBT** (**C**an't **B**e **T**opped) Exposure (PTSD, phobias) **DBT** (**D**e-**B**orderline **T**herapy) Motivational interviewing (addiction) **ABA** (**A**utism, **B**ehavioral **A**nomalies) Family therapy Support groups	ECT ("shockingly effective") TMS (weaker than ECT but ↓ sfx) Biofeedback (variety of disorders) Psychosurgery (not used much anymore)	St. John's wort (depression) SAMe (depression) Omega-3 fatty acids (depression, bipolar) Melatonin (insomnia) **Lifestyle** Nutrition (Mediterranean diet = ↓ depression) Exercise (yoga in particular) Sleep (helps with most things) Emotional support animals (why not?) Acupuncture (↓ pain, no mental health fx) Socializing (helps with most things)

Made in the USA
Las Vegas, NV
07 September 2023

77178272R00154